just one little pill

a novel

lorraine queen

Just One Little Pill copyright © 2025 Lorraine Queen

The moral rights of the author have been asserted

All rights reserved. No part of this publication may be reproduced, distributed, or transmitted in any form or by any means, including photocopying, recording, or other electronic or mechanical methods, without the prior written permission of the publisher, except in the case of brief quotations embodied in critical reviews and certain other non-commercial uses permitted by copyright law.

This is a work of fiction. Names, characters, businesses, places, events, locales, and incidents are either the products of the author's imagination or used in a fictitious manner. Any resemblance to actual persons, living or dead, or actual events is purely coincidental.

First edition June 2025

Cover by Miblart

ISBN:
978-1-0684690-0-8 (e-book)
978-1-0684690-1-5 (print)

Published by One Pill Publishing
Glasgow, Scotland

All profits from the sale of *Just One Little Pill* go to Cancer Research UK

just one little pill

author's note

As a child I was taught shapes and colours. Soon after came shades: sky blue, royal blue, and navy blue. I believe I was in my teens before I realised *navy* referred to the colour of the Royal Navy uniforms.

Sadly, a shade of dark brown was prefixed by another word, beginning with *n*.

I used it with the same innocence and ignorance as *sky*, *royal*, and *navy*, as did my peers.

When I was a little older and realised the derivation of this appellation for dark brown, I was first surprised, then appalled.

In the early seventies we had minstrel shows and *Love Thy Neighbour* on prime-time television, racist symbols on jam jars and in advertisements for coconut bars and sodas... yet none of it was perceived to be offensive by the masses of viewers, programmers, or marketers.

Now when we see or hear such things, we are horrified, and I hope that when you read such references in this book, you, too, will be disgusted by them.

Several people who have helped me with reviewing and

editing have questioned the wisdom of using these offensive terms.

After much consideration I decided it was right to be true to the times of this story. I want readers to be shocked at these terms' use. If not, then we will have learned nothing, made no progress.

If we ignore or gloss over the truth of the past, then we silently condone it.

1 /
phoenix, arizona, october 1999

day 1

AMANDA, FINALLY AT THE FRONT OF THE QUEUE, FLATTENED HERSELF against the wall when she heard the lock switch from *engaged* to *vacant*. She tried smiling as the man squeezed past her in the narrow aisle, but he wouldn't meet her eyes and stared determinedly at the floor. When she stepped into the tiny toilet, she realised why. Good God! She choked back a gag and quickly sprayed some cologne to try and mask the smell. As if she wasn't a big enough mess after fifteen straight hours travelling, now she would smell awful when they finally met face to face. The thought brought back all her turmoil. She swallowed hard and took a deep breath.

'Get a grip, girl,' she chided herself in the mirror. 'There's thirty minutes till the plane lands, so it's your last chance to freshen up before he sees you.'

Hair brushed, mouth rinsed with a minty wash, and make-up swiftly tidied, she peered at her reflection once more. She shook her head to loosen her dark curls. That would have to do. But then, as an afterthought, she spritzed more of the cologne in a little cloud above her head, feeling it lift her spirits as it settled on her hair and shoulders.

All too soon, the pilot announced they were beginning their descent into the Phoenix airport, where the local time was 5:15 p.m. and the weather was twenty-five degrees with clear skies. She was buckled, seat and tray table upright, ready for landing. Her stomach did another flip as she realised this was it. She was going to meet him for the very first time, but was she ready for it?

As she and the other passengers emerged at Arrivals, she deliberately hid behind a large American lady and her husband. It was a little crazy, but Amanda wanted to see him before he saw her. He needed to be looking for her this time. Then she caught sight of him right at the front of the barrier. He was stretching his neck, searching for her amongst the throng pouring through the gate. A small pang of disappointment struck her as she realised he was shorter than she'd expected. He'd looked so broad, strong, and muscular when she saw him on the video cam, and because he was an ex-marine, she'd always imagined he would be tall.

Just then he caught sight of her. He broke into a bright, face-splitting grin, straight white teeth contrasting with his brown skin. Happiness bubbled through her, and all the doubts and fears lifted in that glorious moment of recognition.

She waved and wept with joy. 'Dad! I'm here!'

They rushed towards each other for their first embrace, dodging luggage trolleys and other arrivals. She leaned toward him, but her holdall got between them and she kissed his ear instead of the cheek she'd been aiming for.

He placed a hand on each of her shoulders, and his eyes began to fill as he looked at her. 'You're here, I can't believe it. You're really… I can't tell you…' Shaking his head, he picked up her suitcase and held out his hand to take her bag. Instead, she put her hand in his, and he gently squeezed it. His eyes seemed a mirror image of her own: deep, dark brown. The familiarity was comforting, as was the warmth of his hand. Moments passed as they stood close to each other.

His eyes crinkled as he smiled. 'Let's grab a coffee and start to get to know each other. It's long overdue, baby girl.'

Amanda sat at the table and watched as he bought the coffees. Every few minutes he looked over to her, shaking his head in wonder. She smiled, happy to know he was happy to know her. It had been a long, difficult search. So many years of her life trying to find out the name of the man who had fathered her. By comparison, the months of investigation needed to establish his whereabouts was short, but her impatience had increased with every step as she grew closer. Just as she'd been punching the air with achievement, she'd realised that he might not share her joy of discovery. For weeks, she'd hovered over the information, torn between fantasies of how delighted he would be, then fear that he would reject her. It all seemed foolish now. Of course he would be a good guy. They shared genes; they were of the same bloodline. But she had been enormously relieved when he'd accepted she was who she said she was. Naturally he'd been suspicious at first, but it had been the American Legion who finally helped put them in touch. If she had convinced them she was genuinely Howard Odoms's daughter, then he couldn't deny it. However, it had taken a paternity test to fully convince him, and deep inside, a tiny part of her resented that.

'A milky coffee as requested… Amanda.' He placed it in front of her and sat opposite with both his hands wrapped around a tall mug of black coffee. 'Amanda! You know that's one of my favourite names, right?'

'I'm glad,' she said. 'Amanda Louise Barr, although it should have been Amanda Louise Odoms.'

'Yes, absolutely it should. What was she thinking, keeping you a secret from me? It was a mean, spiteful thing to do! When I think—'

'Stop. No, stop right there, Howard.' She held her hand up, palm facing flat towards him. 'I can't hear a word said against her. She's my mum, and I love her. I was angry and frustrated that she would never tell me your name, but she must have felt she had good reason.'

Howard nodded, took her hand, and bowed his head. She couldn't see the expression on his face, but as his long fingers entwined with hers, she felt as though they were transmitting his love and acceptance of her, his new-found daughter.

Howard held the door of the truck and helped Amanda into the passenger seat. Once he had put her luggage in the back and reattached the cover, he got in and started the engine.

Smiling, he reached over and awkwardly patted her knee. 'Okay?'

Amanda nodded.

They drove in silence until they were clear of the airport traffic and the junctions leading in every direction. Once they were on the highway south towards Tucson, Amanda spoke.

'So, how long were you in Dunoon for?'

'I'd been posted there for two years, but I got shipped home to the States a little earlier than that.'

'Have you ever thought of going back to Scotland?'

'Nope. Never!'

'Sounds as if you didn't like it there.'

'Like it?' He gave a scornful snort. 'I hated it, and they hated us being there – the locals, that is, although they were always happy to take our cash. Anyway, we weren't welcome. Meeting your mum was the first good thing that happened to me. She worked in the pub and was nice. I remember she kinda lit the place up.'

Amanda felt a warm glow when she heard this. All her life she had felt puzzled and resentful that her mother would never refer to her birth father, steadfastly refusing to give even his name. It had taken many years to finally find his name out, and that had given her search a starting point. Now, hearing Howard speak with affection about her mother gave her a boost. She had hated the thought that she could be an unwelcome outcome of a cold one-night stand. She'd grown up feeling loved, but she'd wanted more than that. She'd needed to feel he would have wanted her if he had only known about her. She'd dreamed of being a child conceived in love, not just a mistake. The knowledge of love could wipe away the fear that had gnawed at her throughout her teens. Erase the label she suspected others gave her: the little black bastard of a white woman.

Howard's voice brought her back to the present, and realising she had been drowsing, she sat up and asked him to repeat what he had said.

'Nah, it was just me trying to be a bit of a tour guide. But hey, it's more than three hours to Tombstone. I know you must be pretty tired, so if you want to nap, just go ahead.'

'Oh, I didn't really think about how long a drive we might have once I'd landed. I didn't think of anything much, beyond getting here and meeting you.' She squinted to focus through the darkening sky. All she could make out was the desert scrub and cacti. There was no evidence of a town in sight. 'Is there maybe a hotel or motel we could stop at for the night?' Glancing at her watch, she added, 'It's getting pretty late now, and we could get a fresh start in the morning.'

He agreed. A few miles along the highway, they checked into a Motel 6.

Howard paid for both rooms and lightly kissed her cheek as they said goodnight.

Once inside the small bedroom, Amanda took her mobile from her bag and switched it on. A welcome message from the cell phone network appeared. She hit her message icon and opened a new text window. She tapped *Jamie* into the recipient box and then typed *Arrived ok. Met him. So far so good. In Motel 6 on way to Tucson. Need to sleep.*

She hit send, watched until it signalled the message had been delivered, and then switched the phone off. She kicked off her shoes, stretched out on the bed, and was in an exhausted sleep within seconds.

2 /
dunoon, scotland, january 1972

Diane took the last Christmas bauble and packed it carefully in layers of newspaper in the cardboard box. She had already dragged the big dead tree out to the back garden for the bin men to collect in the morning. Mrs Bissell depended on her to make sure there would be no bad luck this year. The fact that the superstitious landlady was hundreds of miles away, enjoying herself in Benidorm, didn't mean she could let it slide. Diane loved having the big house so empty. No more guests till the end of January, so she and Marion had three blissful weeks without changing beds, laundry, dishes, or early rises. She could hear Marion upstairs now. That lad she'd been seeing was up there with her, so Diane expected she would probably sleep in the back room again tonight. She lifted the big box of decorations and started up the three flights of stairs to put it in the loft.

Diane heard the noises from the top-floor bedroom and had to stifle a giggle as the *uhh*s and *mmmph*s grew louder. There was a slapping sound, and as she stepped onto the top landing, she realised the bedroom door was wide open. Rooted to the spot, she took a shocked breath and held it, unable to let go or drag her eyes away.

He was banging Marion. Really *banging*. Diane had always thought that expression was just another slang term for sex, but he was pounding, *bang, bang, bang*, against Marion's backside. Just then, Marion looked up.

'Fuck off, Diane!' Stretching and twisting from the bed, she reached the edge of the door with her fingertips and slammed it shut.

Diane turned and ran downstairs. One floor down, she remembered to breathe again. The box of decorations was still in her hands. She replayed the image of him standing naked and powerful in front of her and felt excitement build into a fantasy that her inexperience couldn't complete. Unable to settle, she paced around the lounge: looking out the window, switching the television on, then putting it off so she could hear if he was leaving. At last she heard the bedroom door close and his footsteps clattering down.

Diane hurried out and stood in the hall, her back against the wall, and faced the flight of stairs. He slowed as he reached the bottom. Moving close, he pressed his hands against the wall on either side of her.

'Like what you saw, did you, little girl?' And with that he kissed her and pushed his knee between her legs. She felt his hand slide over her breast, first skimming downwards, then pushing upwards, squeezing and pinching her nipple. Abruptly he pulled away and laughed loudly. His teeth were bright and clean; his breath smelt of cigarettes. He winked and undid the latch on the front door. Leaning back, he kissed her again. When the door closed, Diane laughed and breathed; sliding down the wall, she hugged her knees. Only then did she look to the top of the stairs to see fury wrapped in a pink dressing gown. Marion stared down with narrowed eyes.

. . .

Just One Little Pill

It wasn't so much that Marion wasn't speaking to her, more that she'd managed to avoid being anywhere near her for the last three days. As well as being a live-in maid at the boarding house, Marion worked a few shifts in the Anchor Inn. While Mrs Bissell was away, she took every available shift, day and night. Diane stayed in just waiting to hear from him. He'd choose her. She knew he would. He must have felt the connection just as much as she had. On the third day, he rang. As soon as she heard the pips and knew it was a public call box, her heart leapt.

'Dunoon four three seven seven one. Hello.'

'Hey, baby. Are you on your own? I can get away for a few hours tonight.'

Just like that: bold, arrogant, sure of himself and of her. Diane had never known anyone like him. It wasn't just that he was American; after all, Americans were what had drawn Marion and then her to Dunoon in the first place. It wasn't that he was the first black man she'd ever even spoken to, either. It was him – the whole package of exciting, confident, experienced male.

Marion stayed out of their way, deliberately. As soon as Mrs Bissell returned from Spain, Marion handed her notice in, at both the boarding house and the pub. By Valentine's Day she was almost ready to go. While she was packing, Diane tried to talk to her. Not to apologise, just to make sure Marion understood that the force of attraction between Howard and herself was so strong it couldn't be denied by either of them.

Marion laughed. 'Aye, so it is, hen. You two are just made for each other, aren't you?' She rolled up another jumper and pushed it down the edge of the suitcase. Then she stopped, looked up at the ceiling, and let out a deep breath. She turned and sat on the bed, extending her arm to Diane to come and sit beside her.

'Listen, Diane, you're only seventeen. I know you're a smart girl and older than your years in a lot of ways, but you're still young, really young, when it comes to things like this. Your mum only let you come over to Dunoon because I was here to look after you.' She shook her head to stop Diane from interrupting. 'I'm eight years older than you, and we've always said I'm your young auntie. And I am, but believe me, darlin', eight years is a lot at this stage of your life. Don't get carried away with the big rush of hormones you get from discovering sex.'

'It's more than sex, Marion. I love him.'

'Aye, an' he loves the sex, hen. I know he does, but it doesn't mean he loves you.' She turned slightly and held her niece by the shoulders. Looking her straight in the eyes, she asked, 'Did you go on the pill yet?'

'Uh-huh, the very first week we slept together. He told me to.'

'Well, at least that's something. Just watch yourself, will you? Oh, and listen, do not tell your mum I've left.' Marion paused to make sure her niece realised the importance of what she was saying. 'She'll not be happy at you being here on your own. Just don't mention me. I'll write or phone you once I get sorted out in London, and then we can decide the best way to let your mum and dad know.'

Diane nodded and handed Marion her suitcase. As soon as she had waved her off, she ran to the room they had shared and pushed the beds together. She stood back to admire her work and clapped her hands in delight.

3 /
dunoon, scotland, october 1972

'What do you mean, your auntie's a wee bit late?' he asked in bewilderment. Howard Odoms had been posted here for almost two years, and yet this Scottish version of English still confounded him. Diane smiled and lifted a shoulder to her ear. Before he could ask again, she turned and sat astride his lap. Her arms circled his neck, and her fingers traced the skin behind his ears. He shook his head in annoyance.

'What? Don't you know what that means?' she asked. 'I haven't had a red flag recently.'

'God damn it, Diane! Speak English, not this bullshit! Who's your auntie, and what is she late for? Is this some sort of commie thing?'

'My time of the month… my period, it's late.' She dipped her head so he wouldn't see her smile. It could take time for him to come around to the idea, she knew that. But he would get there, maybe even be happy about it.

Suddenly she felt herself land with a thump on the floor. Howard bent over her, grabbed her shoulders, and pushed his face within inches of hers.

'Pregnant? Is that what you're saying? You're fucking pregnant? I thought you were on the pill!' He was almost screaming at her now. Spittle splashed her cheeks.

'I might be, *might* be, that's all I'm saying. I'm a *wee* bit late. I *am* on the pill, but I had to change over to a new one, so there was a bit of a gap.' She held her hand out, and he pulled her onto her feet. This wasn't going quite to plan. Diane knew she would have to play this very carefully or she could end up like Sheila Forsythe. A shudder went through her at the thought: left high and dry with a baby to raise on her own. Even Sheila's parents would have nothing to do with her because the little boy was black. She shook the fear from her mind and focused her best beaming smile at Howard. It seemed to work its usual magic. He pulled her close to him and whispered in her ear.

'You'd better not be, little girl. It would spoil everything. Go find out for sure.'

With that he glanced a kiss on her forehead and left. From her bedroom window Diane watched him stride down the street. *Heaven help me,* she thought with a shudder. She was in trouble now.

He knew the silly little bitch was watching him as he strode down the path. He resisted the temptation to slam the gate behind him, deciding instead to turn and close it gently without looking up at her. This stretch of road was clearly visible from her window, but the beech trees just before the bus stop could give him cover to stop and vent his anger and frustration. He could see the shelter was empty, and he waited until he reached it. He pulled back his foot and kicked the metal panel with such force that the whole structure rattled.

'Calm down. Jeezuz, man, you need to think,' he told himself and relaxed his jaw. He unclenched his fists and stretched his neck left, then right, hearing it pop and crack. He sat on the metal frame where a pane of glass was missing; then, reaching into his pocket, he took out his packet of Marlboros and a cheap lighter. He lit one, inhaled deeply, and slumped forward. Everything about this country was shit. Cold, damp climate; miserable, dumb, ignorant people who didn't want Americans there. Diane was the one comfort he'd had, and now she thought she was going to set him up for a meal ticket? No way. No fucking way, girlie.

Christ, he wanted a drink. He couldn't even get that since he'd been barred after the latest big fight with the dumb locals. There were damn few bars that would serve Americans, and the Anchor was pretty much the only one that served coloureds. Grinding out the cigarette, he looked along the coast road to see if there was a bus heading his way and decided to walk back to the base to give himself some thinking time. He strode downhill, seeing nothing but the toes of his boots as he marched away.

Howard flexed the fingers of his left hand. He still felt pain from the fracture he'd received when the punks had jumped him on his way home last month. He'd been lucky that was all he'd got, but he was a match for any three of those puny cowards. The fracture had been from landing one of his punches, and as soon as he'd felt the pain, he'd run towards the base, knowing that even if they were stupid enough to follow, they could never catch him.

The following Friday afternoon, Howard jumped when he heard the insistent beep to signal his call had been answered. He pressed the coins into the payphone and heard Diane say, 'Dunoon four three seven seven one. Hello.'

'Diane, hi. It's me, honey.' Howard lay back against the door of the telephone kiosk, pushing it open a few inches to let in some fresh air and cover the stink of urine that rose from the concrete floor. 'Listen, hon, Bill's offered to take us into Glasgow tonight with him and Betty. I thought it would do us good to go let our hair down for a while. What do you think?'

'Well… yeah, suppose we could. What time are they leaving?'

'We'll come pick you up at seven, okay? Don't worry about a thing, just get yourself all dressed up and ready for a great night. We are gonna trip the light fantastic, baby doll.'

He stepped out and walked over to a blue Mini at the kerbside. A man in United States Navy uniform stood with a car key dangling from his finger. Howard took it from him.

'Okay, Bill, we're on.'

'You're sure you remember everything I told you?'

Howard tapped his forehead. 'It's all in here, every detail. I'll go collect her at seven and take it from there.' As he withdrew his hand, he looked down at the folded piece of aluminium foil his friend had transferred there. He nodded and slipped it into the breast pocket of his bomber jacket.

Diane sat on the bed, her head resting on the Beatles poster on the wall, and stared at the letter in her hand one last time. Biting down the flash of anger it sparked, she crumpled the cheap paper and allowed herself a small smile as she threw it into the bin in the corner, decorated with the faces of John, Paul, George, and Ringo.

A moment later, twirling in front of the long mirror on the wardrobe door, she happily imagined Howard's face when he saw what she was wearing. He loved her in this, a long lilac dress that tied in a bow behind her neck, exposing her back and shoulders. It gave him easy access to her bare breasts, and this evening she decided to leave her knickers off, too, as a special surprise.

'After tonight, Howard Odoms, you're never going to let me go!' She smiled at her reflection once more, blew kisses at the Beatles poster, and slipped on her coat. Downstairs, she checked the time, knowing she was too early. She threw her new maxi coat over the back of the couch and settled at the window to wait for seven o'clock.

Diane ran out as soon as she saw the car draw up and crossed over to the passenger side. Howard was driving, and no one else was inside.

He leaned over to let her in. 'Hey, baby, Bill got pulled in for an extra shift but didn't want us to miss out, so he loaned me the car and said we should go enjoy ourselves.'

Driving towards the ferry terminal, he once again passed the home-made posters in windows and gardens saying *YANKS GO HOME*. Graffiti on the walls of the beach toilet block echoed the sentiment. Bitterness burned in him at every word; even the fluttering stars and stripes at the ferry did nothing to sweeten it.

Diane glanced at the back seat, noticed his jacket and the small carrier bag beside it.

'Where are we going? What's that bag for? Is it yours?'

Howard leaned over and put a hand on her knee. 'I've planned a little surprise for you, baby.'

'For my birthday? Oh, Howard, I didn't know you'd even remembered!'

Throughout the journey, Diane hugged herself with excitement. Happiness flooded through her: this man had put so much thought into her birthday, even after she'd told him about the baby. He must love her; everything was going to work out. She was sure of that now, and it was the best present she could have ever had. She settled back and began building a picture in her mind of presenting him with a baby that would melt his heart. A little girl with his beautiful dark eyes or a boy who he could teach all those American ball games to. She sighed with contentment and relief.

As they drove through the Glasgow streets, Diane told Howard they were coming to the part of the city where her parents lived. She sat forward and pointed to a row of tenements.

'They're along there, just behind that second lamp post on the right – 321 Jameston Road. I'd like you to meet my parents one day. Soon, maybe?'

'Maybe.' Howard nodded.

'Actually, I feel quite guilty. I've not seen them since Christmas.' She pulled a face. 'Other things on my mind.' She reached over and squeezed his thigh. 'But really, Howard, I'd like you to meet them. They're lovely, and they'd love you.'

'Would they? Do they even know you're seeing me, let alone that I'm black?'

Diane crinkled her nose and shrugged. 'They wouldn't care that you're black. As long as you're not a Proddie!' She threw her head back and laughed. 'I'm kidding, I'm kidding! No, they don't know I've got a boyfriend, but honestly, they're lovely folk. They won't care if you're black, white, or green. If I love you, they will too.'

'What's a Proddie, then, and why would that make a difference?'

Diane took a deep breath and let it out in a sigh. 'Oh, it's Glasgow slang for a Protestant. My mum and dad are Catholic. Well, sort of – Mum more than Dad, but not really very churchy… Anyway, I was just trying to be funny. Don't worry about it.'

'And what about you? Are you churchy?'

'Och no, I haven't been near the chapel in years.' She looked down at her feet for a moment and gave a wistful sigh.

'What? Do you want to go? Is that it?' he asked.

'No, it's just… I was just thinking about my shoes. When I was taking my first communion, Mum bought me a lovely dress and little tiara and veil. I was so excited – all of us were. Most of us were in the same class at school, and for weeks before, we'd all talked about our dresses, how we would wear our hair…'

Howard glanced over to see why she'd stopped talking and was surprised to see her wiping away a tear.

'What's wrong?'

'My shoes. Marion got me my shoes. She had them made specially, in a place in Rutherglen. They were the most beautiful shoes I had ever seen. I felt like a princess. I wore them all the time in the house. I'd have slept in them if I could've. They had little heels, and I felt so grown up. They were covered in sparkles, with a white satin bow.' In the air, her fingers drew the shape of the bow and pointed to the centre. 'There was a diamond in the middle of each of the bows. Not an actual diamond, obviously, but hey, they were real enough for me.'

'God, you're weird, Diane. Why the hell would that make you cry?'

'Because… Marion, y'know? She was good to me. And I've not been very nice to her, have I?'

Ever since February, when Marion left, Diane had steadfastly avoided speaking about her to Howard. Now here she was letting a stupid memory threaten to spoil her lovely night out with him.

She gave herself a shake and forced a smile as she turned to Howard. 'Anyway, she's had plenty of boyfriends, but with you and me, it's different. We're meant to be together.'

They drove quietly for a few more minutes. Diane leaned against the side window. It was fully dark now, but the streets were well lit, and she looked out as the road swept past. Long rows of dark tenement buildings were followed by stretches of tall trees, their stark branches reaching towards the moonlit sky. A disturbing shiver travelled through her body, and she turned to Howard with an anxious expression.

'I do love you, you know.'

He glanced at her and smiled. 'You, too, baby. You too.'

Lorraine Queen

. . .

They drew up at a painted sign that proclaimed *Hillview B&B*. Underneath was a piece of masking tape with *Vacenties* written in black marker pen.

'Listen, babe, I want tonight to be special, so I thought we could get a room and stay over.'

'Really! Oh, that's a lovely idea.' Diane sighed.

'Here's the cash. You go book a room for us. I would go, but you know how people here can get about me.'

Diane kissed his cheek and giggled as she took the money. She waited on the pavement and watched him drive the car around the corner to park where it would be safer. Still smiling, she went inside to book their room.

Howard was perched on the low crumbling wall, smoking, when she came out. He ground the cigarette stub under his boot, and Diane skipped to his side. Arm in arm, they strolled the short distance to the city centre and blended in with the crowds heading for Jo-Jo's Disco.

They danced for hours. Howard had good rhythm but didn't move much. Diane's style was more exuberant. Arms, legs, and hair thrashed in time to the loud music, and she sang all the words at the top of her voice. When Harry Nilsson's 'Without You' started to play, Howard pulled her against his chest. She stopped singing so she could feel his heartbeat. This would be *their song*. As she enjoyed a quiet fantasy of dancing at a distant anniversary, her hand dropped to her belly, and she rubbed to transmit this picture of the future to their little baby. This was going to be her best birthday ever.

. . .

Last orders had been called, and Howard came back after a long wait, carrying a beer and a tall tumbler filled with a viscous yellowy liquid. She gave him a quizzical look.

'What's that when it's at home?'

'Double vodka and fresh pineapple juice. It's almost your eighteenth birthday, babe. Time for a big girl's drink.' He handed her the glass, and she clinked it against his beer bottle.

'Cheers, darlin',' she said and took a large gulp, nodding in approval.

'Come on, babe, let's head out before the crowd. There's only a mouthful left. Drink it up. That's my girl.'

Diane swallowed the last drops of the sweet drink and licked her lips. 'That was lovely. I think I'll make that my drink from now on.'

They headed out to the dark clear night. His arm was around her waist and her head leaned on his shoulder on the short walk to the Hillview room.

4 / tucson, arizona, october 1999

day 2

Amanda was wide awake at 5 a.m. It was far too early to think about waking Howard, so once she had showered and dressed, she slipped out of her room and sat on a bench near the front entrance to watch the sunrise. The excitement of yesterday began to bubble up once again. There was a surreal feeling about all this. Sitting in the early morning sunshine, looking out at this foreign landscape, was part of it, but to know she had finally met her father… She began to laugh, then stopped as she felt it shattered the peaceful silence of the morning.

Moments later she sensed someone over to the far right of the motel. She glanced round and saw her father standing at the other corner of the building. He was quietly watching her.

'Howard… Dad, I didn't think you would be awake yet.'

He made no response, simply continued to stare at her.

'I slept like a baby, but I've been awake since about five o'clock. Well, in London that's like lunchtime, so my body just needs to adjust, yes?'

Howard simply looked down at the ground and scuffed his shoe over the gravel.

'Did you sleep okay?' Amanda had walked over beside him, and at last he looked up and answered with a shake of his head.

'No, too much stuff goin' round in my head.'

'Yes, of course, me too, but I just zonked out.' Niggles of doubt stirred in her. 'But good stuff, right? You're still happy to see me, to meet me?'

'Yeah, meeting you isn't the problem.' He forced a smile. 'How about some breakfast? You hungry?'

She nodded and laughed. 'Always!'

His hands were in the pockets of his jeans, so Amanda slipped her arm through his, and they walked across the car park to the twenty-four-hour McDonald's burger bar next door.

The drive-through was busy, but Howard and Amanda were the only customers sitting inside the restaurant. The enticing smell of meat and onions cooking reminded her that she hadn't really eaten in over twelve hours. She finished her food in just a few minutes, while Howard did little more than pick at his. She sipped at the remains of her orange juice and looked at his solemn expression as he stared into his coffee.

'What's wrong, Howard? Is it me? Have I said something? Is it because I called you Dad?'

He shook his head, looked at her, and gently brushed her hair away from her face. 'Call me what you want, although I can't say I earned the title of Dad. You're a beautiful girl, Amanda, and I'm glad you found me, glad I've met you, but…'

'But?'

'But I can't help thinking it might all be a bit too late. You know?'

'That's not my fault…'

'No, I don't mean that. Nothing's your fault. Look, forget it. Let's get out of here. We've still got a ways to go.'

Fifteen minutes later, they were packed and in Howard's truck, heading south again.

The drive was long and tedious. Amanda thought the low, flat desert landscape with shrubs and cacti alien and strangely beautiful. The horizon was surrounded by distant mountains, soft grey and misty. Although they were traveling forwards, they didn't seem to get any closer to the mountains, and she had a vague feeling they were not moving at all. The truck's cabin was comfortable and cool, thanks to the air conditioning, but the change in Howard's mood unsettled her. He was pensive and said very little. She tried to make conversation but eventually fell silent, leaving him to his thoughts.

They stopped at a roadside diner for lunch, where Amanda tried again to get him talking. 'Is this where you grew up? In Arizona?' she asked, hoping that talking about his childhood might spark some interest in hers.

'No, New Mexico.'

'Oh. The only place in New Mexico I've ever heard of is Albuquerque. Were you near there?'

'No, New Mexico is a big, big place. I lived in a dot on the map in the middle of nowhere.'

Amanda waited for him to expand, but only the sound of the spoon on his cup broke the silence. He wouldn't make eye contact with her, no matter how she tried, and yet she was sure he was staring at her when her gaze was elsewhere.

'I guess Tombstone is pretty remote too. Don't you like big cities?'

'Not much.'

She heard a sigh and realised it had come from her. He seemed like a different man from the one who met her at the airport. Was that really only yesterday?

When she started to ask about why he'd joined the marines, he stood abruptly and said it was time to get going. Back in the truck, she made a few more attempts to get him to talk, but his answers were just monosyllables and shrugs. His unhappiness seemed to deepen as each mile passed, and as Amanda felt it infect her, a little seed of resentment began to sprout.

Before meeting face to face, they had exchanged letters and photographs, then progressed to telephone calls and even a tentative and stilted video call, which had gone very slowly.

Amanda had been the first to suggest she might travel to Arizona and meet him. Howard had initially seemed reluctant, but Amanda's eagerness made it hard to object. Jamie had not been at all happy about her planned journey. Over and over again, he'd tried to make her see what a risk she was taking. For weeks, he'd tried to dissuade her from going; then, changing tack, he'd announced that he would go with her, but she'd firmly vetoed this idea.

Meeting her father was something Amanda was determined to do on her own. Deep down she felt there could be an emotional connection between them, and if there was, she wanted to savour it, to finally fit in a piece of a jigsaw that had been missing all her life. It wasn't Jamie's business. It was too fragile, too personal, to share with anyone, even him.

Now here she was. At the airport, she had been elated. Howard had been, too, but something had changed. She sensed his regret. She wanted him to regret missing her childhood and growing up, but she didn't feel the regret was for missing her past. It seemed to have more to do with his.

'Tell me about your home. Tombstone must be such an exciting place to live.' She heard herself wheedling, trying to elicit a response, and felt like she was coaxing a child to join in at games.

'My place isn't fancy. I mean, I don't live like a slob or anything, but, well… it just needs to be functional…' He trailed off. Amanda wasn't sure what he meant by *functional* and imagined something spartan, even cell-like.

'Hey, no worries. I know how it is with bachelors. I don't expect cushions and frilly curtains.' She kept her voice light and humorous, while inside, her disappointment grew. She'd expected to visit his home, hoped he would make her welcome and let her have a glimpse of his everyday life. However, she had brought American currency so she could stay in a motel, and a brand-new credit card, just in case of emergencies. Jamie had insisted. He'd warned her to keep her guard up until she could get to know her father better, and this morning made her realise he had been right.

Signposts alerted them to a rest area a mile ahead. Minutes later Howard indicated and pulled into the desert car park, where a central building had toilets. Outside, along a little dried-up creek bed, were vending machines and tables with benches attached. There was no shade from the heat of the sun, but Amanda stretched, allowed the warmth to seep through to her bones, and shook the tension out of her shoulders and arms.

'Do you need to use the restroom?' Howard asked. She nodded and, feeling a little happier, went off to freshen up.

When she came out only minutes later, Howard was sitting alone at a table beside the creek bed with his head resting on his arms.

'Are you okay?' She put her hand on his shoulder and was alarmed to see his bloodshot eyes as he raised his head.

'Yup, yes, fine... just tired. I guess it's the emotion of the last couple of days catching up with me. Here, I got you some water from the machine.' He handed her the cold bottle he had been resting his forehead on.

Accepting it gratefully, she sat opposite him and looked down at the dusty gully. Scrawny brown sparrows were scratching in the dirt, picking up crumbs of chips and nuts left by the people using the picnic benches.

'Wherever you go in the world, there are sparrows.' She laughed. 'Here we are in the middle of the desert. Temperatures go over a hundred degrees for months on end, and yet they survive.' She found a packet of crackers in her bag and crumbled them from her fingers onto the ground at the edge of the gully. In a flash, a strange, spindly bird ran from nearby scrub, grabbed one of the sparrows in its beak, and was gone as quickly as it had appeared.

'God! Oh God... what happened? What was that?' Amanda jumped to her feet.

'It's a roadrunner,' he said.

'What? It's *real*? Like the cartoon? Like Wile E. Coyote?' Amanda was still on her feet, scanning the gully, trying to rerun the event in her mind. She looked over at Howard, who confirmed this with a brief nod. She shook her head in disbelief. 'I thought it was just a cartoon. It's real, and it eats *sparrows*?' At that Amanda threw back her head and laughed aloud. She continued to laugh until her voice broke into sobs.

'It's too much, Howard. I can't... I can't do this.'

Howard stood and took her hand, bringing her round to sit down with him.

'I know. I don't think I can do this either.' He looked down at their hands as he spoke. 'I want to, but meeting you, thinking about the time I spent in Scotland... well, it was one of the worst experiences of my life, and believe me, there's been stiff competition.'

She looked at him, sitting with his head bowed. He was asking her to have sympathy for his feelings. A picture of her mother flashed into her mind. Left alone and pregnant, putting her own life on one side to bring up her baby... and now this man was the one feeling sorry for himself. She breathed deeply to clear her mind and asked him quietly, 'You said you were happy to find out about me. You seemed pleased… Why did you agree to me coming over here?'

'I was happy… am happy that you're my daughter. Finding out about you… I thought I could be redeemed for the whole terrible… but there were things that happened, things I don't want to remember.'

Amanda took a deep drink from her bottle of water and handed it to Howard. They slowly walked to where the truck was parked, and Howard stood with the keys in his hand.

'What's it to be, Amanda? South to Tombstone, or back northbound?'

5 /
sky harbor airport, phoenix, arizona, october 1999

day 2

THE MAN GRABBED A SECOND HOLDALL FROM THE LUGGAGE carousel. He carried both bags, and his companion opened two passports at the photograph pages as they headed toward the queue to go through customs.

'Switch the phone on. Are there any more messages?'

'Give me a minute, it's connecting to a local service. Yes, there's three messages.'

'What do they say?'

'These are just giving me rates for calls and texts through AT&T. Wait, the third one's from her.'

'Where is she? Is she okay?'

'Yes, they're heading out for Tombstone today. Said she slept well and feels better now.'

'There's more. What's that at the bottom?'

'It's personal. She's just saying she misses me.'

The queue had moved forwards, and they stepped up to the officer at the immigration booth. A solemn official looked at the young black man with his older white companion.

'Are you travelling together?' Both men nodded vigorously. The official's top lip curled a tiny fraction in an almost imperceptible sneer, but he then checked their visas and customs forms, stamped their passports, and waved them through.

'Right. There's the Hertz desk. I'll do the paperwork, and you go and find a map. See if you can figure out how many Motel 6s there are on the road to Tombstone.'

Each looked at the clock overhead and set his watch to local time.

'It's eleven forty in the morning here. By the time we get the car and drive, it'll be' – he looked at his watch again – 'well, about two o'clock.'

He shook his head and looked at his companion. 'You should have told her to text you more than once a bloody day.'

'It says here she sent this message this morning, and the one we got before we left was the night before, so she is texting more than just at night-time.'

'Jeez, changin' planes, changin' time zones, all this back and forward in time is doing my head in.' He began coughing, grabbed a handkerchief from his pocket, and covered his mouth until the coughing subsided. 'Are you still okay to drive? 'Cause I'm shattered.'

The younger man nodded, and they joined the short line at the car rental desk.

By three thirty they were checked into the same Motel 6 where Amanda had spent the previous night. Jamie had changed into his swimming trunks and gone out to swim in the small pool in an effort to stay awake. After an hour, the older man came outside to find him lying in a lounger, soaking up the late afternoon sunshine.

'Hey, what do you think you're doing? You'd better not fall asleep there.'

'I'm not sleeping. The swim woke me up. But while I'm here and all we can do is wait for Amanda to text me, I'm going to soak up as much of this sun as I can. I want to become as black as my ancestors.'

'Aye, well, just remember that half your ancestors were pale blue! You'd better get some lotion on you.' He laughed and tossed a bright yellow tube of sunscreen to the younger man. Just then he noticed a truck drive towards the motel, coming from the highway's northbound exit.

'Jesus! That looks like it could be his truck. Get back here under the shade in case it's her.'

Both men stood behind the wall, which blocked any view from the car park and front entrance to the motel. They heard a car door close, and the younger man carefully leaned just far enough past the edge of the wall to catch a glimpse of Amanda leaving the truck and walking towards the motel reception.

'It is her. She's coming in.' He swiftly pulled his head back and flattened himself against the wall. 'He's driving away. She must be on her own. What do you think happened?'

'I don't know, do I?'

Jamie was biting his lip and shuffling from foot to foot. 'I'm cold here in the shade. Why don't we go in and ask her how she got on?'

'No. We need to wait. See what she says when she texts you.' He reached behind him and lifted a towel from the back of one of the loungers. 'Here, wrap this around you.'

They waited for another five minutes before venturing back to their room.

6 /
glasgow, scotland, october 1972

As they climbed uphill from Jo-Jo's, Howard paused at the car to collect the carrier bag from the back seat before carefully locking it again. This was not the best of neighbourhoods, and he couldn't run the risk of Bill's car being stolen, although in truth, it would be the anger of his friend's wife that would be hardest to face.

Using the bigger of the two keys on the fob, Diane opened the front door of the B&B and searched the walls for a light switch without success. A bright street lamp was their only illumination. There was a lot of giggling and shushing as they entered the dark lobby and gingerly climbed the three stairs to the corridor. Diane bumped against walls and counted the numbers on the doors as she passed them.

'Four, five... Here we are, Howard. Number six, our little room.' As she turned the key, the heavy wooden fob knocked against the door. Howard put his finger to her lips, telling her to be quiet.

'What? We paid for the room. Why do we need to be quiet?' She stood in front of the unlocked door, blocking his way in. 'Carry me over the threshold, Howard, please?'

Just One Little Pill

'Could we just get inside, Diane? With the beer and dancing, I can barely carry myself. Anyway, I need to piss. Now, move, will you?'

Diane backed into the room, pouting her bottom lip in a show of petulance.

Howard closed the door and looked around the room. 'Where's the john?'

'We passed it, it's down at the end of the hallway.'

'What? We need to share the toilet?' Howard had not expected the facilities to be outside the room. He looked at their shabby surroundings: a low double bed with two flat pillows and a purple nylon quilted spread; a small rug on the linoleum floor with a faded red-and-grey pattern. A bedside cabinet and a scarred wooden wardrobe almost completed the ensemble. There in the corner of the room was the one saving grace: a washstand, pink and chipped but with running water.

'You go first, Howard; I'll go once you come back.'

'What?' He shook himself from stocktaking.

'The bathroom. You go first.'

Once he had left, Diane shivered with excitement at the thought of what was to come. She took a compact from her handbag and tidied her lipstick, rubbed her teeth with her finger, and breathed into her hand to check her breath. She tried to hang her coat in the wardrobe, but there were no hangers, so she folded it and placed it inside on the floor. As Howard came back, she spun round and watched him lock the door. In two steps, she was in his arms, kissing his lips while massaging the front of his trousers with her hand. He reached behind her neck and untied her dress. Holding a breast in each hand, he bent his head and began to bite and suck at the tender skin.

Diane lifted his face to hers and kissed him, then manoeuvred herself to pull down the zip at the side of her dress before beginning to unbuckle his belt. As her dress fell to the floor, she laughed at the shock on his face, thinking it was surprise at her nakedness. She soon realised it was something else and followed his gaze to see blood trickling down her leg.

'No! No, it can't be. The baby! Oh, Howard, our baby! It can't be my period, not now, not after all this time.' She picked up her dress and held it in front of her, seeing his face, tight and frozen in shock. The sound of her crying stirred him into action. He pushed the nylon cover off the bed and handed her the thin sheet.

'Look, take this so you can go to the bathroom and get cleaned up. Don't worry, it'll be fine.'

She wrapped it around herself like a toga, throwing the end over her shoulder. Still quietly sobbing, she opened the door a few inches, checked no one was in the hallway to witness her embarrassment, and looked back at Howard. He nodded, gripped the handle, and closed it behind her without a sound.

Leaning back against the door, he shut his eyes and raged inwardly. He'd been told the pill should start to work in around two hours. His sketchy instructions had also been to add it to a strong drink that would disguise the taste and prevent any sediment from being noticed.

The US military knew situations like this happened. Their fighting forces went the world over. Young men were posted away from home just as they reach their sexual peak. Their boys needed options, and supplying rubber johnnies wasn't going to be enough. This drug was a last resort, unrefined and largely untested, but it worked. Nothing official, just a whisper: You got a girl in trouble? That happened to Joe or Chuck or Hank a while back. Go see the sarge, he'll know what to do.

This time it had been Bill Lundahl, and he knew exactly what to do. Christ, it certainly wasn't the first time. Howard felt a wave of relief when Bill told him it could be sorted. There were barely two months left before he would be posted back to the States, and he wasn't going to get stuck in this damn place because of a pregnant girlfriend.

Fuck! Two hours, they'd said. It wasn't even an hour since she'd had that drink. No way would he go inside her, but she could have managed a blow job before anything started. Fuck! Fuck! Fuck! He didn't want to deal with any of this stuff. There should have been a bathroom in the room; she could have sorted herself out in there. *Oh man, why does all this crap happen to me?*

He took the paper towels from the carrier bag he'd brought with him, made his way along to the bathroom, and knocked quietly on the door. When she finally answered, he had to look down, as she seemed to be bent over and still quietly weeping.

'I'm sorry, so sorry. I want to go home, Howard. Please take me home.'

The naked bulb cast a dim light in the bathroom, but his stomach turned at the bloody mess it revealed. 'Sure, just get cleaned up and come back to the bedroom. Here's some paper towels I found beside the washstand. Use these and bring all the stained stuff back to the room. It'll be all right. Don't worry, Diane.'

'I feel terrible, Howard. I've never had cramps like this in my life.'

'I know, I know. Babe, these things happen. You'll be okay.'

Diane nodded, but he'd turned and headed back along the hall.

Every time she felt she could walk back to the bedroom, cramps doubled her over. Naked and bloody, she crouched in the cold grey bath where clumps of strangers' hair clogged the drain. She turned the tap marked *HOT* to try to wash the steady trickle of blood away. Cold water spluttered out and diluted the blood, spreading it in a greasy film. Feeling frightened and exposed, she held on to the side of the bath and tried to climb out. A fierce pain brought her back to her knees, and she sensed herself pushing and pressing down against her abdomen. Her eyes were closed tight, and the muscles of her neck felt like ropes as she strained and groaned with the effort. Once the pain began to ease, she opened her eyes. There was a dark, bloody clot stuck on top of the drain. A trail of smaller clots led back to her thighs. She put a shaking hand between her legs, and her fingers touched something warm hanging there. Diane's fear turned to panic, and she called out for Howard between sobs and screams.

'Open the door, Diane. Shh, shh, shh. Someone will hear you. Open the door, let me in.' He rapped the door urgently, then realised it was unlocked. Slipping inside, he took care to lock the door behind him.

There was blood on the toilet seat and spotted along the floor. Stained paper towels were scrunched in a pile by the bath. The sight of Diane kneeling in the pool of blood brought a shaft of fear to his insides, and his first instinct was to turn and get as far away as possible. He had not imagined this carnage. Christ, it was really only a late period. She should have gotten rid of it in the toilet and wiped up any overspill with the towels, but this…

He exhaled deeply and snapped into action. Handing her the sheet, he told her, 'Come on. Up you get. Here, wrap yourself in this. Stand up, right, take my hand, and get out of the bath. Stand here.'

Diane followed his orders, quietly sobbing as she watched him scoop up the paper towels to give the floor a cursory wipe before dropping them into the small metal waste bin. He thrust his hand into the bath's drain, clutching at the warm, slippery clot. It took two attempts before he managed to lift everything and drop it into the paper-filled bin. His fingers worked around the bars in the drain to pull and lift out the tangled web of hair, allowing the water to drain away. Still holding the bin, he first checked the hallway was clear, then gently supported Diane as they made their way along to the bedroom.

'Lie down. Just take it easy while I clean up a bit. Okay?'

'Okay, but I want to go home. Please take me home…' Her teeth chattered, and her whole body was shaking. 'Please… I want … my mu… mum.'

Howard looked around the bedroom, checking to see if there was anything more he could take away. He picked up the lilac dress from where it had been dropped.

'Here, put your dress and coat on. You'll feel warmer. Give me that sheet, and I'll get rid of that too.' He helped her into her clothes, then pushed the soiled sheet into the carrier bag and lifted it along with the bin and its bloodied contents. 'Stay here. I'm going to get rid of this stuff. I won't be long. Okay?'

'Okay, but… but you'll come back, Howard, won't you?' Her voice dropped to a husky whisper. 'You'll come and take me home.'

'Yeah, sure, babe. I won't be long.'

Carrying his bloody bundle, he slipped quietly out the room. As he tiptoed along the hall, he heard Diane cry out as contractions once again gripped her body. With a burst of speed, he reached the front door and ran out onto the dark streets.

He kept running all the way to the car and pushed the sodden waste into the trunk, then went straight to the driver's door and slid the key in the lock. His first instinct was to get in the car and drive. Leave, just go and put some distance between himself and all that was happening in room six. Minutes passed before he could push away the urge to run.

It wasn't his fault. Not his fault she got pregnant. It was all her doing, stupid bitch. Bill had told him to give her that pill; he'd said it would sort her out. No way had he thought it was going to be anything like this. Christ! How did he get into a mess like this? Aw, fuck, it would just get worse if he left her there. Better get her to a doc, then get the hell out of it, out of it all.

Then he realised he didn't have a key for the front entrance. Heart racing, he ran back and started pounding on the door. The home-made *Vacenties* sign caught his eye, and he wondered if there were any other occupants. They had made a good deal of noise despite his efforts. Maybe they were the only ones staying there, and Diane certainly couldn't come and let him in.

Think, man! You're a marine, God damn it! You've trained for worse situations than this. Don't let a locked fucking door beat you – ACT!

Looking around, he found a good-sized rock and tapped it twice against the glass panel beside the lock. On the third hit, he smashed it with force, pulling back quickly before his hand followed through. The glass crashed to the floor, and he carefully put his hand through and opened the door.

At that moment, he heard a man shout.

'What the fuck? Stop it, for fuck's sake. Don't dae that! I'm callin' the polis!'

The disembodied voice came closer, attached to a scrawny man in a vest with unfastened trousers clutched to his waist. Howard guessed it must be the boarding house's desk clerk and threw a quick explanation to him.

'I got locked out. My girlfriend is very ill. Room six.'

Without waiting for any reaction, Howard ran upstairs two at a time. The little man followed, shuffling step by step, fastening his trousers as he went.

. . .

Diane lay curled on the bed. Howard stroked her face, but she barely responded. He lifted her easily from the bed. Her dress slopped out from under her maxi coat. Dark and wet, it fell against him, clinging to his trousers. As he turned to leave, the old man reached the door of the room.

'Oh, Christ! Is she dead?'

'No,' said Howard, 'but I need to get her to the hospital.'

The old man looked from Diane to the turmoil visible through the doorway. His hand covered his toothless mouth.

'What did you do to her? What a mess! Get out a' here. I'm no havin' the polis back again.'

The man stepped into the room and looked around. He spotted Diane's handbag on the floor and nudged it with his foot until it was out of sight under the bed. Howard was already halfway down the stairs.

'Where's the nearest A & E?'

'What's an A & E? She's needin' to go to Casualty. Have you got a car?'

'Yes, but I don't know where the hospital is from here.'

'The Royal is only five minutes away.'

'Right, stay here with her till I bring the car round.' He lay her gently on the hall floor, avoiding the broken glass.

'Eh, wait a fuckin' minute, pal! You're no just leavin' her here an' leavin' me to clean up your bloody mess!'

'Shut up, asshole. I can't carry her to the car. I'll need to drive it round here.'

'Aye, well, hurry up then. She's in a bad way.'

Howard was back with the Mini in less than five minutes, and after opening the passenger door, he reached for his wallet and took out a five-pound note.

'Hey, buddy, sorry about the blood and all. This should cover the clean-up.'

The man snatched it from his hand.

'Cover it, my arse! C'mon, pal, give!' His bony little hand stretched out to Howard, fingers beckoning for more cash. Howard took his one remaining five-pound note and put it in the man's outstretched palm, then tightly gripped the hand between his own strong brown ones.

'This is for all your trouble, but we were never here. You never saw me or her. The mess that needs cleaning up is from some hooker who had a bad night with a john. Understand?'

Howard was almost nose to nose with the scowling old face, and seeing the grudging nod of acceptance, he released his grip. The man pulled his hands away with the second note held tightly in his fist.

'Hold the door,' ordered Howard, who carried an unconscious Diane to the car and placed her gently in the seat. He lifted her trailing dress and coat hem, placed them inside, and closed the door as quietly as he dared. Turning back to the man, he demanded directions to the hospital.

'Do a U-turn, go straight along to the lights, turn right, and head down the hill till the next lights. You'll see the Royal across the road. Ye cannae miss it.'

Howard nodded, turned the ignition key, and spun the car off into the night.

Glasgow's Royal Infirmary was easy to find in the small hours of a Saturday morning. Even if there was no light-flashing ambulance to follow, the building itself loomed large and imposing, high on the city's north side. Dark, durable stone was stained with more than a century of smoke and soot. The huge iron gates stood open wide, and three ambulances were parked in the receiving area, where bright yellow lights spilled out of the main doors and all the ground floor windows.

Diane gave a soft groan, the first sound he'd heard from her throughout the short journey.

'Don't worry. We're at the hospital, Diane. You'll be all right now.'

'Mum, please… Mum…' She gave a sob and stopped talking.

Howard barely heard her whispered plea. He drove the Mini straight into the receiving area, swinging it tight to the kerb behind the first ambulance. He jumped out, shouting and running around to Diane's side of the car.

'Help! I've got an injured girl here. She's in a bad way. I need a hand here!'

Howard's deep voice resonated across the space and into the reception area. Suddenly three, four, five people were running toward him. One grabbed a wheelchair, and two young nurses pushed a trolley with a stretcher on top.

Two ambulance men lifted Diane from the car seat and lay her on her side on the stretcher. A blue cellular blanket was pulled over her and a strap fastened around to prevent a fall. This was completed in seconds, and they disappeared into the bright reception and off down a corridor.

One young nurse stayed with Howard.

'Are you hurt? Where are you bleeding from?' she asked him.

'No, no, that's not mine. It's her blood, I'm not injured.'

'You're sure? Okay. Well, just tell me what happened.'

He looked at her. He didn't understand what she was asking at first. Slowly he realised what a dangerous situation he had put himself in by bringing Diane to hospital.

'No, I don't know her. I'd never seen her before…' He looked around, desperate to find some reason for delivering a blood-soaked girl to hospital. 'I was driving… I saw her waving from a bus stop. She was hanging on to the pole. I could see something was very wrong, but…'

Howard began to shake. The young nurse reached out and covered his hand with hers.

'You're in shock.' She patted his hand. Placing an arm around his back, she guided him into the hospital and over to a seat beside an empty bed. With a quick swish, she pulled the curtain around; then she leaned in.

'You stay there and relax… Sorry, what's your name?'

'How… Ah, Bill. Bill Lund… London. Bill London.'

'Well, Bill, you did the right thing, bringing her here. I'll get you some sweet hot tea, then you can tell me what you know.'

With that, she left him sitting on a hard green chair, surrounded by a pink swirly curtain, in a bleak, ancient hospital. He was half a world away from where he belonged, and he began to cry.

7 /
the aftermath

Although Bill Lundahl was an officer of the US Navy, he was attached to the marines to look after their welfare. He was also their dealer. What he supplied were mainly narcotics and amphetamines from the pharmacy. Phantom prescriptions at the base were easy to get hold of. Stocks were shipped over in vast quantities from the States, and no one was required to keep terribly stringent records of how they were dispensed or whom to. Of course, the naval medics demanded their share of the profits, but that still left plenty for Bill to make his life as comfortable as possible. A brand-new Mini for him and many, many driving lessons for his wife, Betty, were a couple of consolations of this posting. Where was the harm? After all, they weren't about to go to war. This was an allied country where the main job was just to be a presence.

Betty feigned ignorance of Bill's illicit earnings but happily boasted about her driving abilities and took every opportunity to coast around in her status symbol, fully coiffured and as visible as possible. Saturday-morning shopping at the town's biggest supermarket was a good way to see and be seen. Bill was on duty at the base, but she had her own set of car keys.

Lorraine Queen

She'd been mildly annoyed to see Howard Odoms had left their Mini at the kerbside instead of in the driveway of their smart semi-detached home. He wasn't a favourite of Betty's. He wasn't even navy, just one of those marines. Everyone knew they were all a bunch of thickos. That's why the darkies joined. They didn't have the same brains as white people. Most of them could barely read and write, but they were fast. You had to give them that: fast, strong, and did what they were told. She'd been upset with Bill for letting Odoms borrow her lovely Mini, anyway, and now he hadn't even had the courtesy to put it back in the right place. Look at the state he'd left it in too! Dirty and spattered with mud. They always kept it shining and spotless. She would make sure Bill took it to the car wash as soon as he got home. As she sat in the driver's seat, her nose crinkled at the unfamiliar smell inside. She shuddered with distaste at the thought of what it might be. *You're a dirty bastard, Howard Odoms,* she thought. *That will be the last time you ever get to use this car. I'll make bloody sure of it.*

Having your shopping packed and taken out to your car by a smart young man was such a civilised service, and Betty always made full use of it.

'The new Mini at the end,' she had declared for all to hear and beckoned imperiously for the boy to follow her. Handbag in the crook of her left arm, she unlocked the boot with her right hand. She lifted it open and was about to step to the side and allow the boy access with the trolley. At the sight of the contents, she gasped and quickly slammed it closed. The trolley boy was looking at her, so she took a moment to help regain her composure.

'Better put it in the back seat this week. My husband… ehm… he must have had a flat tyre, and… well… look, just put it on the back seat, will you?' She pushed a fifty-pence coin into his hand

and looked hard at the boot again before getting in the car and slowly and carefully driving home.

Betty's fury was bordering on the uncontainable, dampened only by the knowledge that Bill wouldn't be within range for at least another couple of hours. Then, just before she turned in to her driveway, she saw Howard Odoms pacing on the opposite side of the street.

She parked and switched off the ignition, watching Howard's approach in the rear-view mirror.

She curled her lip in distaste at the sight. How could Marion Barr have cheapened herself with him? She had always acted like she was a cut above the rest of them. Then she ended up going with this nig-nog, and to crown it all, he went and dumped her! Unbelievable! No wonder she left, stupid cow. No man here would ever touch her after that. Why Bill was still on friendly terms with him, she'd never know, and even less why he would be stupid enough to lend him their beautiful car.

'Oh, Howard.' She took pains to keep her voice light. 'Just the man I wanted to see. Give me a hand into the house with these groceries, will you?'

'Sure.' Howard ground out his cigarette under the toe of his boot and held out his hands to receive the carrier bags.

Betty loaded three bulging carriers into his hands.

'Oh, wait, there's more in the boot.' She pursed her lips and looked him in the eyes. 'Shall we come back for them later?'

Howard looked at his shoes and followed her into the house.

'What the hell did you do?' Betty rasped out the words, fighting to control her anger from being released loudly enough for neighbours to hear. She looked at him standing in her kitchen with his arms still full of her shopping. She didn't wait for an answer. 'How dare you, how bloody *dare* you, use our car for your filthy, sordid affairs? It's gone too far this time. I saw what you left in the boot. The grocery boy at Safeway nearly saw it too!' She heard her own voice and immediately lowered her volume. 'What happened? No! Don't tell me. I don't want involved. Have you still got Bill's keys?'

Howard nodded without meeting her gaze.

'Well, get it out of here. Dispose of the contents of the boot, *then* get it cleaned and polished, inside and out. Do you hear me?'

Again, he nodded dumbly. He turned, placed the carrier bags on the kitchen dresser, and left without looking back.

Betty heard the car engine start up and watched as he reversed out of her driveway and drove away.

Bill wasn't prepared for the tirade his wife unleashed that afternoon. He knew when Betty was truly in a rage: her grandiose manner peeled away and allowed her rasping, aggressive dialect full throttle.

'Ur you aff yer heid? Whit the hell wir ye thinkin', gein' that wee shite oor Mini? Huv ye seen the state he left it in? The stuff in the boot nearly made me boak.'

Clearly, she was angry about something, but in full flow her words were unintelligible. He remained calm and unmoved. He had more to worry about than some incident at Safeway. He held the palm of his hand up and shook his head. 'Whatever's got you all worked up, you need to stop and listen. I've just had a call from a contact of mine in Glasgow. Something's happened. Something terrible.'

Betty paused. She couldn't ask him what he meant, as her own fury had been revving for hours, and the words now crashed and jammed in her throat. Bill continued unprompted.

'A girl died. Diane… Diane Barr, Howard's girlfriend, she's dead.' He pushed past his wife and reached into one cupboard for a glass and another for a bottle of bourbon. Placing both on the counter, he tightened his grip on the bottles and hung his head. Without looking at her, he spoke in slow deliberate words.

'I've put things in motion, called in a few favours. We're going to the States. I'm getting posted back home. It'll be about three weeks till I go. You and the kids will follow… as soon as possible.'

Her wrathful words sputtered and slid away. She carefully watched her husband, trying to connect his extraordinary statements. This morning's bloody discovery pushed back to her consciousness, and fear smothered the embers of her rage.

What the hell was he supposed to do with the bloody stuff? Where could he put it? Jesusfuckinchrist, man. Bill Lundahl was responsible for this; he should be around to help get him out of it. All night he'd raged at his misfortune. He'd been dragged into that godawful mess by the people he'd cared for most. Lundahl was supposed to be his friend, he'd said he could fix things, but all he'd done was stick him right in the middle of a crock of shit. And Diane, she'd said she loved him. Then she went and lied, got herself pregnant, then lied, lied, lied. Christ, she wasn't lying now, poor bitch. She was lucky he'd been smart enough to get her to hospital so fast. Yeah, think fast, act fast: all that training paid off in a crisis. Those medics would have sorted her out.

He continued to drive and then realised he was almost out of gas. He could see the Shell sign up ahead, and as he pulled in, an idea struck him. He went into the forecourt and lifted a jerry can, half filling it with petrol before putting another two pounds' worth into the Mini's tank.

He set the can in the passenger footwell, then drove off the Kilbride Road onto a track he knew led to the reservoir. Once he was a good three miles into wild countryside, he stopped and switched off the engine.

After opening the trunk of the car, he lifted out the metal bin containing the stained sheet and paper towels. The dried blood was dark and accusing. With his fingertips, he began pulling the bed sheet out, allowing the paper towels to fall onto the grass at his feet. He would need to let air get in under the sheet to make sure it fully caught alight; then he could add the paper to the blaze. As the sheet unfolded, he saw something else fall. It rolled down the fabric and landed gently beside the toe of his right shoe.

He stared, pulling his foot back so it lay alone on the soft grass. Diane had just told him last week that she was a bit late. There should only have been a little blob of cells. He knelt and looked at the mass more closely. He could see fingers. Tiny white fingers on a tiny white hand.

Blood pounded at his temples. He knelt in the mud and reached his right hand towards the bloodstained mass but let it hover without touching. His hand began to tremble. He tried to swallow, but bitter acid filled his mouth, and he fell to the side, retching, crying, and clutching at handfuls of cold, wet grass and mud. Reaching for comfort; finding none.

8 /
tucson, arizona, october 1999

day 3

AMANDA WOKE UP IN THE SAME MOTEL ROOM AS BEFORE, HAVING hardly slept. She found herself getting more used to sending texts, and instead of the briefest of messages, she told Jamie about seeing a roadrunner and how tired she was feeling, putting the latter down to the time difference.

When Howard dropped her off yesterday, they had agreed a step back was needed to let emotions cool down. He had gone home to Tombstone after they made vague arrangements to meet and go for lunch today. Amanda was not at all confident he would come. Indeed, she wondered if she would ever see him again. Strangely, after all the effort of tracing him, all the longing to find the man who'd fathered her, she found herself thinking it might be better to just let him go.

She went to reception, poured a lukewarm coffee, and sat with a magazine. Just in case, she told herself. She didn't want to be the one who made their separation final. She heard someone coughing in the corridor behind her, and a shiver went down her spine. Her mother always said it was a sign someone had walked over your grave, and the very thought of her mother sent another shiver through her.

Promptly at one thirty, Howard appeared in the motel reception, just as he had said he would. She really hadn't expected to see him, today or any other day. That thought had given her a deep sense of loss. Yet here he was, and a little flicker of hope was reignited. Perhaps there was a possibility of building a relationship with him.

He didn't smile, but he no longer had the exhausted, defeated look of the previous afternoon. He walked over and stood directly in front of her, hands by his side, as if at attention.

'Could we start again, please? Maybe not from the beginning, but I've had a long, hard look at how I behaved yesterday, and I know I need to be… more up front, more honest about… Dunoon and why I'm so reluctant to let that time in my life resurface.'

Amanda nodded, and he led the way out to his truck.

'Did you sleep any better last night?' she asked him as they set off.

'No, not really. I dozed off a few times, I guess. Too much going around in my head.'

'I know, me too. I hadn't had much to eat and came down to reception about three o'clock this morning and bought some chocolate and crisps from the vending machines.'

He turned to look over at her, shaking his head and frowning in mock seriousness. 'Not very nutritious, young lady.'

Smiling, she replied in the same vein. 'No, Father. I'll try to do better in future.'

'Are you hungry now? Do you want to get some lunch before we head down to Tombstone?'

'Yes, sure, that would be good. I had a snack earlier, but I can always eat.'

• • •

They drove to a large mall, where he parked in the vast car park and led her into a diner called the Lasso Inn. There were a few customers having a late lunch, and the hostess seated them in a booth beside the window. It gave a clear view of the mall and the afternoon shoppers. Amanda was puzzled at the sight of several clusters of elderly people striding past the window, especially when they came back into view for a third time.

Howard laughed when he saw her expression. 'They're mall walkers.' He went on to explain. 'For about four months of the year, it's far too hot here to walk outside, so to be sure they get enough daily exercise, lots of people come into the air-conditioned mall to walk. They often buddy up, so it can be a pretty sociable time too. Plus, of course, it's a heck of a lot cheaper than joining a gym!'

'Oh, that makes sense.' She smiled and nodded. 'Folk at home should try that, but in London it would be to keep out of the rain.'

'Yeah, I remember that rain. I don't know why you Brits don't have webbed feet.'

They ordered lunch and throughout the meal kept the conversation light and general. She told him about her flight and even about the awful stink the man had left in the airplane toilet. He told her about the different states he'd lived in and that the one thing they all had in common was plenty of sunshine, which was one of his reasons for settling here in Arizona.

While they were drinking their coffee, Amanda looked up at him questioningly. He took a deep breath and spread out his hands. 'Okay, Amanda, cards on the table.'

'Only if you're ready. I didn't come all this way to make you uncomfortable.'

'I know. You just wanted to fill in the blanks, meet the father you'd never known. But you always knew you had a father. I didn't know I had a daughter.'

She nodded, and they both fell silent for a few moments to absorb the truth of his words.

Amanda was first to break the silence. 'I didn't know if you were still alive or if there was something terrible about you that made my mum keep us a secret from each other.'

'Sometimes things happen, Amanda. You don't have to be a terrible person to have bad… even really bad things happen to you.'

'You're scaring me, Howa… Dad.'

He stared into his coffee cup and told her how at five years old, he had found himself living in New Mexico with his grandmother. She was old, tired, and struggling to survive. The last thing she had wanted was a grandkid to look after, especially one from her deadbeat son. He'd left the little town ten years earlier when his then girlfriend told him she was pregnant, and then he'd shown up out of nowhere, and with another son in tow.

'That was me. He made all kinds of promises about sending money to her once he was working, which he never did, of course. That was the last any of us ever saw of him, and the worst thing was, he disappeared without making any effort to meet his older son.'

Amanda reached across and touched his arm.

He grimaced and sighed before he continued. 'It's funny how things turn out sometimes, isn't it? I was five when I found out I had a brother. I lost my father and found a brother all in one week!' He smiled with such warmth that Amanda couldn't help smiling back.

'A kind of bad-news-good-news thing, I guess,' she said, and they laughed together. 'Were you close? Your brother and you?'

Howard nodded. Amanda sensed there was more to come and waited until he was ready to continue. The waitress refilled their coffees, and Howard stretched his long fingers around his cup, once again staring into the dark liquid.

'Grandma kept a roof over my head and fed me, but Thomas raised me.'

'What a great brother to have, and of course he'll be my uncle! Do you think I can meet him?'

He bowed his head. 'No. He was killed in Vietnam.'

Amanda closed her eyes and pressed her lips together as if she could pull the words back inside. Instead of this conversation taking the emotion down a notch, his grief was resurfacing. She reached over and tried to hold his hand, but he lifted the cup to his lips in a clear effort to avoid contact. She was rarely at a loss for words, but right now she floundered. Her usual instinct in a difficult situation was to try to lift the mood, but Howard had withdrawn, once again retreating into his own thoughts.

A few moments stretched past; then Howard looked at her with a shrug.

'He was a marine. That's why I joined. I wanted to be like him. He was my hero from the first day we met.'

Howard told her the basic training undergone by the marine corps in America was the longest and toughest of any of the military branches. The physical demands were extraordinary. Each marine spent twelve gruelling weeks pushing their endurance beyond anything they imagined they could achieve. However, the psychological transformation was often even more profound. They needed to be part of a collective, to erase individuality, and when commanded, to respond immediately and unquestioningly. Semper fidelis – always faithful – but to the marine corps, the few, the proud.

He had struggled to complete his basic training but felt his brother's presence urging him on. It had been an effort for him to fit in, to be accepted, but he dug deep and focused on becoming one of the brotherhood, just as Thomas had been. He needed to go to war, to kill those who had taken his brother from him. Then, in

1969, just as Howard was ready to graduate, Nixon announced the beginning of troop withdrawal from Vietnam.

Howard lifted his head and looked Amanda straight in the eyes. Gone was the self-pitying tone. His jaw tightened, and anger strengthened his voice.

'Scotland wasn't where I wanted to go. None of us did. We'd trained for action, fast and furious response. Arriving in a sleepy backwater just didn't cut it.'

Rising abruptly, Howard called the waitress and settled the check. He leaned over and roughly took Amanda by the elbow, guiding her towards the door.

'Come on, let's walk.' His voice was harsh and commanding.

He opened the door and walked through, leaving Amanda to follow. With long brisk strides and arms swinging, he made his way through the centre of the mall. Not even a backward glance to make sure Amanda was following him. Without realising she was mimicking her father, Amanda's jaw tightened, and indignation fuelled her. In moments, she'd caught up with him and grabbed his shoulder.

'Don't you dare stamp off in a sulk and leave me to run behind like a pet dog! You've done nothing but wallow in self-pity and use me as your audience for all your past grievances – when none of them were my fault. I came thousands of miles to meet the man who fathered me, to see if there's any… I don't know… connection between us, any future.'

Howard scowled and opened his mouth to speak, but Amanda pointed her finger to silence him. She shook her head and continued.

'What have you asked me about my life? Why did you encourage me to come all this way? All you've done is sound off about how hard done by you've been. Maybe that's why my mum never told me who you were. Perhaps she realised what a self-centred, selfish man you were, even then.'

'No! No, that's the point. I wasn't a man, I was a boy. A twenty-year-old kid shipped off to a shithole to do a *nothing* job.'

'And that's my fault?'

Howard didn't say anything, just stared at her.

'Right, that's it.' Amanda looked around to determine where the car park might be. 'Let's get the truck and get out of here. I've had enough.'

'Suits me,' Howard muttered under his breath. He pointed to the exit at the farthest end of the mall, and they walked in silence.

Amanda bit down on her fury during the short journey back to the motel. She should have listened to Jamie. What a waste. All this time and money with nothing but bitter disappointment to show for it. Worse still, now that she knew what a shit he was, she couldn't even enjoy the fantasies of having him be a loving family man who would welcome her into his life.

She expected Howard to drop her at the main door of the motel and was surprised when he drew into a parking space. Lifting the door handle, she prepared to leave, fully intending to slam the truck door behind her as a final close to their stunted relationship.

'Wait.' Howard's voice was even and calm. 'I thought we could take the tour of Davis Air Force Base tomorrow. I worked there once, a while back. What time do you want me to pick you up?'

'What?' She was so taken aback, it came out in a shaky falsetto. She turned to look at his face to see if he was serious or had indeed taken leave of his senses. His expression made her think it was the latter.

'I'm trying here. Come on, Amanda, don't be so quick to strike me out.'

'Oh… what… you're unbelievable, do you know that?'

'I do know that, Amanda.' He smiled. 'When you tore me a new one back at the mall, I realised you're a chip off the old block. You're *my* daughter.' He threw his head back and laughed with such abandon that Amanda got caught up and began laughing too.

9 /
glasgow, scotland, december 1972

Marion looked down at her sleeping baby, feeling each breath comfort her. Those dark eyelashes curled up from her soft, pudgy little cheeks. A warm flood of emotion spread through her. Her beautiful girl. The greatest achievement of her life and the best thing Dunoon had ever given her. She had to hold on to that knowledge. What lay at the end of this long journey would be hellish, she knew that, but it couldn't be put off any longer.

Diane hadn't answered her first letter. That wasn't surprising. It was a lot for a young girl to come to terms with, so she'd persevered and sent another two letters before finally deciding to telephone. Mrs Bissell told her what had happened.

She'd picked up the phone to call Davy and Ina at least a dozen times. Running through in her head what she would say, how she could start. An apology, of course, but it was so weak, so inadequate. Sheila had been a great help, a real pal. She'd offered to watch Amanda so she could travel to Glasgow and speak to her brother and sister-in-law face to face, but Marion couldn't bear to be separated from her baby. She was still nursing her and didn't want to put her onto bottles yet, she told her friend. The truth was that holding Amanda gave her strength.

Lorraine Queen

The taxi stopped outside the familiar close in Jameston Road. The driver lifted her bags onto the pavement and helped her out of the cab. Marion paid him, adding a ten-pence tip, and stood looking up at the first floor. White net curtains criss-crossed all three panes of the big bay window, and a vase of orange plastic chrysanthemums sat in the centre. She had a powerful temptation to turn and take the taxi back to the station, but she knew that this time, there was no running away. With the baby safely cradled in her sling around the front of Marion's body, she lifted the navy pram bag with all Amanda's paraphernalia and kissed her head before standing at the entrance of the close, gathering all the courage she possessed.

Inside, Davy poured another two large measures of whisky, adding a token splash of water before handing one to his wife. Ina sat in the chair beside the electric fire, watching the hypnotic flicker of the red bulb below the dusty plastic coals. The ring of the doorbell brought her round from her thoughts, and she narrowed her eyes at her husband.

'Who's that?'

'Don't know. I'll go and see.'

He placed his glass on the mantelpiece, walked to the hall, and opened the heavy wooden door. Marion stood in front of him quietly, stroking the baby. Davy shook his head at her. He motioned for her to leave with the back of his hand and mouthed the word *go*.

'Who is it, Davy?'

'Nobody, hen. They've got the wrong house.' He began to close the door, but Marion put her hand out and stopped him.

'Ina, it's me. It's Marion…'

Davy closed his eyes and hung his head in defeat. He opened the door so Marion could step inside.

As Marion entered the kitchen, Ina rose from the fireside chair and took a step towards her. 'Oh, it's you, is it? Ah wondered when you'd finally show your face.'

'I didn't know, Ina. I only found out last week. I'm sorry.' She turned to her brother. 'I'm so sorry. I still can't… Ina, I'm sorry. Please, please believe me. I didn't know.'

'You left her. You left… left ma lassie to die. She was only in Dunoon because of you.' Ina stepped towards Marion, but Davy quickly got between the two women.

'Right, hear her out, Ina. It must've taken a lot for her to come here, an' it looks as though she's had… well, maybe she's been through stuff as well.' He motioned with his head towards the sleeping infant.

'Well, she's fuckin' lucky she's no' been through what I've been through.' Ina turned back to the fireside, lifted the whisky glass, and finished the rest of the drink in one gulp. 'She walks in here wi' a baby an' we're supposed to say… what? *Oh, come in an' let's have a wee catch-up.* Well, I don't bloody think so!'

Marion let her brother take the baby gently from her. He laid her on the bed in the recess, expertly slipped off the sling, and turned her, still sleeping, onto her side. Only then did Amanda's dark skin colour register with him, and he looked over to see if his wife had noticed. Standing up, he held his arms open to Marion, and she fell against him. She exhaled with a whimper and sobbed quietly onto her big brother's chest. Ina tutted and shuddered. Then, sitting back in her chair, she wrapped her arms around herself so tightly she could barely breathe.

After a few moments, Marion let go of Davy and rubbed her eyes. 'She's due her next feed soon. I'd better go and splash my face.' She gave him a weak smile, and as she left the room, Ina rose and followed her.

'It's all right for you, isn't it? You've got *your* wee girl. My wee girl's gone, bleedin' to death in a cold hospital, losing *her* baby!'

Ina's voice was a low, rasping whisper. She punctuated her words with a pounding fist on her own chest. 'You were supposed to keep an eye on her. Make sure she was okay. *Oh, she'll be fine, Ina. Don't worry, Ina, I'll keep her out of trouble!*' Her voice broke in a sob. 'You couldn't even keep yourself out of trouble!'

'Right, come on now, Ina. It doesn't help anyone for you to get all worked up again. Come on.' Davy steered his wife back into the kitchen.

Marion sat on the fireside chair opposite Ina and looked down at Amanda as the baby suckled, her big dark eyes watching her. Marion had spent many nights in this room. When Diane was little, she'd babysit to let her brother and sister-in-law have a night out. She had even made this her home for a few months after their mother passed away, before deciding to go to Dunoon to work and, if she was honest, to have some fun with the Americans posted there. A mixture of cigarette smoke and all the usual cooking smells of the big kitchen enveloped her, but there was no comfort in their familiarity now.

Davy busied himself in the tiny scullery making tea, careful to avoid seeing his sister's breast. Ina finished another whisky. Marion glanced at her sister-in-law, scared to make eye contact and invite another tirade. She could feel Ina's resentment pulsing across the room to her. The older woman's lips were tight, a pulse twitched at her temple, and her bloodshot eyes were drooping.

Suddenly, she stood and leaned towards Marion. 'I cannae even look at you. I'm goin' to ma bed.' Her words were slurred, and she turned and made her way unsteadily to the door. Her shoulder banged against the door frame, and she turned back as if to say something. Instead, she shook her head and went out, slamming the door behind her.

Marion looked at her brother, letting the physical change in him register properly for the first time. He was stooped like an old man, clothes crumpled, and with unshaven patches of stubble on his cheek and neck. He'd always kept himself smart, a virtue instilled in him by their mother and reinforced during his time in national service. There were a good twelve years between them, but her big brother could easily pass for her father now.

Davy didn't acknowledge Ina's departure from the room. He busied himself making tea until he was sure Marion had finished feeding the baby. He placed the mug on the mantelpiece and nodded towards the door.

'She'll be better in the morning. Whisky makes her worse, but it's the only way she can get some sleep.' He had taken Amanda and was rubbing her back to help her break wind while Marion adjusted her cardigan and drank her tea. 'You and the wee one can sleep in the recess.' He said with a half smile, 'It's nice and cosy in there.'

'Tell me what happened, Davy. At least tell me what you can… if you're able to talk about it?' She watched her brother's jaw clench, and he stopped rubbing the baby's back.

He slowly shook his head and swallowed hard. 'The police came to the door. Four in the mornin', pitch black. Ina didn't want me to answer it.' He hugged the baby closer, rubbing his cheek against her hair before continuing. 'Two big polis standing there. We couldn't take in what they were sayin' at first. You know? Just wakened out of a sleep, and they're sayin' we need to go to the Royal. That our Diane's ill and it's serious. Well, you know it's serious when the police are at the door.'

Amanda gave a loud burp. Marion and Davy looked at her in surprise. They had almost forgotten she was there.

Davy lifted the baby from his chest and smiled at her. 'That's a girl! You needed that, didn't you, darling?'

Marion took the baby from his lap. 'Let me get her changed and settled. Then we can talk some more.'

Davy watched for a while, then rose and washed up the few cups and plates stacked by the sink in the scullery. After a few minutes, he dropped his hands in the basin of water and started to cry. Marion came over, leaned her head on his shoulder, and began rubbing his back just as he had with the baby.

Settled in front of the fire, they spoke in whispers so as not to disturb little Amanda. Perhaps also because it seemed a gentler way to speak of such harsh truths. Diane had barely been conscious by the time they arrived at the hospital. All the blood transfusions and medication had failed to stop the haemorrhage in time. Doctors had explained that she'd miscarried at about fourteen weeks into the pregnancy. She must have delivered before arriving at the hospital, for they hadn't found the... you know... foetus. Davy drew a shuddering breath as he told Marion this part.

'I keep thinking about her going through that. Delivering that wee thing out in the cold, all alone at a bus stop!'

'What? A bus stop? What was she doing at a bus stop? In Glasgow at that time of night, on her own?'

'The wee nurse said she thought she was trying to get home. She wanted her mum.' Davy got up and poured himself a large whisky from an almost empty bottle. He held it up towards Marion to inquire if she wanted what was left. When she shook her head, he poured the remainder into his own glass. 'A young guy – called London, but he was American, one of your black ones—' He gave a little nod towards the bed where the baby was sleeping. 'Anyway, he'd driven her to Casualty. He'd seen her at the bus stop and knew she needed help. She was really confused. Apparently thought he was a taxi. Asked him to bring her here. Thank God he remembered the address, otherwise they'd never have got us to the hospital in time to say our goodbyes.' Tears spilled into his whisky. 'She knew we were there at the end. That's something. She didn't die alone. Our wee girl didn't die alone…'

Marion hadn't expected to be able to sleep, but the journey and emotions had drained her. She awoke confused, feeling unfamiliar with the bed, the sounds, and the smells of this house. Amanda was gone! The safe space she had created for the baby in the corner of the mattress was empty. She sat up quickly and scanned the room. Standing by the window was Ina. She was holding the baby, rocking her in her arms, kissing her forehead and singing quietly to her.

> Go to sleep, my little piccaninny
> Mumma's gonna smack you if you don't
> Hush-a-bye, rock-a-bye
> Mumma's little baby
> Mumma's little alli-balli-boo

Marion vaguely remembered the song from her own childhood. Now she felt uncomfortable, even a little angry at it being sung to her beautiful Amanda, but Ina seemed to be soothing herself more than the baby, so Marion pushed her disquiet to the back of her mind and let it be.

10 /
london, england, december 1972

Marion wound the key on the back of the musical bunny and placed it at the bottom of her daughter's cot. She left the door ajar, and the gentle sound of Brahms's 'Lullaby' drifted into the kitchen. Sitting at the table across from her friend, she picked up her mug and cupped her hand around it.

'My tea's a bit cold now. How's yours, Sheila?'

'Almost done, but I never refuse a cuppa!' She held out her mug and continued rolling the small pram back and forth as she spoke. 'It's great to get peace to enjoy one for a wee change.'

Marion leaned over to look in the pram and smiled at the sleeping baby, who almost filled the space.

'You're not going to get much longer out of that pram.'

'I know, he gets bigger by the day. You'd think I was feeding him fertiliser!' Sheila looked down at her big baby boy with an affectionate smile. Marion could hear the pride in her voice. 'I'll tell you, though, he keeps me on my toes day and night. He's still holding on to the furniture, but it'll not be long till he's walking on his own, and then' – Sheila held her arms up in surrender and laughed – 'I'll not have a minute to call my own.' She looked at her son again, and her smile changed to a worried frown. 'Those big teeth at the back are coming through just now, and the wee soul isn't having an easy time with them.' Sheila shook her head. 'What if I hadn't kept him, Marion? What if I'd done as they wanted and gave him up for adoption? Oh, my God, I can't bear to think what I'd be like without him!'

Marion placed a fresh mug of tea in front of her and leaned over to hug her.

'You were really brave, especially after all you'd been through. You were stronger than me, Sheila. You didn't know anyone down here. At least when I came down, I could count on you to help me. Where would I be without you?'

'Och, listen, we're both well out of there. There was no future for us. The locals despised us. The Americans ignored us. Mine… Well, he didn't know anything about what was happening, and thank the Lord he made it home, but no one thinks about the girls left to deal with the aftermath. As for that Howard of yours, well…'

Staring into her cup, Marion sighed. Sheila reached over and covered her hand with her own.

'I'm sorry. I shouldn't have mentioned him. Don't think about it. There's nothing you can do. You can't turn the clock back, Marion. You went to see them, and now they know about wee Amanda, they'll understand why you left.'

Marion looked her friend in the eye and shook her head. 'Ina needs to blame someone, and it's me. I get that. In fact, I agree! It was me who brought him to the house, me that walked away and left them to it…' She held her hand up to stop her friend's objections before they could start. She continued, 'Davy? Well, Davy is broken-hearted, the same as Ina, but he's blaming himself. He feels he should have done something to protect her. I think because it happened so close to their house, he… I don't know… he feels he should have sensed she was in danger or something. Daft, isn't it?' She paused, and looking down into her cold tea, bit her lip. 'It *is* my fault, though, Sheila. I left her there in Dunoon. I'd promised to look after her, but… I left her there.'

'But you were expecting a baby, you had to leave…'

Marion interrupted. 'No, it's more than that, Sheila. I wrote and told her about the baby coming and that it was Howard's child. Diane must have been already pregnant, so she knew… she knew about Amanda. She must have got my letter before… before…'

'Come on, Marion, you have nothing to feel responsible for. Diane knew her own mind, knew what she wanted, and she wanted him.'

'I should have told her I was pregnant by him when I was leaving Dunoon. Maybe she wouldn't have kept seeing him…'

'You know she was daft about him. You couldn't have stopped her seeing him. Marion, stop trying to find an excuse for feeling guilty. It doesn't help, believe me. How guilty do you think I felt after Samuel was beaten up? God helped me to realise I wasn't responsible, those thugs were. In the same way, you're not responsible for the tragedy that befell Diane. Let the blame lie where it belongs… and that's not with you.'

Marion gave her friend's hand a squeeze and thanked her, but she didn't look convinced.

Sheila smiled sympathetically, but before she could add anything more, her little boy began to stir and snuffle. 'I knew the peace was too good to last,' she said. Then she gave her friend a quick hug and left.

Marion cleared the tea things away, then reached into her cardigan pocket and pulled out a piece of impressively headed paper. She unfolded it and read it for the third time that morning.

No longer stationed in Scotland… national security prevents… unable to disclose his current location… Marion narrowed her eyes and peered at the bold insignia of the United States Marine Corps. Bastards!

Good Samaritan? A guy called London, my arse! she thought. She knew it was Howard. No way had some random black American just happened to drive by and pick Diane up. The Lundahls' Mini was a dead giveaway. It was him, she knew it, and she would find out what had happened. That selfish bastard would pay, one day.

Two floors down, Sheila Forsythe unlocked the door of her flat and pulled the pram in behind her. It almost filled the hallway, making it difficult to get to the door of the only bedroom. She unbuckled the reins and lifted her son from his pram. He was fully awake now and managing to push his fist in his mouth and grizzle simultaneously.

'Is your mouth hurtin', darlin'? Aww, don't worry, let's get you your dinner and then Mummy will put some teething powder on your gums. Just don't bite me when I'm trying to reach the sore bits!'

She laughed at her own joke and gave her son a cuddle. 'This is only one step away from me talking to myself, Jamie. Thank heavens we've got Auntie Marion and Amanda to keep us company now.' She ruffled his tight curls and planted kisses all over his head and down to his neck before he struggled to push her away.

Jamie was bathed and settled in his cot by eight thirty. Sheila finished brushing her teeth and checked the door was fully locked and bolted before squeezing past her son's cot and kneeling in the small space between it and her own single bed. Leaning on the soft candlewick bedspread, she clasped her hands and began her whispered prayer.

Her mother's voice resonated in her head.

God doesn't want to read your mind, Sheila Anne Forsythe. Speak out loud for the Lord to hear. As a child that had puzzled her. If God was 'all knowing, all seeing', then why couldn't she just pray inside her head? But the habit had stuck nevertheless.

'Dear Lord, forgive me my sins. I have been good today. I tried to comfort Marion as she struggles with her conscience. You sent her to me in my time of need, and without her love and friendship, I wouldn't have found my way back to you. Help me to guide her on the right path. Allow me to be the friend to her that she has been to me. Look after my lovely Samuel. Lord, help him, wherever he may be. Bless my son, Jamie, save him, and keep him. And bless me, oh Lord, that I may stay strong and carry out your work. Yours is the power and the glory, forever. Amen.'

As a child, she had thought her parents' faith was the only true way to worship the Lord God Almighty, but growing up she had rebelled against them and their church. Starting work in the local Woolworths had given her enough money to rent a room and move out of their home, with its forbidding regime. The following year, after her eighteenth birthday, she also started working four evenings a week in the town's disreputable Anchor Inn. Bolstered by the admiration of all the virile young men both in and outside the pub, she had gained in self-confidence with each passing day. Now she could buy fashionable clothes, pluck her eyebrows, and wear make-up.

Sheila had blossomed, loving her new freedom, her new look, and most of all her new-found popularity. Then she'd fallen in love. Samuel was much quieter than most of the boisterous American customers in the bar. He had a few friends but often sat alone and watched her from the corner stool at the bar. She made sure she served him whenever he needed to order a drink.

'Another cola, Samuel?'

'Pepsi-Cola, please, Sheila.' And he smiled. 'Pepsi-Cola saved my grandpappy's life, and to drink any other soda would just seem damned ungrateful, now, wouldn't it?'

Samuel had given her several versions of the tale of the metal

Pepsi sign that had saved his grandfather from a bullet, but she believed there must be some truth in it and had laughed with him at each and every telling. Samuel never drank beer or spirits, and she was sure he only came along to the Anchor to see her and flirt a little. After a few weeks, he would wait till closing time and ask if he could see her home. At the end of her early shift, she left the bar just after eight o'clock, when it was still light outside, so it wasn't that she needed an escort, but she revelled in his gentlemanly attentions.

Sheila, inexperienced and naive, began dating him exclusively and felt his need to have sex with her was an expression of his love. In the late evening sunshine, he took her virginity in a secluded back street. It began as a clandestine kiss and cuddle as he walked her home after finishing work. His passion quickly escalated out of her control. She wanted to ask him to wait, to get back to her room for some privacy and comfort. Her back was against the door of one of a row of lock-up garages, with a padlock pressed into her side, but in a few moments her protests became endearments as she gave in to the excitement of being wanted so urgently. For fifteen minutes, both were wrapped in their own world, unaware that they were being watched.

Ally Grant's bedroom window overlooked the garages, and he often enjoyed a free show of courting couples having a groping session in what they believed was a secluded and private place. This was the first time he'd seen one of the black Yanks there, and with a Dunoon lassie. He shouted to his older brother. Within minutes the brothers had gathered three friends, and they lay in wait till the young couple were leaving by the only access road.

One boy held a struggling Sheila to stop her getting into the fray, his hand over her mouth to muffle her screams. The other four punched and pulled the serviceman till he was on the ground trying to roll onto his side and pull his knees up to protect himself. Three of them held him, one wrenching his arms above his head, two others grabbing an ankle each, pulling his legs wide apart. When he was open and unprotected, Ally began kicking him to the cheers and encouragement of his friends.

'Ya fuckin' dirty black bastard! You'll no be fuckin' any of oor lassies for a while, will ye, Sambo?' His boot landed in the serviceman's groin time after time, moved on to stamp on his belly, and then finished by aiming his last blows to his face. Releasing a hysterical Sheila, the five men then ran down the street towards the seafront, laughing and congratulating each other. It was all over in less than five violent, life-changing minutes. Sheila knelt by the side of her damaged love, stroking his face, alternating between telling him it would be okay and screaming at the top of her lungs for someone to help them.

It was Marion who had come to the hospital. It was Marion who had comforted her in the aftermath of the attack. Samuel's physical injuries were serious, but it was the severe stroke he suffered hours later that left him with disabilities that would never fully mend. He had been moved to sick bay at the US base as soon as he was stable. Then, almost overnight, he was shipped back to hospital in the States, where he could receive the best treatment. His brother and sister were waiting there, anxious to see him.

Traumatised and unable to work, Sheila had to give up her room and move back to the purgatory of her parent's home. They were appalled to have a succession of policemen and officers from the naval base turn up at their door to question their daughter. Sheila couldn't or wouldn't answer any of the questions. The minister and elders from her parents' church assembled in their home to pray for her redemption. Sheila stayed withdrawn and unresponsive.

Then she found out she was pregnant. Her parents called the wrath of God on her when she told them, finally sending her from their home and condemning her to the fires of Hell for turning away from the Lord.

Marion had taken her back to stay at the guest house, where she spent days alone in the room. Her friend brought small, tasty meals up to her, but Sheila barely touched any of them. Then the following weekend Marion had found the room empty. Hours later, when Sheila returned, there was a spring in her step and a lightness that transformed her from the sad, dejected girl of the previous months. She told her friend that she had picked up a Gideons Bible from the bedside drawer and she felt hope. For the first time in almost four crazy, manic years, Sheila could see a way forward. She had gone to the Methodist church and asked for the Lord's forgiveness and the church's help. They gave it. Jesus had saved her, but it was her friend Marion who had made it possible.

11 /
london, england, october 1978

Jamie struggled, trying to avoid having his shirt buttoned. At the kitchen door, Amanda stood straight as a die, her school uniform perfect, clutching her carefully packed bag. She watched him with a tiny scowl, which did more to tame him than any of his mother's pleas for cooperation. Finally, he was dressed. The waistband of his trousers seemed undecided about accepting the bottom of his school shirt, but he was tidy enough. Sheila stood back and looked from one child to the other, satisfied at what she had spent the last ninety minutes achieving. Both were fed and dressed, and they were in time to leave for school. No small feat where her darling big son was concerned.

'Okay, we might make it to the gate before the bell this morning. Now, have you both got everything?' They nodded at her. 'Right, let's go before something else happens.'

As they reached the gates of Castlehill School, Sheila crouched in front of the children. 'Amanda, you know your mum will be back tomorrow, and I'll tell her what a good girl you've been and that you got all your homework right. She'll be so proud of you, and it'll help her feel better.' Sheila gave Amanda a little kiss on her forehead and then turned to her own son. 'Right, my lad, you

Just One Little Pill

do your best, and at three o'clock go and collect Amanda and bring her here. I'll be waiting for you.' With that she aimed a kiss at his forehead, just catching him before he ducked to try and avoid it.

'Mum, I'm too big for that, don't embarrass me...' With that he ran off into the crowd of boys outside his classroom. Amanda smiled at Sheila and skipped off to the far corner where her friends were gathered.

Oh Lord, Sheila thought, *I love those two. Still, it'll be nice to have Marion back tomorrow.* She glanced at her watch. The funeral would start an hour from now. 'Poor souls. Bless them, dear God, help them through their troubles. Amen.'

When a girl looked at her strangely, Sheila realised she'd been overheard. She shrugged and set off across the road to catch her bus to work.

The day passed slowly for Sheila. Every hour she looked at the clock and imagined what was happening up in Glasgow, what stage the funeral was at. How was Marion bearing up? How would Davy cope with losing his wife now as well as their daughter? Her greatest worry was that Marion would want to move back to Scotland and live with her brother. She couldn't bear to lose her. She had made friends with her colleagues at the office and some of the other single mothers in the block, but her relationship with Marion was on a different level. Only Marion had known her in her wild days at the Anchor and knew what she'd been through *that* night, but most of all, only Marion had helped her. God had made sure she had a friend in her darkest hour. His guidance had sent her to the Methodists. These were the people who gave practical help to unmarried mothers and their babies. Then, in a miraculous turn of fate, Sheila was the one who had been able to help Marion. They couldn't lose each other now.

By nine o'clock both children were asleep in the twin beds. Sheila looked down at these two little innocents: so alike with their big brown eyes, dark curls, and skin the colour of milk chocolate. Different in nature and build but inseparable. The four of them were a family. A close, loving family. Sheila couldn't bear to think of anything breaking them apart.

The funeral service wasn't well attended. Ina had avoided, even spurned, all efforts at contact by friends or relatives in the last years of her life. After losing her daughter, her only solace had been her husband, Davy, and whisky. Whisky numbed her, blurred memories, and let her slip into a dreamless sleep. For those first few agonising weeks, the doctor had prescribed sleeping pills and tranquilisers. She had swallowed them gratefully, washing them down with neat whisky just to be sure. Gradually her doctor had withdrawn the sleeping pills but continued to give her repeat prescriptions for the powerful tranquilisers, and Ina had kept increasing her dose. Davy had seen his wife slipping further and further away from him. He lost her to a misty blurred stupor where she was never fully aware and often barely conscious. He had been tempted to go down the same path, but the need to care for his wife gave him a reason to keep going. The doctor had put cause of death as pneumonia, but everyone knew her heart had been broken with grief for her child.

Marion had come up from London on the train. Davy had sent a short letter with details of the funeral arrangements and enclosed a postal order for ten pounds. She knew he would have loved to see his little niece, but Amanda had school, and anyway, a funeral was no place for a five-year-old. Deciding to leave her with Sheila was better all round, and the two youngsters were thrilled to be having a sleepover.

A few of Ina's neighbours had come along to the funeral. Her brother and his wife lived in Canada and couldn't make the trip, but Ina's older sister, Chrissie, travelled up from her home in

Kelso. It was hard to believe the sisters were related. Ina had been a strikingly beautiful woman before tragedy ravaged her health, with bright blue eyes, fine bone structure, and a ready smile. Although her sister was only two years older, deep lines pulled down from her mouth, giving her a set look of disapproval that matched the scowl of her eyes.

Along with Davy, Marion and Chrissie were the only people on the front row, and throughout the service, Marion had felt that scowl focused on her and worried that Chrissie was looking to reopen old wounds.

At the cemetery, Marion couldn't bear the sight of the open grave. Diane's remains were down there, and the thought of her lying in the dark, wet dirt made Marion feel dizzy. She forced herself to stay upright, and it helped to focus on the white marble headstone. Over and over, she read the words etched clearly in gold.

> Diane Marie Barr
> Beloved daughter
> She brightened our lives
> Shining now in heaven
> Born 2nd November 1954
> Taken from us
> 28th October 1972

She held tightly to Davy's arm, frightened of seeing his face, knowing she had to be strong for him. If he could hold his emotions in check, then surely she could too.

They made a forlorn little group in the limousine. Chrissie, eyes closed and lips tightly pursed, the lines on her face a road map to misery. Davy sitting, hands clasped in front of him, staring resolutely at the floor. And herself, eyes fixed on the back of the driver's neck, willing the angry red boil at his hairline to burst and release some of the unbearable tension.

A luncheon was laid on for the mourners at a hotel near the crematorium. In such a small gathering, it was increasingly difficult to avoid Chrissie, who had tried several times to take Marion on one side and speak to her alone. When the waitress went over to discuss something with Davy and Chrissie, Marion took the opportunity to speak with her old friend and employer Mrs Bissell, whom she had seen briefly at the graveside.

They greeted each other with an affectionate embrace, and after they had expressed how glad they were to see each other, Mrs Bissell handed Marion a brown carrier bag she had been clasping all morning. Marion looked inside and gasped as she recognised the contents. Her hands shook as she reached inside and lifted out a blue leather handbag.

'Sit down, Marion, dear. I know this must be a shock for you.'

Marion reached behind her and, finding a chair, sat. She held the carrier tightly.

'This is Diane's.' She shook her head in confusion. 'Surely this should have gone to Davy with her other belongings?'

The smartly dressed woman sat knee to knee with her and took both hands in hers.

'No, no, that's the problem, dear. A man brought it to me almost a month after Diane had…' She bit her lip and left the sentence unfinished. 'I'm so sorry, Marion. I didn't know what to do with it. You were down in London, and I didn't want to give it to Ina or Davy and reopen wounds.'

'It's okay, Mrs Bissell, but I just don't understand how he came to your place with it.'

'He was so dirty and smelled a bit. I really just wanted to get him away from my door. I should have asked him more questions, but… he was trying to get me to pay him for it. I gave him the money and was glad to be rid of him.'

'Start at the beginning and tell me what he said. Please, Mrs Bissell, this could be important.'

The older woman took a deep breath and glanced around to make sure no one could overhear. 'I opened the front door, and he stood there holding the handbag up level with his face. *Recognise this, do you?* he said. I had no idea who he was or what he was talking about, but when I tried to close the door, he put his foot in the doorway.'

Marion patted her hand and nodded encouragement for her to go on.

'Well,' Mrs Bissell continued, 'he said, *She left this in my place when the Yank rushed her to the hospital. I thought you might make it worth my while to bring it back for her.* That's when I realised he could be talking about... Diane.' She said the girl's name in an almost inaudible whisper. 'So, I asked him when this was. *Friday twenty-seventh October,* he said, as certain as you like.'

Marion paled at her words, even though she had recognised Diane's handbag right away. A blue leather shoulder bag with an appliqué pattern on the front flap. It was the one she had bought her niece for Christmas. She took the package and put it on the floor behind her feet.

'Thanks, Mrs Bissell. You did the right thing, waiting until you could give it to me. How much did he want? I'll pay you back.'

'Oh, I wouldn't take it from you, dear. Anyway, I beat him down. Told him it was all I had in my purse. To tell you the truth, I'd have given a lot more to get him off my property before any of my residents saw him!'

'Did he say what *his place* was?'

'Yes, dear. A hotel, he said, just like mine! Blooming cheek of it!' Pursed lips and flared nostrils showed the older woman's outrage at the comparison.

'A hotel?'

'Yes, although from the look of him it would be lucky to

qualify as a dosshouse!' She glanced at the ceiling as if trying to remember more detail. 'Hillside or Hilltop or something. There was definitely a *hill* in it.'

'Okay,' said Marion, 'well. Thanks for bringing it to me, and again, thank you so much for coming along for Ina.' They both stood, and Marion gave her old employer a hug. 'You've always been so good to me… and to our Diane. I can never thank you enough for all you've done.'

'Oh, Marion, we're family, no matter how distant. And you and Davy have been through so much. Poor Ina, may she rest in peace, is out of all her pain now. You just look after yourself.'

Mrs Bissell buttoned her coat, put on her black leather gloves, and walked over to offer her condolences to Davy.

While her brother was busy with the other mourners, Marion lifted the package and slipped into the ladies. After locking the cubicle behind her, she opened the bag and looked at the contents. The first thing she saw was the perfume: Tabu. Diane had loved the strong, distinctive scent. Carefully, she lifted out the spray. It was almost empty. She sprayed the few drops that lurked at the bottom of the bottle, allowing herself a heady swim in the past. The dark blue purse had no money, not even a copper, but tucked within the pocket were two library cards. Marion saw they were made out to the Dunoon hotel address and realised that was why the man had taken the bag there.

From the bottom of the bag she lifted out a brown tortoiseshell compact and a lipstick. She remembered it was called Pink Meringue, and it brought Diane back to her so vividly that she could swear she was in the cubicle with her. She kissed the compact and lipstick, then placed them back in the handbag, enveloped by a sense of guilt as strong as the scent of the perfume.

Today, after burying Ina and talking to Mrs Bissell and now feeling so close to Diane, she knew she had to take this rare chance and speak with someone at the naval base. Boosting her impetus to act, there came a loud pounding on the cubicle door, accompanied by the unmistakeable crackle of Chrissie's voice.

'Is anybody in here? Marion, is that you?'

Marion burst from the cubicle and threw an apology. 'Sorry, Chrissie. Got to rush. Tell Davy I'll be back later. Bye.'

'Mrs Bissell, wait!' Marion ran down the steps of the hotel and caught up with the older woman just as she was about to start her car. 'Could you give me a lift over to Dunoon, please? There's a couple of things I want to try and do before I go back.'

12 / revelations

THE JOURNEY TO GREENOCK AND OVER ON THE CAR FERRY TOOK almost an hour. Mrs Bissell happily brought Marion up to date with all the local news and gossip. By the time they docked, she was fully caught up on the affairs, marriages, divorces, and other scandals of the last five years. At the ferry terminal, she thanked Mrs Bissell and hailed a taxi. One particular little nugget of information had resonated with her, and she quickly decided on a slight detour from her original destination.

Betty Lundahl had gone over to live in America with her husband, Bill, but within the last year she and their two children had come back and were staying with her mother. Mrs Bissell had been happy to speculate on the reason, but for the moment that was all she could do, as Betty had given nothing away.

When Betty answered the door, she took a few moments to recognise her friend.

'Jesus… Marion?' She took a step back and for a second seemed to consider closing the door again. 'I wasn't expecting to see you. It must be… what, six years? You look great, though. Come on in.' She held the door wide and gestured towards the kitchen. 'The kids are at school, so we'll get peace to talk. Come on through. I'll put the kettle on.'

Marion let her talk uninterrupted for the first ten minutes and soon remembered how self-absorbed Betty had always been. Finally, she asked what Marion was doing back in Dunoon after all this time. When Marion told her about Ina's funeral, a strange look passed over Betty's face, and she sat down on the chair at the opposite side of the table.

'Diane's mum?'

'Yes, her mum and my sister-in-law.'

'I'm sorry, so sorry, Marion.' Betty closed her eyes and placed her palms together. She looked as though she was about to pray.

'Did you know Ina?'

'Not directly, no, but...' Betty stood and walked over to the window so her back was to Marion. 'Things happened that affected me.'

'What things? Diane? Are you talking about what happened to Diane?'

'Not *just* Diane, but yes, Diane, me, my family... and I suppose Ina as well, now.'

Marion wanted to ask her what she was talking about but held back. Betty turned and looked at her.

'Do you know how wonderful my life was in Florida?' Marion shook her head but still didn't speak. Betty continued, 'We had great living quarters, twenty minutes from the beach. The kids each had their own room, and we had *three* bathrooms. Three! I'd pack a wee picnic, and we'd go to the beach at the weekends. Barry was learning to play basketball, 'cause he's tall, my Barry, like his daddy.' Betty opened a pack of cigarettes and offered it to Marion. Shaking her head, Marion silently refused. Betty lit hers with the kitchen matches, blew the smoke towards the ceiling, and went on. 'I loved it there. The other wives on the base were so nice. They welcomed me into all their clubs, and I did voluntary work...'

'Betty, why are you back here with the kids? Where's Bill?'

Betty's eyes became cold, and her mouth set in a thin line. She stubbed her cigarette out in the ashtray, then covered her face with her hands.

'Jail. Bill's in jail.'

Marion could see it had been difficult for her to admit the reason for her loss of status, but once it was out in the open, Betty wasted no time in loading the arsenal with Bill's misdeeds. The more she told Marion of the frightening and sordid story, the more Betty painted herself as the innocent, unwittingly caught in the crossfire.

Betty Lundahl's bitterness over her changed circumstances spilled out in bile and spite. This was mainly directed at her ex-husband, but if there was anyone else she could rope in, she would happily do it, and Howard Odoms was firmly in her sights. He had egged Bill on, had been one of the main links in the distribution chain. She stressed that Odoms was the one who'd sought out her husband for *something* that would help him out of the mess he said he was in with Diane. By this time her Bill was in too deep to refuse. Not that she was making excuses for her husband, but in the beginning, he had just been trying to help relieve the boredom of a few of the servicemen. Word had quickly spread, and before long he'd been the go-to guy for all the men on the base, and they, in turn, would be happy to share their perk-me-ups with their dates – whether the women knew it or not.

Thankfully, the train back to London was quiet that evening. The last two days had sent everything spinning and colliding in

Marion's head. She reached into her overnight case and brought out Diane's blue shoulder bag, needing to hold it again to be sure she hadn't just dreamt it. The funeral service for Ina had been so personal and moving, dwelling on her childhood, marriage, and of course motherhood. It had brought memories of Diane sharply into focus for Marion, and then when she'd seen Mrs Bissell and this handbag, she'd felt ashamed and guilty – feelings she'd worked hard to move on from, only now they were even stronger. She had known for years there was far more to Diane's death than a tragic miscarriage. Other than a few letters to the US Marine Corps, she'd not pursued it, distracting herself with bringing up her daughter and making a life for them in London. Dunoon had seemed a long way away, and with each passing year, the distance grew. Now, it was as though she had been dropped from a great height, straight back into the time that had radically changed the direction of her life – of so many lives.

She brought the bag up to her face and wept softly into the scent of the leather.

Where did he take you, Diane? What did he give you? Did he tell you to take it? Did you even know you'd taken it? It's a bloody shame. I know about the drugs. Surely you wouldn't be that stupid… You were on the pill. You told me you were on the pill. You were tryin' to get pregnant, weren't you… He wasn't marriage material, I could've told you that… I should have told you that…

Marion wiped her face and blew her nose. She needed to think clearly. She wasn't sure who her grief was really for. Ina's death had triggered this backward look; then getting this bag had been like a slap in the face from Diane. That was really what had pushed her to go back to Dunoon. Then Betty! Stuck-up cow. Well, she wasn't so stuck-up now, back with her mother in the same house she grew up in.

Marion tucked the haunting handbag back in her luggage and forced herself to consider her options. Who should she tell? Could she report it to the Americans? Now that Bill Lundahl was locked up and clearly involved in peddling drugs, they would be forced to investigate. But would they? What other proof was there? Look at what had happened when poor Samuel was beaten. It got swept under the carpet. That's where it all started, really. That's how she got involved with that bloody Howard Odoms in the first place.

She stared out of the window and, as the miles clattered past, remembered the time when she'd thought Howard Odoms was just a conceited shit who sometimes came into the bar. Shame she had let him wheedle his way into her affections, but then she wouldn't have Amanda, would she? She had wanted a baby so much back then. All right, Howard wouldn't have been her first choice to have a baby with, but he had shown his softer side. Two, sometimes three times a week after Samuel was hurt, he would call round to see how Sheila was, and that softened her feelings for him. Then the night of the big fight, she'd helped him get away from those bloody Dunoon boys. Bursting into the Anchor with bats, crowbars, even knives – bloody knives! Someone could have been killed…

Just as well the Americans outnumbered them, although half the stupid eejits were still outside, unable to get up the stairs and in the door fast enough. He was some fighter, Howard, you had to give him that. Roaring like a lion, jumping over tables, throwing himself into the midst of the worst of it. It had been fierce and bloody, but amazingly, it had all been over in a few quick minutes. Howard had taken some blows, but nothing compared to the damage he and the others inflicted on the local boys. They'd scattered, and most of the Americans had hurried back to base before the authorities arrived. Howard couldn't run; he could barely walk because a chunk had been gouged out of his leg and his hand was damaged. Marion helped him down to the cellar and, returning to the bar as the police arrived, swore that there was no one left in there except her and the other barmaid, who was crying hysterically in the arms of a sympathetic young constable.

Later, left to lock up, Marion had gone to tell Howard the coast was clear, but putting her arm round to help him up had turned into an embrace before either of them had stopped to think. Their adrenaline levels were high, and sex in that dark, dusty cellar was the most exhilarating she had ever had. Even after all these years, she found herself breathing faster and biting her lip at the thought of it.

Throughout the train journey back to London, the memories and revelations circled in her head, turning into a pounding knot. But, above all, Betty's tale of the contents of the car boot replayed until she thought she would scream.

She'd tell Sheila. It would help because the very telling of the story would force her to unravel the facts to explain everything she'd found out. And she could trust Sheila. She'd always trusted her.

It was late by the time she got back to Sheila's flat. Both children were fast asleep in the little bedroom. Marion haltingly told her everything. Saying it aloud made it even more horrifying. Sheila sat, mouth agape, eyes open even wider.

'Dear God, dear God...' Sheila clasped her hands, closed her eyes, and rocked back and forth. 'Dear God, I know Diane's soul will be in your safekeeping. May she be at peace and be reunited with the soul of her unborn baby. Please help us to find it in our hearts to forgive the sinners who caused this. Amen.'

'Well, God might forgive them, Sheila, but I won't.' Fists clenched, Marion beat the table. 'He poisoned her! Whatever it was, it killed her! Odoms has caused enough grief in our family.

Him, Lundahl, and all those bloody Yanks that cover up and run away. They might not have been at war with us, but they dropped plenty of emotional fucking bombs to change our lives forever.' She swiped at the tears spilling down her face with her hands still clenched in fists, then, realising how loud she had become, lowered her voice. 'Do you know what frightens me more than anything?'

Sheila shook her head.

'He's Amanda's father.' She kept silent to allow her friend to sense the depth of her concern. 'If I had told him I was expecting, he might have given me some of that poison.'

'No!' Sheila gasped. 'You wouldn't have taken it 'cause you weren't as naive as Diane. You wouldn't have let him talk you into experimenting with drugs.'

'We don't know that he did talk her into taking anything. Diane meant to get pregnant. She wanted that baby. I don't think she would have willingly taken anything, but he could easily have slipped her a Mickey Finn.' Marion took a deep breath. 'And if he could do that with Diane, then he could have done it with me.'

On the table in front of them lay Diane's blue handbag. Marion lifted it, went to the sideboard, slid out a secret drawer, and pulled out some letters.

'One thing all this has taught me is that my Amanda must never know who her father is. Never!' With that she thrust the papers inside the handbag and gave it to her friend. 'I don't want these in the house, Sheila. Please take them, put them somewhere safe. Somewhere I don't know about. And it needs to be where Amanda won't accidently come across them.'

Sheila took the bundle from her friend and nodded.

'What if she wants to know about her father? Once she's a bit older, she'll ask questions, won't she?'

'I'll tell her I don't know. She can believe I was a hippy into free love or a wee slag who slept around. I don't care what she thinks of me, I just don't want her to ever meet that murdering bastard!'

Sheila made soothing noises and got up, saying she'd make more tea, but Marion pulled a bottle of wine from her luggage and lifted two glasses from the shelf.

'Come on, hen. While the kids are asleep, we can have a wee drink. God knows I need one.'

The women raised a full glass each, and Marion toasted. 'To our wonderful children. Though they'll never know their fathers, they can be thankful they've got such great mothers!' They clinked glasses and sat back on the couch together.

On the other side of the door stood a seven-year-old boy. His pyjama trousers stuck damply to his legs and his bare feet were in a small puddle.

13 / tombstone, arizona, october 1999

day 4

'I'd always planned to take you to where I live, Amanda. There's a small problem, though. I don't always live alone.'

'Well, I never thought you'd be living like a monk. Come on, Howard. Having a daughter is new to you, but I've been all grown up for quite a long time now.' She laughed at his wry nod and wanted to keep him talking so went on. 'How long have you lived in Tombstone? As soon as I found out you lived there, I wondered what had brought you to such a tiny, isolated place.'

'Most of the places I've lived are isolated. Arizona and New Mexico are vast states. The whole of Britain would fit in many times over. Sure, there are cities, but that's never appealed to me. No, I bummed around for a long time after I got discharged. I drank a bit, too, you know?'

'Do you still drink? I've only seen you take water or coffee – lots of coffee!'

'Nah, I stopped drinking almost four years ago, completely this time.' He glanced over at her. 'There were a few false starts,' he admitted with a shrug.

. . .

The town of Tombstone was almost at Arizona's border with Mexico. The tourist attractions dominated everything, geared around the old Wild West in general and the infamous shoot-out at the OK Corral in particular. As Howard drove in, Amanda was excited to glimpse Boothill cemetery. Then, as they headed farther into the town, she could barely contain herself at the sight of a stagecoach drawn by a pair of horses passing on the other side of the street.

'Oh, wow! Do you actually live here? It's like stepping back in time, or not really in time, but into one of the old cowboy movies. I'm half expecting John Wayne to stroll along the street!'

'Well, when you live in a place like this, you kinda stop seein' things the way the tourists do.'

'Do you work here? Are you one of the actors in the shoot-out?'

Howard smiled and shook his head. 'No, I'm one of the few folks here that's not involved in the tourist attractions. They're all professional actors. I still count myself as a United States Marine, always have. I guess I always will.'

He parked the truck at the roadside, led the way into a small trailer park just off Fourth Street, and stopped at the first trailer on the right, a distinctive red and white. He opened the door of his home and stood back to let her enter before him.

The air was a little stale inside, and although everything was neat and tidy, it reminded Amanda of a larger version of a caravan she'd stayed in as a child. Her mother and Aunt Sheila had hired a residential van just outside Broadstairs for two weeks when she and Jamie were children. Looking around her father's home, she recognised a similar layout. The kitchen and lounge were one large room, but with the dark wood units, brown seat covers, and half-closed blinds, the overall effect was gloomy, unlike in the holiday van, where the light had streamed in. No clutter, no photographs or ornaments. In fact, if anything, the rooms were sparse. The kitchen area looked spotless, but there were different pieces of medical apparatus visible in the lounge area, and through the open door of the first bedroom, she could see a tray full of medicine bottles on the bedside table and a walking frame beside the door.

'Are you ill, Howard? Were you wounded when you were in the marines?'

'Me? No,' he replied and seemed happy to leave his answer at that, but Amanda's expression demanded more. 'It's my buddy's stuff. He stays with me some of the time.'

They sat at the compact dining table and drank coffee. He wanted to show her around the town that had become his home, but she wanted to talk. Here seemed ideal. This was a place where he could feel most comfortable and at ease. She was also getting impatient for him to ask about her. He'd made no effort to find out anything about her upbringing, career, or boyfriends. In fact he'd shown very little interest in her life altogether.

'Perhaps I could fill in a few details about me, Howard?' She saw relief flit quickly across his features and wondered if he had felt she was only here to find out about him. He looked eager for her to continue, as if he'd just realised the spotlight could fall on someone else.

She shrugged and turned her palms outwards, showing she'd nothing to hide, but she wasn't sure where to begin.

'We lived in a tiny flat when I was really young, just me and Mum, but Jamie and his mum lived in the same block.' Amanda stared out the window, thinking back to scenes from her childhood. 'It was fine. I suppose, looking back, it could be a bit of a rough area, but as kids we weren't aware of anything bad. Well, nothing worse than getting into trouble for not doing homework, that kind of thing, and I always had Jamie to look after me.'

'Who's Jamie?'

'Oh, Jamie's… Jamie. We were like brother and sister when we were little. We kind of grew up together when we lived in the flats. His mum, I call her Auntie, was a single mother, too, and she was friends with my mum from way back, even before we moved to London.' Amanda paused for a moment, smiling as she remembered happy times growing up. 'Then later, Mum's brother moved down from Glasgow and eventually he bought a house in Peckham, and we went there to live with him.'

'How old were you then?'

'I was almost twelve.'

'So, a new home, new school, new friends?'

'Well, yes. Moving schools was hard. I never really settled in at Kennington High. Not many black faces, and I always felt like the odd one out.'

'Were you bullied?'

She shrugged. 'A little bit at first. I stood up to them, though, and in the end… well, I think they were a bit afraid of me. They called me "the savage".' She could see his expression change and quickly continued before he had time to ask more about school. 'Don't get me wrong, though, I loved living with Uncle Davy. There was a garden, and we all had our own room. Then he bought a car too. All of this was new to me. He made Mum take driving lessons, and then she got to use the car, probably more than he used it.' Her face was shining as she told him this, but then a shadow passed and she became serious again. 'I missed Jamie, though. We missed each other a lot. There were visits – every summer and at Christmas we all got together at Uncle Davy's – but we'd been used to seeing each other every day, so it was a big change. Then we both went our separate ways when we started at uni, and the gap between us got bigger and bigger.'

'It sounds a bit like you still miss him.'

She slowly shook her head and smiled. 'No, we met up again

at his mum's wedding, and… kind of saw each other differently… romantically. That was almost six years ago, now. We live together. We'll probably get married one day. He wasn't happy that I came over here on my own. To be honest, he didn't want me to come at all. He said, "You can't miss what you never had." But you can.'

Howard shifted in his seat and took a breath before leaning towards her with an earnest expression. 'Yeah, I suppose you can, but if you don't know what you're missing, you can make stuff up to fill the gap. Is that what you did, Amanda? Have I disappointed you?'

Amanda shrugged. 'I don't know. Sometimes, yes, you have. You push me away, close in on yourself. You've been thousands of miles away from me all my life. I wanted you to seize the chance for us to bond… connect. We can't make up for the lost years, but I'd hoped we could make the best of the time ahead of us.'

Howard pushed the coffee cups aside and clasped both her hands in his. 'Any family I had, I lost. A mother I barely remember, a father who dumped me, a grandma who didn't want me. Then there was my brother, who was everything to me, ripped out of my life. Now, at my age, I'm presented with a daughter. Not just any old daughter, but one who is beautiful and smart! I've been conditioned, Amanda. It's hard for me to let my guard down, to let anyone get close again.'

'Well, Howard, I hope you'll give it a try, for me?'

He looked at her and then smiled and nodded, but she didn't feel entirely convinced.

They spent the rest of that afternoon visiting all the attractions in Tombstone. A few locals seemed to know Howard and nodded an acknowledgement or, in the case of the cowboys, touched their hat and muttered 'Ma'am.' No one made conversation, and he didn't introduce Amanda to anyone. She was thrilled by the re-enacted gunfight at the OK Corral and had her photograph taken with both the goodies and the baddies, though she much preferred the jokey manner of those bad boys, the Clantons. The famous Boothill was something she definitely wanted to see, and of course she had to take a stagecoach ride. Howard hadn't wanted to go on that, said he'd done it once and that was enough, but Amanda insisted. Eating ice cream as they walked back towards the trailer park, she began to laugh.

'Look at us, Howard!' She turned to him and flashed a broad grin that was a mirror image of his own rarely seen one. 'We're having a fun father-daughter day out, even down to eating ice cream together! Who'd have thought it, eh?'

He nodded his agreement, smiling at the turnaround this day had brought.

Just as they approached the entrance of the RV park, she noticed a building facing it with insignia displayed on the wall. Above the door, it said *American Legion*. She stopped and turned to him.

'This is it, isn't it?' She pointed to the circular badge at the right-hand side of the entrance. 'This is where you work. That's how I was able to find you.'

'Yeah, this is it.' He went silent, turned to the garbage bin at the side of the street, and dumped what was left of his ice cream. 'C'mon, let's head back.'

Amanda couldn't understand what had triggered the abrupt change in mood yet again.

'Wait, Howard, wait.' She caught up with him and pulled him round to face her. 'What's wrong? Don't you want to take me in and introduce me? Your long-lost daughter, the family you didn't know you had?'

'No. Come on, we need to get you back to the motel. We can

go to a nice restaurant for dinner in Tucson. The prices here are hiked up for the tourists.'

'But doesn't the Legion do food? Can't we go there?'

'Not just now. Come on, Amanda, just leave it, will you?' There was a sharp edge to his voice she didn't like. Without saying anything, she followed him towards the truck, shaking her head and wondering what had slammed his emotional door this time.

That evening, seated in the booth of a large steakhouse, they both opted for burgers and beer and smiled at their taste in food being so alike. They enjoyed a more relaxed meal than on any occasion previously. The conversation was light and impersonal. They compared American words to British ones: *pavement* for *road*, and *sidewalk* for *pavement*. Different brand names for the same confections: Three Musketeers, Milky Way, Mars Bars. These were well known to both under different guises, which also led them to decide she'd inherited her father's sweet tooth. Though she declared that was one gene she wished he'd kept to himself, they nevertheless went on to order chocolate brownies with ice cream.

Howard looked up from his dessert and began to laugh. Amanda was puzzled: Why was he pointing at her with his spoon? He couldn't tell her what was so amusing for a few moments till he caught his breath again.

'Your teeth.' Again he pointed towards her mouth using his spoon. 'They're all black bits! You look like a picture of a wicked witch!' Again he roared with laughter.

She bristled. He couldn't know, but at school the drama group had put on a performance of *The Wizard of Oz*. Amanda had longed to be Dorothy. She knew all the songs, she could dance, and she'd watched the movie at home at least ten times.

During casting, she had stood in the school's assembly hall

waiting to audition as Dorothy. She even brought a little toy dog she'd stuffed into a basket as her prop. When they called 'Next,' she'd walked out onstage. In the front row sat the drama teacher, the head of English, and a teaching assistant. All three fell silent when Amanda took centre stage; then simultaneously, they began to snigger.

'No, dear, you're black. Dorothy isn't black.' They began to chuckle again, but this time tried to cover it with genteel coughs. 'Why don't you come back and audition tomorrow? We're casting the Wicked Witch then.' The three members of staff whispered in a huddle; then the drama teacher announced, 'Tell you what, Amanda dear, you don't need to audition. You have the part.'

It took Howard a while to realise Amanda wasn't sharing his laughter, and when she told him about the audition, he felt a familiar old anger tighten in his gut. Amanda saw his hands close into fists and the expression in his eyes darken.

'You, too, huh?' she asked.

'Me too? Oh yes, me, too, for sure.'

'But I thought in the marines you were all like brothers?'

'If we were in a war zone, yes, everyone would have your back, absolutely. But remember, we were stuck in an allied country, in the middle of nowhere. We were trained and ready to fight but basically meant to keep the peace with the protesters, even though we had to be in a state of readiness if the call should come.'

'Against the Russians?'

'The Russkies, the Chinese… anyone. But it never came.'

'Thank goodness.'

'Yeah, but still we were all trapped there, together, lots of us from all over. Looking for somewhere to belong. Sometimes joining the marines, or any of the forces, was the only way out, the best chance at a future away from what we grew up with. Guys stuck with their own kind. Rednecks, cowboys, street punks from the big cities. Back then, there were a few Mexicans. There's a lot more Hispanics now. In Scotland, about twenty of us were black, and we all knew each other. Looked out for our brothers, you know?'

Amanda nodded, waiting to see if he would go on. He shook his head, then turned and looked off to the distance.

'Bastards. We were there to support them. We hadn't invaded, we weren't at war with them, but they hated us.'

'Who?'

'The locals, that's who! That's who we did battle with. Fucking guerrilla warfare! Waiting to jump on any of us out on our own. Attacking the one place we could go for a bit of entertainment off the base. They allowed dogs into the pubs, but not men. Black men like us were kept separate!' Howard's voice had become louder and more strident with each phrase he uttered. Soon all the other diners had turned to stare. Their young waiter came over, shuffling nervously from foot to foot, the spots on his chin reddening on his pale face. He waited for a moment, then asked if they needed anything more or if they would like the check.

Howard stood up, and with his face barely an inch from the young boy's, growled, 'Yeah, get the check... *boy!*'

The waiter stood stock still for several moments. Amanda didn't know what to do and watched Howard, trying to predict his next move. He was staring at the young man with an intensity that worried her. Just as she decided to step in and try to break the tension, the waiter spoke up.

'I'll bring your check right over, sir. My name's Randy, and it's been a pleasure to serve you this evening.' With that he turned and walked toward the cash desk.

'Howard!' Amanda spoke to him in a hissed whisper. 'How could you? He's only a kid. Probably working here to pay for college. He didn't do anything worse than walk over here when you were mad about something in the past!'

'But it's not. You're proof it's not in the past. You're the generation after me, and it's still hurting. Look how quickly the memory of those assholes putting you down resurfaced! The wound may have scabbed over, but a single word, *witch*, and it's bleeding again.'

Randy was standing a few paces behind Howard, holding a small plate with the check weighted down by two pieces of peppermint candy. As soon as Howard stopped speaking, he stepped forward and placed the plate on the table.

'Here you are, sir. I'll be happy to sort that for you when you're ready. No rush, though. Would you care for more coffee?'

Amanda had already taken money out to pay for the meal and added an extra ten-dollar tip. Howard was still glowering at the waiter, so she placed the cash on the plate, stood, and slid round the booth towards Howard, forcing him to move too.

'Thanks, Randy, that's fine. Everything's good, thank you.' She took Howard by the arm and steered him towards the door.

This time Amanda silently simmered. A knot of tension had formed in her stomach. It wasn't the memory of the discrimination that caused it but Howard's outburst at the young waiter. Unable to trust herself to speak in case she lost control and shouted – or, worse still, cried – she didn't say a word, didn't even look in his direction. She could see her father glancing towards her, waiting for her to comment. His total self-absorption couldn't be ignored by her any longer. She knew he was waiting for her to sympathise with him over how unfairly he felt Dunoon had treated him. He was nearly fifty years old and yet still carried that chip on his shoulder about how he'd been treated by others. Amanda had faced prejudice, too, but she didn't allow herself to be a victim of it. She hadn't been raised that way.

Her mother had taught that if you treat others fairly, you should expect to be treated with the same respect. When she was a youngster, justice had been swift when she overstepped the line.

It was a lesson she had learned well. When they were children, Jamie had given in to her every demand. Any toy she wanted, he gave her; whatever game she wanted to play, he played. Amanda was smaller and younger, but he gave in to her wishes every time. Until Marion caught her.

When she was four, they were building houses with Lego. Five-year-old Jamie was the labourer and general dogsbody, while little Amanda was designer, architect, and director of operations. A vital piece had gotten stuck behind the radiator, and she demanded Jamie squeeze his hand under it to retrieve the missing piece. Twice he tried but had to withdraw as the pipe behind was so hot his hand was getting burnt. Amanda needed that part. She demanded he try again, told him it was his fault it was stuck there, anyway, and he'd better get it out or she would never play with him again. Just as Jamie, with a trembling lip, was about to try for the third time, they heard a slow round of applause.

Her mother stood at the kitchen doorway, clapping her hands in mock appreciation. 'What a performance, little lady! Who made you queen for a day?'

Amanda scowled at her mother, who walked over to the window, slipped the tea towel from her arm, and dropped one end behind the radiator. Grasping the towel top and bottom, she slid it sideways, pushing the building block out the side gap, where it fell onto the carpet.

'Right, madam, get this Lego put in the case and tidy all the mess up. Jamie, son, you come in the kitchen, and we'll get your hand sorted.'

The tone of her mother's voice told Amanda there would be no negotiation, so she set about her task without argument. Once Jamie was settled in front of the television with a biscuit and juice, Amanda was taken into the bedroom, stood in front of her bed, and told that the way she had treated Jamie was very naughty. Her mother asked how she would feel if Jamie had made her put a hand behind a hot radiator. The telling thing was when she was asked how she would feel if a bigger boy made Jamie hurt himself. Amanda began to cry at the very thought of it.

'You wouldn't like it, would you?' said Marion, and the little girl shook her head so vigorously her curls bounced and brushed the tears off her cheeks. She would not be allowed to play with Jamie for three days, and there would be no television or sweets until the weekend. Three days go by very slowly for a kiddie of that age, and Amanda would never forget how isolated that punishment made her feel. She told Jamie how sorry she was and hugged and kissed him to underline her apology.

When Auntie Sheila came to collect Jamie that afternoon, she overheard her mum telling her what had happened. Marion spoke in an angry whisper. 'God knows her father must be in there somewhere, Sheila, but she's *my* daughter, and I'll be damned if any of his cruel streak will be allowed room to grow.'

Now, looking across at her father, she shivered at the memory of her mother's words.

She didn't feel angry; even her shock at his behaviour towards the waiter had dwindled. All that was left was a cold stone of disappointment. Years of dreams and wishes for her father came together in a brittle realisation: what an unworthy specimen this man was. Half her DNA came from him. This selfish failure was the truth she'd spun her fantasies around. On the way back to her motel, she looked over at him sitting in the driver's seat of his truck and saw him warming his self-righteousness. All those years, and still he couldn't move beyond past injustices.

At the age of twenty-seven, she'd finally managed to find this man. But right now, she felt grateful to her mother for keeping his identity from her. She'd often resented her mother's obstinate refusal to tell her who had fathered her, and now she could begin to understand why.

She wanted to go home. Back to where she felt wanted, loved, and familiar. She wanted her house, her mum, and Uncle Davy, and most of all she wanted Jamie.

In the time it took to drive back to her motel, she accepted the fact that she didn't want to pursue any meaningful relationship with her father. It was done. She'd found him and put together the missing pieces of how she'd come about. Most of them, at least. The only thing that still puzzled her was how her mother could have had a relationship with this man in the first place. She'd been in her twenties when Amanda had been conceived. Old enough and, from what Amanda could determine, experienced enough to have been on the pill. It made her squirm to think of her mother having sex at all, but even if she had been young and a bit promiscuous, she'd never have one-night stands. From the little she did know, her parents had been seeing each other for several months before Marion knew Amanda was on the way.

'It's not late, Howard. They have free coffee in reception. Come in, and let's see if we can talk without any more drama.'

The lounge area was deserted, and they settled in the farthest corner on two comfortable couches, shielded from view by the motel's enormous fake plants. Howard held his coffee and put the plastic stirrer in his mouth like a cigarette.

'I still miss it, smoking.' Sitting back, he took the stick from his lips and pretended to exhale smoke. 'You saw the oxygen in the trailer. Can't smoke around that stuff. It was easier just to give it up completely. Never was any good at rationing myself. All or nothing, that's me.'

Amanda smiled an acknowledgement. She wanted to ask him about the relationship with her mother. This was the last thing she needed him to explain. After that, she could turn around and go home. Not satisfied, certainly not happy, but… What? Vindicated? Justified? Yes, maybe justified for all the detective work she had put herself and others through. Right to have spent so much of their hard-earned cash on this trip. She'd push Howard to tell her what had brought them together. How did it all start?

She thought talking about Dunoon again would bring back the self-pitying Howard she had begun to despise, but for the moment he seemed willing to speak about the early days of his posting. He told her how he had made friends with a few others at the base and one man he became real close with, even going as far as to say he became like a new brother.

Of all the pubs in the town, only three served Americans, and the Anchor Inn was the sole bar where black Americans were welcome. His friend didn't drink but agreed to go along with Howard because the two of them enjoyed each other's company. The prices were double what the locals paid in their bars, but the atmosphere was sociable, and the barmaids were pretty.

His friend was immediately taken with one of the barmaids and would sit nursing his soda, watching her work, and listening to her sweet voice. She clearly liked him too. He was taller than any of the others and had a soft southern drawl that girls loved. He asked to escort her home after the bar closed, and they soon became a couple.

'Do you know what they did to him?' Howard looked across at Amanda but didn't wait for a reply. 'They jumped him. Ten of them, when he was on his own. Ten of those *brave* Scottish punks beat the shit out of him. Left him for dead.' His eyes flashed with anger. 'It took a goddamn miracle to save him, and he lived, but… no, things were never the same again.'

'That's terrible, Howard. I hope they were thrown in jail for a long time.'

He sat back in his chair and shook his head, snorting with derision. 'Jail? No, not a single one of them were ever prosecuted. They all had alibis in each other. Our goddamn top brass decided to let it slide rather than stir up more trouble.' He pursed his lips in frustration. 'He was shipped back home for treatment, and I lost another brother.'

Amanda looked at him closely, trying to understand what his poor friend's fate had to do with her mother.

'I'm getting to that,' he snapped at her, although she hadn't asked aloud. 'The girl was there when the beating happened. She was hysterical. Your mum looked after her. Not just that night but for months afterwards. My friend couldn't tell us who was responsible, but the girl could. I started to go visit her. Sure, to comfort her. She wasn't the one who had caused this, not really, but she didn't want to give me any names. She had been born and raised in that damn place and seemed to still feel some kinda loyalty to those bastards.' Howard paused for a moment and swept his hand across his face. 'I had to know. You get that, right?'

A faint uneasiness nudged at Amanda, but she shrugged it off and said nothing, giving him free rein to continue.

'Yeah, there had to be some sort of justice, and no one else was doing anything. Not the military police, and certainly not the local force... so it was up to us – his brothers.'

'But you didn't know who was responsible, did you?'

'Not for a while, but they were all in it together, you know? If they didn't land the blows, they helped cover up for those that did.'

'So, all-out warfare? Did the marines just do battle with every man in Dunoon?'

He tutted and shook his head derisively. 'No, we're not animals. We still have a code.'

Amanda raised an eyebrow but decided against challenging his pride. 'So, my mum...?'

'Well, I got to know your mother when I was seeing her friend to try to find out the names of the punks. She was cute and sweet, caring for her friend like that. Anyway, we started to get close, and one night they burst into the bar, looking for a fight.'

'Who did?'

'Some of the Scots boys. Idiots! Too stupid to realise they were dealing with a trained fighting force! Waving knives and home-made weapons… Look, a tyre iron ripped into my leg.' He pulled up the hem of his trousers and showed her a large scar just above the ankle bone. 'When the cops came, I couldn't get away, and that's when she… your mother hid me in the cellar. We were both hyped up with all the fighting, and when she came down to let me know it was safe, well… one thing led to another.'

'But it wasn't a one-off, was it? You kept seeing each other, didn't you?'

'Yeah, sure we did. It suited both of us. We were good together. She had a room in a boarding house where she did some work, and we went back there a lot.'

'How long did you see each other for?'

Howard shrugged and shook his head. 'Not sure… A while.'

'So why did you split up? She didn't tell you when she found out she was expecting me. Was it over by that time between you?'

'I don't know, really. I don't know when she realised she was pregnant. Even if she had told me, I couldn't have been sure it was mine – not back then. I'd met someone else and moved on. Your mother didn't put up any sort of a fight. In fact, I didn't even see her again once I started seeing the other girl. So' – he shrugged – 'I thought we'd both realised the relationship had run its course.'

'You went off with another girl? Just went off without talking to my mum? You didn't even end things properly? No wonder she didn't tell you she was pregnant.' Amanda's voice rose. She was struggling to keep her temper under control, feeling anger on behalf of her mother at this callous individual who could just move on without a word – no explanation, no apology.

'Wait now. Just hold on there, girlie. Your mother was supposed to be on the pill. I don't know how you came to be, but I sure as hell wasn't out to make babies with her. She was a barmaid, for Chrissake, and don't be thinkin' she was any kind of virgin when we got togeth—'

His head bounced to the side as Amanda stood and gave him a resounding slap across his cheek. Immediately, he too was on his feet and face to face with her, fury making his eyes bulge, a vein at his temple pulsing above where she had caught him with the force of the blow. His fists were clenched, and his lips had disappeared in an angry grimace.

'You don't get to do that!' He ground the words out through his teeth. 'I'm a fucking marine. I could snap you in a second!' He demonstrated, clicking his fingers in her face.

She raised herself onto her toes, leaned forward, and snarled inches from his face.

'You're a disgrace, that's what you are. A fucking marine' – she mimicked him – 'a fucking machine, more like! I've no idea what attracted my mum to you in the first place, but I will not listen to you putting her down to try and excuse your behaviour. You're nothing but a selfish…' She drew a deep breath. 'The only good thing you've ever done for her or me is be a sperm donor!'

His eyes twitched and his lips twisted as he tried to bring his rage under control. He began to spit out words: 'You don't know me…'

Amanda turned and strode towards the lift. She had barely gone three paces when fingers closed around her arm and she spun to face a furious Howard.

'Take your hands off me!'

'Not until you listen to me, to my side of things. Don't think you can burst into my life, turn it inside out, then slap me and walk away.' He dropped his grip on her arm, but they remained standing, faces just inches apart. 'You have no idea what I've been through, in Dumb-noon or afterwards. When I was first contacted to verify I had fathered a child back in 1972, I thought it was a cruel joke. I felt sick.' He threw his head back, closed his eyes, and slowly blew his breath out through pursed lips before continuing in a more controlled tone. 'The first thing I wanted to do was go out and get drunk, really deep-down drunk. Do you know how hard it was for me to resist falling back down that tunnel? No, of course you don't. You wanted to find your father. You never asked yourself if your father wanted you!'

'I have a right to know—' she began, but Howard raised his voice once more, drowning her out.

'My life was a living fucking nightmare… for years! Finally, I get myself sorted, know who I am. I find a peaceful way of living, being settled. I mattered. At last, I mattered in this world. Then you come and stomp all over it, over me. Where's my fucking peace now?'

Suddenly, they were both silent. Howard turned and walked out the glass doors to the car park. He slammed the door of his truck, then reversed from the space. Grinding it into first gear, he didn't glance at a small white sedan that raced into the drop-off space at reception or at the tall, young black man who tumbled from the passenger side and raced towards the motel.

14 /
london, england, summer 1983

THE WAITER SHOWED THEM TO A TABLE ON THE PAVEMENT JUST outside the door. Marion smiled at him as he pulled the chair out. Ronnie seated himself opposite, scraping the black metal legs along the paving stones. Even at this time of the evening, it was still hot, and they were glad of the shade the overhead canopy gave them. Marion pushed her sunglasses to the top of her head, sweeping her fringe off her forehead, and enjoyed feeling a wisp of breeze on her face. Once they were settled at the tiny table, the waiter handed them each a large menu and pointed out the specials in a bad Italian accent.

The couple stifled a giggle as they looked at each other over the top of the cardboard. Ronnie lowered his menu and addressed the waiter with a solemn expression.

'Bella, bella. Due vini si prega!' He waved his hands extravagantly and rolled his head and shoulders in rhythm to the sing-song tone of his voice.

Marion couldn't contain herself any longer and grabbed her napkin to mask the spluttering laughter, disguising it as a coughing fit.

'Your accent was miles better than his,' she said, still laughing minutes later when they were each holding a glass of red wine.

'What can I tell you? I am a man of the world, after all. Let's not tell him I've never been further than Dagenham!' He lifted his glass towards her in a salute.

'My lips are sealed… Well, apart from drinking this wine and eating my lasagne when it gets here!' She lifted her glass to him, but he wasn't looking at her face. His eyes were wandering over her cleavage, which was spotted with beads of sweat in the hot evening sun.

'Hey! It's unlucky to toast someone without looking them in the eye! Up here, mate!'

'What? Oh, sorry, it's just… No, sorry…' He cleared his throat. 'Unlucky? I didn't know you were superstitious.'

She shrugged. 'A long time ago I worked with a lady who was very superstitious; some of it must have rubbed off on me, I suppose.' She was still holding her glass up to clink against his.

'Cheers, my lovely,' he said, tipping the rim of his wine glass against hers. He leaned over the table to emphasise staring directly into her eyes, and then crossed his own to look down his nose.

'That's better,' she said. 'No need to ask what was going through your mind.'

'Can you blame me? I've waited a long time for this evening.'

Marion shook her head and, placing her elbows on the table, balanced her chin on her hands.

'Not as long as me, Ronnie. It's so long since I've had' – she leaned in towards him and lowered her voice to a whisper – '*sex*, that I don't know if I remember how to do it.'

'Ah, sweetheart, it's like riding a—'

She quickly placed her fingers on his lips to stop him finishing his words. 'Don't you dare say it!' she told him sternly as he began kissing her fingertips. 'Where I come from, calling a girl a' – again she whispered – '*bike* is like calling her a prossie, a tart.' Her voice rose in a parody of shocked aristocracy. 'A woman of easy virtue!'

'No bleedin' danger of that, Marion Barr. There's nothing easy about your virtue.'

'Well, that might not have always been the case, Ronnie. How do you think I got my Amanda?'

'So, what changed? What turned you into this *born-again* virgin?'

Marion looked at him and sighed. How could she tell him about her life in Dunoon? This lovely man who made her laugh, who was kind, considerate, and patient. How could he understand he was exactly the opposite of the last man she had slept with?

She held out her empty wine glass, and he poured her what little was left of the bottle. Smiling, she half closed her eyes. 'If talking about my last lover is your idea of foreplay, then I've got to tell you… you're gonna be a lonely, lonely boy tonight.'

'Nope, you're right. Forget I asked. I'm going right back to staring at your boobs and fantasising about licking that trickle of sweat to see where it leads!' He opened his eyes wide and rubbed his hands together, miming lust.

She was glad he was back to joking around again; she felt more comfortable with him that way. Speaking about past mistakes might cast a different mood on the whole evening. In fact, she was frightened he could see her in a whole new light. They'd been friends for a long time, and he'd never made a secret of how much he fancied her, but his friendship was all she wanted or had space for in her life when they first met and for a long time afterwards. She wasn't sure when she realised her feelings had changed. He'd had girlfriends before, nothing that lasted more than a few weeks, but then he'd begun to date the new receptionist where they both worked.

Marion knew exactly when Ronnie and the receptionist had first slept together. The looks between them as they stepped out of the elevator together were unmistakeable. A sudden twist of jealousy had taken her breath away. She hadn't felt pain like that in many years. Back then, she had walked away. He hadn't been worth fighting for, but Ronnie… no, this time she was staying. This time the other girl could walk away.

Marion squinted as the late August sunshine streamed in, and a small sigh escaped before she could stop it. She shouldn't feel sad. It was a nice house and had loads more room than the flat, with a garden at the back, and she and Amanda each had their own room. She had a new double bed for the first time in her life. Amanda's room had their old twin beds, but that was so she could have friends to stay over. Turning to avoid the dazzling sunshine, Marion watched her daughter from the bedroom door. Amanda was sitting on top of her desk, leaning her head against the window frame. Probably watching for her uncle Davy to get back from dropping Jamie and Sheila off.

'You'll see him again soon.'

Amanda turned to face her, tears spilled from her big brown eyes, and a shuddering sob broke free.

A few swift steps took Marion to her daughter's side. 'Aww, sweetheart, don't cry. He'll be back before you know it, an' you'll be bossing him about again in no time.' Marion cradled her daughter's shoulders and buried her face in the soft dark curls. 'Shh, shh. There, there, darlin'. Look at your lovely room. You've got a new school that's just down the road, and you'll soon make loads of new friends.' Marion stroked her hair one more time, then, standing back, held her at arm's length so Amanda had to look at her. 'Right, enough now. I don't want your uncle Davy seein' you all upset. He's doing all this for us. He's uprooted himself and moved down here so we can have a lovely house and you can go to a better school.'

'I don't want to go to that school. I don't know anybody, and they all stared at me when we went to enrol. You saw them, I know you did.'

Marion hugged her daughter tightly, then bent so their faces were inches apart. 'Listen to me, Amanda, you are my clever, beautiful girl, and that school will be lucky to have you. Believe in yourself, and remember, if you treat people with respect, you can expect to be treated that way too.' She moved her mouth to her daughter's ear and whispered, 'But if anyone gives you any shit… then they'll have me to deal with. Okay?'

Amanda opened her mouth to speak but thought better of it and just sniffed loudly and let out a deep sigh. She nodded to her mother.

'Right, go wash your face and hands. Uncle Davy's bringing fish suppers back for tea. Go on… and cheer up. That's an order, miss.'

Amanda managed a crooked smile before running to the bathroom to freshen up.

Marion looked around the little bedroom. She felt like having a wee cry herself. Eleven years in the flat; all the worry of raising her baby on her own. Making every penny do the work of two. Stuff other folk didn't want; rummaging in bargain bins and charity shops. It should have been awful, but it wasn't. Yes, it had been hard, but plenty of the neighbours were single mums too. The church had moved them there once their babies were six months, so they all faced the same challenges, but faced them with others who understood and helped.

Couldn't get credit? Liz on the eighth floor had a brother who would co-sign for you. Doctor wouldn't prescribe the pill for you? Register with the one Alice went to; he was young and more understanding. There would always be someone to turn to. And of course there was Sheila. She'd been better than any sister and sometimes more like a mother to Marion.

Their kids had been raised together and shared a bond even distance wouldn't break. Jamie and Amanda were simply two of the huge variety of kids in the area. Racist remarks weren't unknown, but they certainly didn't cut as deep there. That was a part of London where the melting pot of nationalities produced nicknames for boys like Gandy, whose family were among the first to come to Britain when Idi Amin expelled the Ugandan Asians. There were Packy and Jammy, boys whose families came from Bangladesh and Jamaica, and Hammy, who was a young Jewish boy whose full name was Abraham – but even his mother had been heard to refer to him this way when calling him to come home.

Jamie was a big strong boy the others looked up to and was known as Jay or sometimes J-man, and when he spoke, the others listened. Everyone knew he and Amanda were close. Some had mistaken them for brother and sister when they were very young, but Jamie had told everyone they were cousins because it was easier than a long explanation. It meant Amanda always had Jamie's protection, and Marion had never had to worry about her being bullied or picked on. Here at the new school, in a new area, it would be different. Her daughter would have to learn to fend for herself.

Movement outside the window caught her eye, and she saw the big blue car draw up. Her brother got out, trying to balance a package of hot fish suppers and a bottle of cola that he had tucked under his arm so he could turn and lock the car door. She would go and help soon, but for a few moments she stood watching him, appreciating just how lucky she was and crossing her fingers that it would last.

15 / peckham, london, england, december 1983

MARION, AMANDA, AND DAVY HAD SWITCHED OFF THE MAIN LIGHTS and stood admiring the colourful, twinkling fairy lights. The tree looked wonderful.

'Och, girls, that's beautiful. It's been a long time since I've seen such a great tree.'

Marion looked over to her brother to see if memories were upsetting him, but his expression wasn't visible in the pulsing colours. She stepped over and linked arms with him.

'Aye, and there's nothing to beat the smell of a real tree. This one's a beauty, isn't it, Amanda?'

'It's really nice.' Amanda gave a deep sigh. 'The girls in my class all have artificial ones, and they've had them up for ages. Why did we have to wait till now?'

'Because real ones don't last forever, but they're definitely worth the wait. Aren't they, Davy?'

He laughed and turned to switch the lamps back on. 'Aye, an' if you know you only have something for a short time, you appreciate it all the more. Your pals will be dragging the same tree out the loft year after year, an' each time it'll be that bit less sparkly. A wee bit less magical.'

Just One Little Pill

'Right! Come on, we need to get the beds changed and the camp bed set up for Jamie in your uncle Davy's room. Move, please, there's loads to do.'

Marion shepherded them from the living room and made her way upstairs, lifting a folded pile of bedding from the armchair as she passed. Sheila and Jamie were arriving later that evening and spending all of Christmas and New Year with them. Ronnie would be joining them, too, but wouldn't arrive until Christmas morning, and that would mean another reshuffle with beds. She felt a tingle at the very thought of him. They had only been a couple since June, but their friendship had started many years before, when Marion joined the company. She still marvelled at how uninterested she had been in him sexually for all that time; she now struggled to keep her hands to herself whenever he was near. He was in her mind constantly. She would go over things he had said to her, the touch of his hands, the way his eyebrow was crooked and made him look quizzical. His hair covered it most of the time, but when they lay quietly together, she studied every nuance of his features, his hands, his smooth chest with only four hairs sprouting strangely in the centre.

She pushed the pillow into the fresh slip and imagined him lying on it, looking at her.

Okay, today was Friday. Only two more days till Christmas, and then she would see him, be with him. It had been tricky, sounding out Davy and Amanda to see how they would feel if Ronnie slept with her when he stayed over. She was wary of Amanda particularly, taking it badly, feeling pushed out. Everyone had known about the change in her feelings for Ronnie from the first night they went out on a real date. No one had been negative in any way; quite the opposite. Sheila had even laughed and applauded when Marion told her.

'Thank the Lord!' she had exclaimed, looking to the sky. 'It's

117

about time too. You deserve to find someone, someone nice who'll treat you well and make you happy, and Ronnie's lovely.'

He is lovely, thought Marion, *always happy and trying to make others laugh and be happy too.* There was a warmth to him that she felt so comfortable and protected by. On the rare occasions she allowed herself to compare him to men from previous relationships, Ronnie's character shone even brighter in her estimations.

The torn Christmas paper had been balled up, crammed into one of the big gift bags and pushed in at the side of the couch along with empty packaging and boxes from Amanda's and Jamie's gifts. The television in the corner of the room was still on and had been since early morning. Jamie's gifts were scattered throughout the lounge, but Amanda's were stacked neatly under the tree. All except for her Cabbage Patch doll, which she hugged in front of herself as she sat on the floor with her back propped against Davy's armchair.

Amanda watched her mum flutter and giggle around that Ronnie guy. He was nice enough, always gave her one of the new pound coins when he saw her, but she wasn't sure she was ready for things to get more serious between the two of them. She was still struggling to cope with moving here to Uncle Davy's house.

Out of the corner of her eye, she noticed Jamie waggling his eyebrows to get her attention. He jerked his head backwards, and she realised he wanted her to go into the kitchen.

'I'm going to get some more cola. Anyone need anything while I'm in there?' She looked around the room.

'No thanks, hen. I couldn't manage another bite, although maybe another wee bottle of beer for me to sip on would be all right.' Davy smiled at his niece and handed her an empty bottle.

Amanda carefully sat her new doll out of harm's way and headed into the hall, where Jamie caught up with her.

'Come on, quick.' He put a hand on her back and gently pushed to hurry her along. Closing the kitchen door behind him, he put his finger to his lips. Amanda shook her head and skewed her face to question him. Without a word, Jamie lifted an open bottle of cola and handed it to her, nodding to get her to taste it.

She sipped it gingerly, and Jamie's face broke into a broad grin. 'Bacardi!' His body bobbed up and down in soundless mirth.

Amanda thrust the bottle back at him and shook her head. 'No thanks, I'll just stick to ordinary cola.' Then she looked at his face more closely. 'Have you had some?'

Jamie nodded and covered his mouth with his hand but allowed a snorting noise to escape through his nose.

'Oh-oh, your mum better not find out. She'll kill you.'

'Nup, she's got no idea. She's had about six gins herself. Go on, have some. It'll cheer you up. What's wrong with you, anyway? D'you not like your presents?'

'Nothing's wrong, and of course I liked my presents.' Her expression brightened. 'Did you see my new baby?'

'Yeah, it's an ugly-looking thing.'

'It is not! I love it. She's mine, and I've got the birth certificate to prove it.' This brought back a frown. 'I've got all her papers. She's adopted… just like I'll be.'

Jamie was stunned; then, gathering himself again, he grunted, 'Who would adopt you? Your mum wouldn't part with you. That's just a daft thing to say.'

'No, it's not!' Amanda stood as tall as she could and faced up to Jamie, although her nose barely reached his chin. 'If Mum marries Ronnie, he'll want to adopt me so I'll never find my real dad.'

'Well, your real dad is a dirty rotten shit, so you don't want to find him anyway.'

Amanda fell back in shock, bumping into the kitchen table, which was serving as a temporary bar. Two of the empty beer bottles started to wobble and were about to fall when Davy appeared and caught them.

'What's going on here?' Davy placed the bottles back on the table and looked from Amanda to Jamie. 'Who's a shit?'

Both youngsters looked at the floor, mumbling and turning away from each other.

'Come on, it's Christmas Day, for Chrissake. You shouldn't be arguing today of all days. In fact, you two shouldn't be arguing at all. It's weeks since you've seen each other. 'Mon, shake an' be pals again.'

Amanda looked up at her uncle with a fierce expression pulling at her face. *No, Davy, no, Go away. Mind your own business.* Then she looked over at Jamie, willing him to meet her gaze, but he was still concentrating on scuffing his shoes on the floor. Who did he think he was, talking about her father like that? She wanted to scream at him, tell him he was wrong, but she couldn't say a thing while Davy was there. Without a word, she stamped out of the kitchen and upstairs to her room.

'What's up wi' her?' Davy looked sternly at Jamie. 'Who's the dirty rotten shit you don't want her to find?'

Jamie began to retch. He put his hand to his mouth, and Davy quickly spun him around to lean over the kitchen sink. The boy heaved and vomited for the next few minutes, struggling to catch his breath, as Davy ran the taps to cover the noise, then lifted a wooden spoon from the draining board and used the handle to poke the solids down the drain.

'Here, drink this.' Davy thrust a glass of water at him. He wrung out a tea towel and placed the cool cloth on the back of the boy's neck.

Jamie sipped the water and studied the glass, mumbling his thanks.

'What's happened? Is everything okay?' Marion had opened

the kitchen door and stood looking in. Ronnie was just behind her.

'Ach, the boy's been eating too much chocolate and other rubbish on top of all the excitement. He's been a wee bit sick, but now he's got it up, he's feeling a lot better. Aren't you, son?'

Jamie nodded, still not meeting anyone's gaze. He pulled the damp tea towel from his neck and buried his face in it. All three adults watched him, then exchanged glances with each other.

'What? There's something else. Tell me.' Marion's expression was determined and fixed hard on her brother.

'He and Amanda had a bit of a fall out. I think that was the last straw for this one's upset stomach.' He gently put his arm round the boy's shoulders, which sloped dejectedly. 'Go and say goodnight to your mum, then get up to bed. Everything'll be better in the morning.' He gave him a gentle push. 'Go on, I'll be up soon myself.'

Marion and Ronnie stepped back to let him through and said goodnight as he passed. Rolling her eyes and shaking her head, Marion took Ronnie's hand and pulled him into the kitchen.

'We'll clear up the rest of the dishes and pots, Davy. Sheila is sound asleep in front of the telly. See if you can get her to go up to bed as well.'

Once the couple were alone in the kitchen, they began to lift some of the trash and debris from the day's festivities. A little later, as one turned towards the sink and the other towards the refrigerator, they met midway. Without any other part of their bodies touching, their lips met and softly kissed.

'Merry Christmas, Miss Barr.'

'Merry Christmas to you, too, Mr Spencer.'

'Is there mistletoe?'

'Who needs mistletoe?'

They emptied their hands of the chores and moved into a deep embrace. Making the most of this little piece of privacy, they indulged in their first passionate kiss of the day.

Totally absorbed in enjoying each other's body, they were deaf to the sound of someone coming downstairs.

'Mum, Auntie Sheila's snoring…'

Before either of them could stop her, Amanda had run from the room, and all they could hear was her feet dashing away.

Marion sat on the edge of the table and covered her face. Ronnie bent down to speak to the back of her hands.

'Do you want me to go and talk with her?'

'No! God, no. That's the worst thing you could do.' She stood up and buttoned his shirt. 'No, you finish tidying here, and I'll meet you in the bedroom once I've calmed her down. It's not as if she didn't know we're dating. She's eleven, not four years old. Besides, she likes you. She'll be fine. She just wasn't expecting to find us… all dishevelled!' She giggled and went upstairs.

Amanda sat cross-legged on her bed, cuddling her new doll. She heard her mother's footsteps and knew she was coming to talk to her. Well, she didn't want to hear it all again. How special Ronnie was, how it didn't change how much she loved her, how grown-ups get lonely, and blah and blah and blah! She pulled the covers over her head and curled up just as Mum entered.

'Amanda,' she whispered. 'Amanda. I know you're still awake. Come on, pet, I don't want to wake Auntie Sheila.' A loud snore from the other bed was the only response. 'Okay, be like that, Amanda. We can talk about it tomorrow, just remember, I love you very much. Oh, and merry Christmas.' Mum quietly closed the door.

Amanda pulled her dolly closer and whispered angrily into her pillow. 'This is the worst Christmas ever!'

. . .

Next morning Jamie opened one eye, then quickly closed it as a stream of light lasered into the back of his skull. His mouth had a sour fur coating inside. The camp bed he was on had a dip in the middle, so levering his long legs over the edge required coordination that was a challenge for him this morning. It was easier to lean over and roll onto the floor, which invited him to stay for a while.

He hadn't meant to groan out loud, but knew he must have when he heard Davy's voice.

'Aye, I'll bet you're full of the joys today, Jamie boy!'

'What time is it?' His voice sounded alien, hoarse and sticky.

'Time you were out your pit and getting fresh air into your lungs.' A bright red sweatshirt flew toward him, but he couldn't manage to catch it, and it landed fully on top of his head.

'Right, give your face a quick wash and put your clothes on. We're going for a good walk. It'll set you up to face the day.'

Jamie reluctantly forced his legs to move and allowed them to lead the rest of his body into the bathroom. Within ten minutes he was cocooned in his parka and he and Davy were heading down the street towards the waste ground behind the church.

'Did you tell anyone?' he asked without lifting his chin above his collar.

'Tell anyone what? That you'd been drinking? No, no need. You feel bad enough without having women nagging at you as well.'

'Yeah… thanks, but no. I meant about what I said to Amanda.'

Davy sighed. After a pause, he stopped and turned to face the young boy.

'I wanted to ask you about that…'

Guilt and alcohol are a potent mix for anyone, but especially for a twelve-year-old boy. Jamie shivered even though he was wrapped in warm clothes and only his eyes and nose were exposed to the cold December air.

He gulped and shook his head, hoping that Davy would let it go and not ask him anything more about his outburst last night. The expression in the older man's eyes made that hope fade fast. His head still hurt, and he wished he could think more clearly about just how much he could get away with saying and how much he could leave out. The calculation wouldn't click into place. Every time he tried to form a thought, it fell out his mouth in an inane 'Buhh.'

Davy sat on a low wall and pulled Jamie down beside him.

'Right, just start at the beginning, son. Do you know who Amanda's real dad is?'

Jamie shook his head. That made it hurt even more. He made a silent prayer asking forgiveness and pleading for this punishment to stop.

'But you told Amanda he was "a dirty rotten shit", so how would you know that?'

He shrugged but saw Davy's face bearing down on him. He looked determined, and Jamie knew he was going to have to give him something.

'I heard Mum and Marion talking one time. They said he poisoned someone, another girl, I think. She died.'

Davy pulled back, a stunned look on his face. Whatever he'd expected Jamie to say, it hadn't been that.

'Who was the girl, Jamie? Do you know her name? You can tell me. I promise I won't tell Amanda.' Then, after a pause, he added, 'Or your mum and Marion, I promise. I just need to know.'

Jamie twisted his mouth, wishing he had kept it shut last night. Davy looked strange. His eyes were bright, as if he might cry. His hands were clasped together and pressed against his mouth, but he didn't look as though he was going to pray.

Jamie felt frightened. Davy was always so easy-going. He

never nagged him and always took his side if Mum was telling him off. He decided he didn't want to say any more, wished he hadn't said anything in the first place. God would forgive a white lie if it was to stop someone feeling bad, and Davy looked as though he was feeling really bad right now.

'I don't know, they didn't say a name.' All at once his headache eased, and he knew God approved and loved him once again.

Davy sat on the bottom stair and slowly untied his bootlaces. Hearing about Amanda's father had rocked him. He had been so sure the big secret was that Jamie and Amanda had the same father. He pulled off one of his boots and let it drop. No one had ever said as much, but the two kids were so alike. Born just a year apart, each mother falling pregnant in Dunoon to a black American who turned his back on her. Well, it was difficult not to draw conclusions. He hadn't been the only one who thought that. He and Ina had discussed it many times before she sank into her last, fatal depression. They had been surprised when they saw Marion had a baby, although it did explain why she'd left Dunoon and their Diane. He held his other muddy boot and looked up at the door in front of him. He thought back to his home in Glasgow. Seeing his sister at their door carrying baby Amanda had been a shock, and one that was compounded when they saw the baby was coloured. After all, how many darkies were there in Dunoon?

But now… poison… and the poor girl who died. Davy felt his old shock and pain return with gut-wrenching force. How had her parents felt? Dear God, his life had changed forever the night they lost Diane. His grief was a black leaden caul that stayed with him. When prodded, it shifted and cut him off from rational thought, leaving him feeling chilled and alone.

He firmly turned away from that painful train of thought and forced himself to concentrate on the here and now. Jamie had told him all he knew, but Marion knew the whole story. She must. She would know who the girl was. Maybe the evil bastard was in jail; maybe that's why he hadn't been able to stand by Marion when she told him she was pregnant. Lots of maybes, damn few answers.

Sheila had known all week that something was wrong with her son. He kept trying to go for walks on his own, and whenever Sheila or one of the others said they fancied going, too, he changed his mind and retreated to his bed. This had always been a fear of hers. She knew that one day he would start to develop feelings, needs, urges that she just wasn't equipped to explain or help him understand.

As a toddler, he would pull his little tassel until it was red and upright. The first time this happened she had panicked and run to Marion for help. Her response had been to slap his hand and tell him firmly to stop it, that he would hurt himself. After that Sheila found that if she took both his hands in hers and prayed, that eventually he would forget about this fascinating toy and be distracted by something else. She couldn't do that now, though.

Maybe Davy could talk to him. Give him a few words of wisdom about the physical side of love. Tell him about the changes his body was beginning to go through. She'd thought those would happen at some point in the far distant future, but suddenly here they were, and somehow Davy no longer seemed like the right man for the job. Jamie had been avoiding him all afternoon. Not an easy task while they were all living in one house and Davy and Jamie were sharing a bedroom.

With a sigh, she considered her naked hands. There had been a time when she had hoped Davy might ask her to come and live with them in Peckham, and not just as a friend. Sure, he was a lot older than her, but he was dependable, and more important, he was kind. She didn't think he would be all that bothered about intimate stuff. After all, he was nearly fifty, and since he'd lost Ina… Well, that was probably all behind him now. It wasn't as if she wanted it. Even those kinds of scenes on TV made her switch channels or leave the room. Thinking about how Jamie had come about was too tied up with the horror that followed. That was a route she absolutely couldn't travel. Davy seemed happy to have them over for weekends, Christmas, or birthday celebrations, but as nice as he always was, he hadn't shown any sign of particularly wanting her companionship.

She looked over at the giggling couple cuddling on the couch. She was glad for Marion. It had been a long time since she'd been with any man. If Sheila was really honest with herself, she had been a little jealous of how popular Marion had been in Dunoon. It had always been easy for Marion to talk to men – anyone, really – and she was never short of company. That was one of the reasons her relationship with Howard Odoms had been such a shock. Marion hadn't been very keen on that particular American when he came into the bar. He would sit beside a sunny and friendly Samuel and be the surly and morose counterpart to his friend. Over the years, she had questioned Marion about what had changed her attitude to Howard Odoms and found it difficult to imagine the concerned and sympathetic character that Marion said he had become in the aftermath of Samuel's attack. But that was such a long time ago, too long for Marion to deny herself the company of an attentive man.

Ronnie was just what Marion needed, even if it had taken her a few years to realise it. They were pretending to watch Top of the Pops reprise the hits of 1983. Perhaps she could ask him to speak with Jamie. She quickly discounted that idea. He was a nice guy and all that, but he was a stranger to her boy, and anyway, asking him would be mortifying. No, maybe the minister or that nice new verger at work would be best. After all, they probably had some training in discussing delicate matters.

Yes, she decided, that was the thing to do. As soon as the New Year was over and they were back home, she would speak with Mr Barbour or Mr Cairns, and they would sort it all out for her. Mr Cairns was nice. He always smiled and shared his flask of tea with her. He'd tried to share his sandwiches, but Sheila couldn't develop a taste for brown bread spread with Bovril, so she began making extra and sharing hers with him, something she looked forward to every day. Spending over a week away from him made her realise how much she enjoyed their little chats. She would ask him to speak to Jamie once they went home. He would handle it well.

She gave a silent prayer of thanks for guiding her decision and pushed her way on to the couch, smiling as Boy George and Culture Club mimed through their big hit of the summer.

16 / peckham, london, england, january 1984

Davy watched Marion stroke her daughter's hair as they sat together on the couch. Amanda had her French book open on her lap and was haltingly reading the words with a strong London accent. It struck him as funny that he didn't hear her English accent until she was reading a foreign language; then suddenly he could hear nothing else, despite the unfamiliarity of the words. Between the three of them they spanned a chasm of regional accents: Davy, with his broad Glaswegian, which had never changed, to Marion, who still used Scottish words and expressions, though her pronunciation was practically BBC now. Amanda, born and raised in the heart of the city, was a Londoner through and through.

As he looked at them, he wondered again about Amanda's father. What kind of accent did he have? American, yes, but was he from the Deep South, a hard man from the Bronx, or maybe one of those surfers like the Beach Boys? Well, okay, that wasn't very likely, but Motown, maybe? They were mostly darkies in those groups. But then if he'd been a singer or musician, he wouldn't have joined the bloody military, would he? It was full of misfits and no-good gits. Fuck up, then fuck off!

He could feel himself going down that path again, working himself up into a temper of injustice, only to hit the wall of frustration just a short distance in. Who the hell was the poor wee soul that man had poisoned? Ever since he'd overheard Jamie at Christmas, it kept reverberating in his brain. There was something about it that bit into him. He needed to talk to Marion. Once she was alone, he would make her a cup of tea and get her to talk to him. Accents: he'd start with accents. She wouldn't see that coming, and then he'd ask her. Yes, now was a good time. She was settled, happy that Amanda had come on so well, happy that she and Ronnie were together and in love. The past wouldn't hurt her now. She could talk about it now.

Marion glanced over at him and smiled. She kissed Amanda's head.

'Well done, but that's enough for tonight. I don't want you pushing so much homework in one side of your brain that stuff falls out the other side. Go get ready for bed, and I'll be up in a few minutes.'

'Night, Uncle Davy.' She stopped at the door and turned and blew a kiss at him. He caught it and slapped it on his cheek.

'Night, Amanda. Sleep tight, don't let the bugs bite, and if they bite…'

'Bite them back!' Amanda smiled at their evening ritual and headed upstairs.

Davy turned to his sister. 'You go up and get her settled down, hen. I'll put the kettle on.'

He watched Marion lift the books and papers off the coffee table, put them into Amanda's school backpack, and head towards the door.

'That would be lovely, Davy. I could just murder a cup of tea. How about a wee bit of toast to go with it?'

'Aye, good idea. I'll have it ready for you in a jiffy.'

'Thanks. You're a smashing brother, the best.' And with that she headed upstairs to her daughter's room.

He poured the boiling water into the teapot, placed it on the tray beside the mugs and a plate of hot buttered toast, and carried it through to the lounge. Soft footsteps were coming downstairs. Instead of going over to his usual armchair by the fireplace, he sat on the couch and stirred both the mugs of tea.

Without glancing up as his sister entered the room, he announced, 'Your supper awaits, ma'am.'

'What a man!' she declared and sat beside him, helping herself to a piece of toast.

'Aye, well, I wanted to talk to you about something, an' it's a bit sensitive, so I thought I'd better butter you up a bit.' He offered her another piece of toast, and she laughed.

'Oh, you know me too well, Davy. Hot toast and a cup of tea, and I'm an open book.' She took a bite of her toast and looked up at Davy's face. Laying her mug and toast on the tray, she leaned back on the couch, half turning so she was facing him.

'What is it? You're not ill, are you?'

'No, nothing like that. It's just... Look, there's no point in going all round the houses. I always thought Jamie and Amanda were brother and sister, but they're not, are they?'

Marion gasped at this startling query. She hadn't thought about Amanda's father in a long time, very deliberately. As for Davy thinking she and Sheila had become pregnant by the same man... Well, it had never entered her head that he could have thought that. She jumped off the couch, crossed to the other side of the room, and stared straight at her brother.

'No, absolutely not. They have separate, very different fathers. Very different.' Her voice was shaking. 'I don't know what could ever have made you think that.' She coughed, once, twice, and then began to choke.

Davy ran to her side and began pounding her back with his

fist, but she twisted away from him and ran to the kitchen. She was leaning against the sink and holding a glass of water by the time he reached her. He rubbed her back, gently this time, and shook his head.

'You okay now, hen?' He took a deep breath and closed his eyes. 'Christ knows I'm no loss to the diplomatic service. I'm sorry, Marion. I didn't mean to just come out with it like that. Are you sure you're okay now?'

She nodded and let him guide her back to the lounge. She sat in the armchair, and Davy knelt in front of her.

'So, there was more than one black man in Dunoon back then. Okay, I shouldn't have jumped to conclusions. Sorry, really, sorry, I don't want to upset you. It's just that I heard something… I wondered…'

'You heard what?'

Davy leaned back a little, hearing the challenge in her tone.

'I heard he was a bad yin.'

'He was, probably still is. If he had been a good one, I would have wanted Amanda to know him, but I knew he was no good, and I was right, more right than I could have possibly known at the time.' Marion's voice had strengthened with each word. She stood up, strode past her kneeling brother, and headed for the door. She paused, holding it open, and without turning around told him, 'Amanda is *my* daughter. The man who made it possible for me to have her has no idea she exists.' She turned and stared hard at Davy. 'It needs to stay that way, for her sake. Understand?'

Davy couldn't speak but nodded and watched his sister sweep out of the room on a wave of purpose he hadn't realised she possessed.

17 /
peckham, london, england, january 1987

Marion had been feeling irritable all morning. She'd snapped at Ronnie before he left for work and then apologised, blaming it on her hormones. He'd responded with a wink and a big daft grin that made her roll her eyes. They'd agreed to keep their secret for a little while longer, but he seemed incapable of masking his delight and had spent the last few weeks beaming at everyone.

Now the noises from the transistor radio her brother was trying to tune in were giving her a headache. The reception was fading in and out, and little snatches of commentary were masked by noise the crowd was making. There was often singing or chanting at the game, but this was strange: it sounded like 'Ooo, ooo, ooo.' Her annoyance grew as she watched her brother move the radio from his ear to his mouth, shouting at it with an aggression she'd rarely heard before.

'What's going on, Davy?' She massaged her temples in an effort to ease the pounding in her head.

'Shh!' he hissed as he waved his hand towards her without moving his gaze from the radio. 'I'm trying to make out what they're sayin', and all I can hear is the bloody crowd chantin'.' He held the radio towards the window and turned the volume up again. 'Listen to that. They've had to delay the game to clear the pitch. Bananas! They're throwing them onto the pitch. That's bloody ridiculous, so it is.' He shook the radio to demonstrate his anger. 'Listen! *"Go back to the jungle"* – God's sake, just get on an' play the bloody game, will you.'

Marion pursed her lips and turned to her daughter, sitting with her book forgotten in her lap. Marion lifted the book and ushered Amanda towards the door.

'Come on, Amanda, upstairs and get your room tidied. Maybe once your uncle has finished listening to his game, we can go out for a while.' She watched her daughter leave, then waited until she heard the bedroom door closing before she turned to her brother and said in an angry whisper, 'Put that radio down. I can't believe you could be so thick!'

Startled, he put the radio down on the sofa and looked at her, puzzlement furrowing his face.

'What?'

'*What?* What do you bloody well think? Have you even noticed that your niece was sitting right there?' She pointed to the empty chair. 'How could you let her hear all that? You're turning the sound up and shouting like you're at the ground. Christ! As if football isn't bad enough with all the sectarian crap, but now those morons are making monkey noises and throwing bananas onto the pitch because there's a *black* man playing? Are you totally insensitive or just plain bloody stupid?'

'Oh, Christ, I'm sorry, hen. I never thought. I don't even think about Amanda's colour, it jist disnae occur to me.' Holding his arms wide in apology, he went on. 'I didn't know there would be all that horrible stuff about the bananas. That poor guy. Even a bloody Rangers player doesn't deserve that.'

'No, and my daughter doesn't deserve to have the uncle she looks up to start behaving like a bigoted, idiotic racist!'

'Hey! I'm not racist, and I'm not a bigot, either, come to that. I wasn't condoning any of that stuff. I was the one objectin' to it!' He firmly turned the dial on the radio to off and flung himself onto the couch, folding his arms and scowling.

'Right, well, don't go in the huff. We've had a nice quiet New Year, and we've still got the weekend in front of us. Let's go out and make the most of it.'

He let out a sigh. 'You're right, Marion. I've made my life down here now. There's nothing left for me in Glasgow, but I do miss my team. I really loved going to the old firm games. The atmosphere… But the nasty religious stuff… Nah, I don't miss that. An' now the Rangers have signed a darkie. Well, that's just gave them another stick to hit them with.'

'I know, Davy. God knows I don't begrudge you a football game, and all the shouting and name-calling has bugger all to do with religion or colour. It's pure bile. It was like that in Dunoon. The local boys hated all the Americans, but there was a smaller group of coloured servicemen, and they were an easier target.'

'Was Amanda's father one of the targets? Is that why you fell for him? You always had a weakness for lame ducks.'

'Huh. Believe me, Howard was no lame duck. No, his best friend was the one the locals pounced on.'

Shock hit Marion like a punch as she realised she'd said more than she'd ever intended.

What a rotten day this had been. She turned and looked at the luminous dial on the bedside clock. Almost 1 a.m. Ronnie snored gently, and she nudged his side to make him move position. He obliged with a splutter and grunt, which made her smile. All evening he'd asked her what was wrong, and she'd fobbed him off with weak excuses. Every time she thought about how she had revealed Howard's name to her brother, she felt her chest tighten. She wanted Ronnie to know about all that had happened back in

Dunoon, but it was so tightly bundled up in her mind. If she started to poke holes in it, then it would all seep out. She couldn't have Amanda know the truth about her father. Ronnie was such a good influence on her life – on both their lives – and she wouldn't allow it to be tainted. Leave the past where it lay.

But... Davy, oh God, Davy. Why was he so interested in Amanda's father? He'd asked a few times now, thinking he was so subtle. Aye, subtle as cymbals! Then today, without even thinking about it, she'd told him Howard's name. Unbelievable! How could she just come right out with it like that? If he ever found out who Howard was, he might make the connection to the man he thought had *heroically* delivered Diane to the hospital. She recalled how he'd said he once thought Amanda and Jamie were brother and sister. But Amanda's brother or sister would have been Diane's baby, Davy's grandchild.

Suddenly she jumped from bed, wakening Ronnie and running towards the bathroom. Then the whole household woke as she vomited noisily.

Ronnie leaned out of the half-opened bathroom door and whispered to Davy.

'Better call an ambulance, Davy. There's a bit of spotting, but I think we should get her to hospital to be on the safe side.'

Marion had been taken into a side room, and they were allowed to wait in the corridor, where a few hard plastic chairs stood in a line against the wall. They had been there for almost an hour, and occasionally one of them would sit on the edge of a chair, then jump up again whenever anyone walked towards them. Soon they were all standing, leaning against the wall or each other for support. Ronnie put his arm around Amanda and buried his face in her dark curls.

'She'll be all right, sweetie. That's the main thing. She'll be all right.' Lifting his head, he sniffed loudly and rubbed his eyes to stem the threatening tears.

He looked over at Davy. His face was drained of colour, eyes wide and staring. Ronnie spoke quietly to him.

'It might be for the best, Davy. It was so early. The little one wasn't ready to come into this world.' He drew in a long slow breath. 'As long as Marion is okay, that's the main thing, isn't it?' His voice caught as he said these words. These weren't his. He heard this sort of thing said about miscarriages. When you work with a dozen women, you pick up snippets of kitchen sink wisdom.

Suddenly Ronnie let out a loud sob. His face crumpled, and he tried to cover it with his hands. Amanda turned and put her arms around him, patting his back to comfort him as he cried on her shoulder.

Davy stood motionless. Still propped against the wall, no longer seeing the people in front of him, he was in a different hospital in a different city.

He could hear Ina. The needle was taped to Diane's hand, and tears were splashing onto it. His tears. She was so small and pale, disappearing into the white sheets. Disappearing, fading, leaving… Ina was telling her to stay, be brave.

'Don't leave us, don't leave us, Diane…'

'We're here, darling. Mum and Dad are right here with you. You're getting more blood, Diane. You'll feel stronger in a minute. Every drop will help you, every drop…' Ina talking, trying to keep Diane with them, keeping her own hysteria at bay. He couldn't speak. He just wept.

Then the nurse. 'We did everything we could…'

'We did everything we could. I'm so sorry, Mr Spencer.' The nurse laid her hand on Ronnie's shoulder. 'Your wife's very tired, but she's asking for you.'

'What about the baby?' Ronnie's eyes were pleading for the right answer, but the nurse just shook her head.

'Come on, I'll take you through. Just you though, she needs to rest.'

He took Amanda's hand and gently squeezed, then turned to Davy and asked, 'Will you stay with Amanda, please?'

Davy nodded and stretched out his hand, watching as the girl's slim dark fingers clasped his own. The warmth of her touch brought him back to the present.

It was almost six o'clock when they got back to the house. Ronnie was slumped in an armchair with his eyes closed. Amanda had been sent to bed to try for a little sleep, and Davy retreated to the solitude of the kitchen. Marion would be okay. They would probably send her home later today. She'd miscarried, but thank God, she hadn't had the complications that Diane had. Strange how a woman of almost forty could come through that okay – well, physically, anyway – but his wee lassie who'd been a healthy seventeen-year-old had bled to death. Right there in the hospital. Doctors and nurses doing everything they could, pumping blood in as fast as it was coming out, and yet she hadn't made it. Hardly a sick day in her life then...

His eyes clamped shut to wipe the picture from his mind. He'd filled the kettle and put it on with a vague notion of making tea. Lost in his memories, he was still holding the handle when it began to boil. A murmur of steam scalded his wrist and jolted him back into the present. As he ran cold water over the burn, his thoughts sharpened, processing and joining little snippets he'd pushed away, frightened of being overwhelmed if it all tumbled in together. The nurse who had spoken to Ronnie today became the nurse who had tried to offer them comfort after Diane was gone.

'She was trying to get home to you…' Each piece came with jagged edges. Fitting them together cut and hurt. 'Trying to hail a taxi…' 'What a shock that guy must have got…' 'A young American in his wee Mini…' 'He was *black* as well… Just shows you…'

Davy turned off the cold water and stared at the red weal across his wrist.

He was black! Young. American… A Mini isn't a taxi. Why would Diane have been at a bus stop near the infirmary? However she'd travelled into Glasgow, she wouldn't have been anywhere near a bus stop up there.

The nurse's voice changed. He heard Jamie's wee frightened voice confess when he'd overheard his mum and Marion talking about Amanda's father. 'He poisoned someone, another girl. She died…' *She died.* Diane died. His healthy young daughter had died. Amanda's father had been American. He'd been black. He'd been in Dunoon. Diane had been living in Dunoon. Diane had been pregnant, so…

An anguished cry burst from his lungs, loud, tearing, hurting. Ronnie rushed in.

'What's wrong? What happened?'

Davy spun, shook his head. 'Scalded myself. It's okay. I overreacted. I'm okay.'

'Let me see.'

As Ronnie reached over to take his wrist, Davy turned and fled from the kitchen. His jacket was still lying at the bottom of the stairs, and he grabbed it with one hand as he opened the front door. He walked to the pavement, turned right, and began to run.

Around the edge of the cemetery were some clusters of trees, probably left there to shield the new houses' view of the headstones. A low, broad stump offered Davy a flat place to sit and pull himself together. Ignoring the dampness of the wood, he sat with his elbows on his knees, head in hands.

Come on, man, pull yourself together. It's been fifteen years, for God's sake. You're letting your imagination rule your head. All you've got are bits and pieces of gossip, and you're using them to glue the facts together, jumping to all the wrong conclusions. His inner voice fought for control, but in his heart Davy was sure he was on the right track. All his instincts were screaming at him. Diane had been poisoned... something she'd been given had caused her death... someone was to blame... the same man that had fathered Amanda? This guy Howard? Yes, he had poisoned a girl. He had poisoned a girl, and she'd died...

Marion could see the sadness etched on Ronnie's face when he picked her up from hospital. They could barely speak to each other for fear of tearing the fragile membrane containing their grief. Deep inside, Marion was holding back the guilt that was threatening to overwhelm her. They had been so happy when she discovered she was pregnant. These wonderful tests you can buy over the counter these days, showing that glorious double line. They'd looked at it together, arms round each other, hugging their joy. This baby had been so different, right from the start. Well, it would have two parents who wanted it, apart from anything else.

Finding out Amanda was on the way had been such a different experience. She had completely misjudged Howard Odoms, misjudged so many things. When her friend Betty fell pregnant, Bill had been pleased. Betty had got her happy family. Yes, Marion had been envious – not that she would want Bill Lundahl, but he'd given Betty everything she wanted. After what had happened to Sheila, she did think, *Well, at least she'll have her baby.*

That had been the start of it, really. A longing for a baby. It had changed from a want, a dream for some time in the future, to a need. A damn shame that had been when Howard Odoms was worming his way into her affections. He'd always seemed so arrogant in the bar, snapping his fingers at them for service. Marion had hated that. Her dislike of him had grown with every click.

After Sheila moved into the guest house with Marion, he'd kept coming around. At first it was to talk to Sheila, but then he'd started to show his gentle side. He was compassionate, tender… Then, when they began having sex? Well, it was unlike any other man she'd ever been with. She'd wanted this man's baby. Pity that man hadn't wanted her any longer. The bastard had walked from her bed straight into Diane's arms.

She'd fallen with Amanda within a week of coming off the pill. An easy pregnancy with a beautiful healthy daughter she'd loved instantly, but now…

Ronnie caught her glancing over at him and smiled encouragingly.

'Not far now,' he said, and took his hand from the steering wheel to give hers a quick squeeze.

She smiled weakly at him, then turned her head away and fell back into her dark thoughts. He deserved a child of his own. As soon as he had moved in with her, the old longing for a baby had swamped her again. A baby they could have together. A brother or sister for Amanda to complete their little family circle. But she had lost their baby. Her body hadn't nurtured Ronnie's baby. She had let him down. She felt as though her guilt was nestling in her womb, filling the space where their baby should have been.

'Almost home, darling.' Ronnie's voice brought her thoughts back to the present, and she realised they were turning into their street.

He parked the car so close to the front path that Marion thought for a moment he was going to drive it through the garden and up to the door. He opened the passenger door and held out his hand. She was perfectly able to walk unaided, but holding on to him was comforting for both of them. She could see Davy and Sheila at the window. Amanda had opened the front door and was smiling determinedly.

She counted three vases of flowers in the lounge, and there had been a small posy on the hall table too. Tea, biscuits, brandy were softly offered, along with questions about how tired she felt and whether she needed to lie down for a while. She looked at her feet, wondering if she could run away in a pair of slippers and how far she might get in the icy rain. The affection and concern of the people she loved was stifling.

'No, thank you. No tea, no brandy, and absolutely no wee lie down.' She turned to Ronnie, who was sitting close beside her on the sofa with his arm around her shoulders. 'Honestly, I'm okay. I managed to sleep in the hospital. They gave me something. What I really want now is to go for a shower.' As she began to stand, three pairs of hands came to assist. 'Stop! I'm capable of standing and walking up the stairs.' Their wounded expressions tempered her tone. 'Sorry. It's just… I don't mean to be crabbit, and I know you're all doing your best, but let me come to terms with it all in my own way. What I really want – need – is a hot shower and then… fresh air.' She turned to Ronnie. 'Fancy a walk?'

He nodded and stood back as she made her way across the room.

Davy watched from the armchair, fists clenched in his lap. His had not been one of the pairs of hands offering to assist. Relief that Marion was all right was battling with his revelation that she could know who was responsible for Diane's death – Diane's murder! But she was his sister. How could she have kept something like that to herself? They had always been close. Surely she would have told him… There was a buzzing in his ears, and he squeezed his eyes shut, feeling as though they were about to explode from their sockets. As his thoughts brewed and darkened, young Amanda came and slouched onto the floor at his side, placing her head on the broad arm of the chair. Instinctively he lifted his hand and tenderly stroked her cheek.

A new realisation struck him. This man he was conjuring hatred for: he was Amanda's father.

The first time he had held his niece as a tiny infant, he'd felt a memory of holding his own baby daughter eighteen years earlier. A fragile bond had begun to form. In his profound loss, Amanda became God's consolation gift. A reason to keep going. He loved this child – separately from his Diane, but he did love her and wanted to protect her. This insight helped him realise why Marion might have kept her terrible knowledge buried inside for all those years.

Davy took a deep breath and slowly released it, forcing himself to relax the tight muscles in his shoulders. He tried to reconcile his dark thoughts about his sister's role in this. Part of him still wanted to stand up and demand answers right now, but how could he? She'd been through enough. No, he decided, he would bide his time. He would figure it out. Marion didn't kill Diane. He would direct his anger where it belonged; then he would decide what to do.

Sitting forward, he bent and kissed Amanda's head. Then, ruffling her curls, he stood and looked over to where Sheila was sitting with her head bowed and whispering a little prayer.

'Come on, Sheila,' he said, pointing at the clock on the unit. 'I'll give you a lift home. Let's give Marion a bit of space, eh?'

Sheila nodded and came over to the chair to kiss Amanda.

'Tell your mum I'm praying for her. Do you want to come with us? You could come up and say hello to Jamie. Well, if he's in, that is.' She turned to Davy and shook her head. 'He's out all the time just now. Don't know what he's up to half the time.'

'No, Auntie Sheila, I'll stay here and make Mum something to eat when she feels up to it. Tell Jamie I said hi.' Amanda leaned over, brushed a quick kiss on her aunt's cheek, and gave Davy a half wave before she went towards the kitchen.

Sheila sat quietly as he drove north on Friary Road. He'd said he wanted to avoid the traffic heading towards the busy high street. Everyone who had cash or credit left after Christmas would be down there squabbling over the best of the bargains in the sales.

'You didn't have to drive me home, Davy. I could've got the bus or hopped on the underground.'

'It's okay. I kind of hoped to ask you something anyway.'

Sheila's heart quickened for a moment. She waited for him to say more, but he seemed intent on the traffic lights up ahead.

'What was it you wanted to ask?' She regretted the words almost before they left her mouth. Maybe he was going to ask her out. She'd hoped for that at one time, but oh, please, don't let him, not now! She had Joseph now. God had answered her prayer but, in his wisdom, sent her the man she needed, not the one she'd been willing to settle for. No, she should do something. Say something to head off his question. They couldn't be stuck in this car for another forty minutes with that awkwardness between them.

'Did Marion tell you I was seeing someone now?' He still sat like a stone, staring at the red lights, so she took a breath and went on. 'Yes, he's the new verger at the church. He took me to see *Crocodile Dundee* last year. Well, it wasn't a year ago. November…'

Sheila kept talking, hoping to avoid any silence that would give him an opening.

She paused for a breath just as they drove out of the Rotherhithe Tunnel, and Davy took his chance to speak.

'Sheila, tell me, what happened back in Dunoon? Who got my Diane pregnant?' He started with his voice firm and clear, but then it fell away to a stilted whisper. 'Was she… raped?'

Sheila gasped. Dunoon was so far away from what she'd

expected him to ask, it had come in under her radar and scored a direct hit. Winded, she scrabbled for her thoughts.

'Dunoon!' Her voice came out in a squeak. 'No, I don't know. I'd come down here to have Jamie before… Davy, why would you ask *me* this? I can't help you.'

'Who can I ask, Sheila?' His grip on the steering wheel tightened. 'I thought it was all a horrible twist of nature. She was only seventeen, her life had just started, but she miscarried. Lost her baby, then her own life.' Tears misted his eyes.

He swallowed to clear his throat before he could speak again. 'Tell me, Sheila. You know what happened. Marion told you.'

'She wasn't raped, Davy. That's one less thing to torment yourself with. Diane fell for the guy, loved him. I think that was why she got pregnant: she wanted him to marry her. More than that… I can't help you, Davy. I'll pray for you, though. God will help you find your peace.'

He kept looking straight ahead, blinking the tears away. The lights finally changed to amber, and he released the handbrake, letting the car ease forward slowly to allow time for the light to turn green. He lifted his left arm and wiped his face with the sleeve of his jacket.

The last thing she heard was her own scream and a deafening clash of metal.

18 /
tombstone, arizona, october 1999

day 4

HOWARD SEETHED ON THE DRIVE BACK TO TOMBSTONE. SHE WAS HER mother's daughter all right. Bitch! Turns up in his life, boiling up all the thoughts and memories he'd buried long ago, then has the nerve to slap him and walk away! His face twisted with anger. Ever since her first letter, he hadn't slept properly. Lying for hours with images flashing into his head, unable to shut them down. His conscious mind knew she was Marion's baby. Marion? He could barely remember her. All she had really been was a means to get to the truth about Samuel's attackers. Well, that and a warm body – warm and willing. He rolled down the truck window and spat onto the dust and sand.

Somehow Marion and Diane had become intertwined in his mind. It was Diane's child he felt was coming back to him. At first, he'd been frightened. No, not frightened: he was a goddamn marine, trained for combat. Fear wasn't what he'd felt. Fuck! He wanted a drink. He rolled the window down again and let the heat invade the truck's cabin. No, it hadn't been fear. Apprehension; anxiety, maybe. Whatever it was, it churned in his mind and innards. She did remind him of Diane, though. Diane with her adoring eyes. She had loved him; she would forgive him for what happened. She would understand it all had gone too far. He hadn't been ready to lose her. Christ, he'd tried to save her. He'd gotten her to that hospital with no thought of his own safety. An American hospital could have saved her. Fucking Scotland.

'Shit!' he yelled to let out some of the building pressure, forgetting the window was open. Tourists turned and looked at him. He closed it quickly.

He pulled his truck into the trailer park and recognised a large car parked in his spot. Sitting with the engine idling, he tried to clear his thoughts and decide what to do. They weren't supposed to come today. He'd arranged to have this week clear. Fuck it! He put the truck in reverse, turned, and headed back onto the main road out of Tombstone.

The town of Saint David was just a few miles down the highway. More a small family town than the tourist attraction of Tombstone, it boasted a high school, a post office, and a couple of grocery stores. Howard hadn't taken much notice of it, even though he'd driven through at least four times a week. He might have stopped for gas once or twice, but beyond the amenities lining the road, he had no clue what was there.

Where the hell were all the bars in this town? Plenty of diners where you could get a beer, but he needed liquor, hard liquor. It was her goddamn fault. She'd pushed and pushed until all his rage surfaced again. Sonofabitch! Four years he'd been dry. Four fucking years of damping down the fury, the taunting voices. Four years without any booze to shut it all out. Then she turned up. God damn it!

His eyes hurt. He rubbed at them to clear his vision. A row of cafés and shops were coming up on the left. If there was no bar, then there would surely be a liquor store. He rubbed his eyes again. He signalled and pulled into the turn lane.

The loud crunching of metal startled him. He suddenly realised he was over the turn lane and onto the oncoming traffic. A big blue Chevy had swerved but clipped his wing. Howard rested his head on the steering wheel and thought, *For fuck's sake, can this day get any worse?* Jeez, now the guy was coming over to him.

'Hey, buddy. You okay?'

'*Okay?* No thanks to you!' Climbing down from his cabin, he bent to inspect the damage. 'Look at my truck! You fucking asshole!'

'Calm down, man. You were the one who came into my lane! My car came off worse than your goddamn truck!' The man's voice escalated from enquiring to outraged in seconds. 'Have you been drinking?' Without waiting for an answer, he pointed his finger in Howard's face. 'I'm calling the cops, you jerk.'

By now others had come over from the parking lot in front of the shops.

'Hey, buddy, I saw what happened. He just pulled right out in front of you. No way you could have avoided him.'

Other voices added their assent to the vocal witness.

Howard drew himself up and tried to take control of the situation.

'Look, sorry, I apologise, okay? It was my fault. I haven't been drinking, I just... Sorry, I had something on my mind. I just lost my daughter.'

A gasp went round the small crowd, and the other driver stepped forward and offered Howard his hand.

'Jeez, man, that's heavy. Say, why don't we move our cars into the lot, and we can exchange insurance details. They're only lumps of metal, after all. It's people that matter.'

Howard nodded and got back in the truck. He started the engine, put it in drive, and slowly moved forward into the large rectangular car park in front of the stores. Once he was past the entrance, he put his foot down and accelerated out of the exit on the right-hand side, then left along the residential street leading back to the highway.

He knew he couldn't speed. The last thing he needed right now would be to get stopped by traffic cops. Vanessa could handle it for him. He just needed to get back to Tombstone. Hopefully she hadn't left yet.

He sighed with relief when he saw her car still parked in front of the trailer. She would take care of it. She was good at sorting out other people's messes. After all, he'd helped her out for all this time now.

The trailer door was unlocked, and Howard ducked as he stepped in. He was in no danger of hitting his head, but ducking was habit now.

'Hi. I didn't expect to see you two today.'

Vanessa was on her cell phone and barely acknowledged his entrance, but the long gangly man on the couch grinned broadly and leaned forward to shake Howard's hand.

'Howard!' he exclaimed. 'My brother!' He pumped Howard's hand with vigorous enthusiasm. 'Oh my, I never thought I'd see you again!' Howard forced a brief smile and covered the man's hand with his own, giving it an encouraging squeeze, and then gently removed it.

'Yes, Samuel, it's me, buddy. Good to see you.'

Vanessa clicked off her phone, dropped it into her purse, and walked three steps to stand between the two men. Howard leaned past her and gestured to Samuel to sit back down at the window again.

'I told you I had things to do this week.' He could hear the irritation rising in his voice and schooled himself to take it down to a friendlier tone, knowing he needed this woman's help to deal with the traffic incident. 'Anyway, I'm here now.'

'Right. Listen, my office called. A meeting had to be rescheduled, and I have to be there.'

'So, what were you going to do with Samuel if I hadn't come back? You can't leave him here on his own again. You do know that, right?'

'Right.' She turned away and began rearranging things in her purse, then finally brought out a bunch of keys. 'No, of course not. This is an emergency, though. I'll be back in about two hours. I thought maybe I could leave him at the Legion.'

'You know he won't stay there unless I'm working. The others can't watch over him, and if… no, *when* he wanders off, they can't go chase after him.' *Okay, stop lecturing her.* Forcing a semblance of a smile, he shrugged. 'I need some help from you as well now. Seems I was a bit slow off the mark making a turn this morning. I was over in Saint David's. Bumped a car. No big deal, but the driver seemed a bit spaced out to me. Wasn't making sense, so I drove over here…'

'You left the scene of an accident? Really? You know, Howard, that wasn't your smartest move.'

'It wasn't a real *accident*. No one was hurt. A fender-bender, that's all.'

'Okay.' She was shaking her head and pursing her lips as she reached towards the door handle. 'If they get in touch, just refer them to me.' She opened the door to leave, then, as an afterthought, turned to the smiling man still sitting quietly by the window. 'Bye, Samuel. I'll be back later. You be good for Howard, won't you?'

'Sure will, sis.' His smile grew even broader, and he looked at Howard, excitement shining in his eyes.

Howard knew Vanessa would just have left Samuel on his own if he hadn't turned up. She'd done it before. She was responsible for her brother: Howard helped with his care, but she was the one who ultimately decided if he could live outside the care facilities. Not that he blamed her. It could be tough looking after a grown man who behaved like a big, happy puppy.

The medics had done all they could for Samuel physically. Sure, he still needed a shitload of pills and potions, and his leg would always give him trouble, but it was his brain that had received the worst of the long-term damage. Samuel had been twenty-four when he was beaten by the punks, and he'd never be any older in his head. He remembered his sister, Howard, and other people from before the beating, but there was no short-term memory at all. He even needed to be taken to the restroom. He could urinate by himself but in those few minutes could lose track of where he was, even how to get out of the toilet. Still, at least Samuel was happy – super happy! Any of the bad stuff that had happened to him had been wiped clean. Maybe that wasn't such a terrible way to be. It certainly beat feeling so twisted up and angry all the time.

'Come on, buddy.' Howard held the tall man by the elbow and helped support him as he unfolded himself from the seat. 'We need to get ourselves a burger.'

'Oh, yeah. I like burgers and fries. Can I have fries and a Pepsi-Cola? I always drink Pepsi-Cola. It saved my grandpappy's life. Did you know that, Howard?'

'Oh, I think you mentioned it to me once or twice, Samuel.'

'Yup. Why would I drink anything else?'

Howard stood on the dirt in front of the trailer door and held Samuel's hand to steady him as he stepped onto the disabled walkway. He felt his heart lighten as he looked at his guileless smiling face. How could this man be so content with his past when his own strangled and haunted him?

Amanda had puzzled him. What did she want from him? Had she believed there was a big new family where she would be welcomed with open arms? The thought that she might need a kidney donor or something had crossed his mind, but that was uncharitable. Although if he'd turned out to have money, she surely would have tried a bit harder to get along with him.

His hand went to where she had slapped him. A lesser man would have put her in her place. Early in his training, he'd had to learn to make split-second decisions: foe or civilian, strike or hold. That had stood him in good stead when she lashed out at him. He worked at his jaw. Samuel was looking at him.

'Women, huh?' Howard gave Samuel's back a playful slap. 'Too much kissin'll wear me out!'

The tall man laughed. 'Too much kissin', yeah, too much.'

19 /
london, england, january 1987

Twice the nurse had hurried past his room. Davy pressed the buzzer again, hoping it would bring her in faster. He wanted to shout, but that would require a deep breath, and pain strangled anything above a rasping whisper. Moments later, though, the nurse bustled in, carrying a small cup with three white capsules.

'Aye, about time.' His voice came out in a low growl.

She laid the cup on the locker and checked the bag of liquid hooked on the stand beside his bed.

'Mr Barr, you need to calm yourself. I promise I'll find out how your friend is as soon as she's out of surgery.'

'What kind of pills are these? Don't try to knock me out, not till I find out how Sheila is!'

'They're for your pain, Mr Barr, and a mild sedative just to help you rest. You've had quite a bashing yourself, you know. Now, please lie still. You've got a drain in your chest, and I don't want it disturbed.'

He felt drowsy but fought against sleep. Just rested his eyes, relieved that the pain in his leg and head had subsided. Voices dipped in and out of his hearing. Medical words in crisp efficient tones, sympathetic murmurings from a woman's voice he didn't recognise. He strained to focus and saw the back of an orderly's uniform leave the side of his bed. Dark shapes in the room came into his field of vision, but his eyes closed once again, unable to resist the pull of sleep.

The blood pressure cuff inflated, gripping the top of his arm, rousing him to consciousness once again. He turned to look at it and saw two men sitting at the side of his bed. He wanted to ask them who they were, but a phlegmy grunt was all that came out.

One of the men leaned forward and took his hand. A shiver of fear brought their faces into a sharper focus. The taller of the two was young Jamie. The older man he didn't know, and it was he who was holding Davy's hand and speaking slowly and softly to him.

'Mr Barr… Davy, please don't worry. You've had a few bumps and knocks, but you'll be back on your feet in no time at all… just weeks and you'll be fine.'

'Sheila?' He looked at Jamie and knew he understood who he was asking about even though his voice was still hoarse. 'Is your mum okay?'

Jamie looked down at his feet and shook his head.

Davy cried out, and the man patted his hand and said, 'No, no, Sheila's alive, thank the Lord. The other car hit her side of your car, though, and I'm afraid her injuries are' – he looked over to Jamie, then back to Davy – 'well, her recovery is going to be much longer and more difficult.'

A frantic guilt gripped him. He reached out and gasped, 'She's not going to die? Jamie! She's not going to die, is she?'

'No.' Jamie lifted his head, and his eyes were full of tears. 'No, but it'll be a long time before she gets better. They cut off her leg…' And with that, his tears and anguish spilled out.

Just One Little Pill

• • •

Jamie knew Mr Cairns… Joseph… was all right, but he always felt he had to be *well behaved* when he was around, and that didn't sit well with a boy of sixteen. His mum thought he was wonderful, and he made her happy, so he was willing to put up with him – for a bit, anyway. He cringed, remembering the attempt Cairns had made to speak to him about *grown-up things*! Jeez, that had been horrible. What a twat. Jamie could have told him a few things. Laughing, he thought of Holy Joe's description of wanking. *'Giving yourself a lonely pleasure'*.

His mum was going to be in hospital for months, between recovering from the injuries and the operation. There would be rehab after that too. No way had he wanted to stay with Mr… Joseph all that time. Christ, the last fortnight had been the longest of his life. Thank fuck old Davy had spoken up. He'd felt guilty about the crash, even though it hadn't been his fault. He wanted him to move in with him over in Peckham, once he got out of hospital, but apart from it being a tight squeeze, there was no way Jamie could manage to get over to school every day, and there were some big exams coming up. He was nearly sixteen and knew he could manage fine on his own in the flat, but Davy moving in with him made sense, he supposed. At least he wouldn't have to do the shopping and cooking, but on the downside, an empty flat would have been pretty good for a few parties or having a chick over. No need for *lonely pleasures* then.

Sheila and Jamie still lived in the same block of flats the church had placed her in after she left the mother and baby home. They had outgrown the tiny one-bedroom quickly and been lucky enough to be rehoused in a two-bedroom on a lower floor. Now she had the space and privacy her son needed but without having to move away from all their friends and neighbours in this tight-knit community.

Davy heaved the bulging case onto the bed, making sure the wheels didn't mark the bedcovers. The effort started another coughing fit. Sitting heavily on the bed, he pulled out his handkerchief and spat into it. The phlegm wasn't so bad now. All those years he'd smoked with barely a hint of a cough, and now, years after stopping, he got all these problems after a car crash. Weird. Definitely weird.

He sat back and looked around the room. Sheila had pink bedding, lace curtains, and a dressing table covered in bottles of perfume, lotions, and potions. Photographs hung all over the walls and in frames on her bedside table. Lots of Jamie as a baby and toddler. School portrait. Some with Sheila. Quite a few also had Marion and Amanda in them. High on the wall above all the photographs was a large crucifix with the figure of Jesus looking down on them.

'Sorry, pal' – Davy pulled the dressing table stool over and stood on it to reach the crucifix – 'but you'll need to come down from there if I'm going to get any sleep. Don't worry, I'll put you back before Sheila gets home.' He nestled the plaster figure into one of the bedside drawers. Spotting a Bible already in there, he smiled: 'Oh, look, you'll have something to read while you're waiting.' He laughed heartily at this mock conversation and turned to the door, where Jamie stood, smiling too.

'Aye, I can live with all the frills and stuff, but the big guy on the cross was always a bit grisly for my taste.' He stepped over and put a friendly arm round the boy's shoulders. 'I'll hang him back up before your mother comes home. She'll never know he was gone.' The two of them walked into the kitchen, heads together, laughing.

20 / london, england, 29 april 1987

Sheila had taken over three months to recover sufficiently to be able to manoeuvre her way around on crutches. The main problem was her flat was on the third floor. The building had two lifts, but they rarely worked, so it was totally impractical for her to go back there. Joseph had visited her almost every day. Marion and Ronnie had popped in as often as they could, and Amanda was usually with them, but if Jamie was there, too, Amanda would quietly stand off to the side or volunteer to go to the machine for hot drinks. Davy brought Jamie to visit her two evenings every week, and always on Saturdays and Sundays. He had been such a pillar of strength to her. She knew Jamie was well cared for and happier in his own home with Davy than he ever would have been in the church house with Joseph.

She had been moved to the Rehabilitation Unit eight long weeks ago, and having the opportunity to go home was tantalisingly close. Now she looked around her bed at the smiling faces and offered a private prayer of thanks for all these wonderful people.

'It's high time Ronnie and I got our own place, anyway.'

Marion was in the seat closest to the bed, patting her hand and nodding with each word to emphasise her determination.

'But... but I couldn't let you all turn your lives upside down like that. Joseph, tell them.' She looked over to where he stood with his Bible in his hands, smiling back at her.

'Jamie's school...' Her voice was weak. This could be the answer to all her prayers, but she had a heavy burden of guilt at how much disruption it would cause in everyone else's life.

Davy stepped forward and leaned over the end of the bed. 'It's done, Sheila. It's all sorted. You don't have to worry about a thing except getting better.' He looked over his shoulder to where Jamie stood and nodded to him. 'Your big boy and I have been getting' along great. Sure we have, son. I can give him a lift to school in the mornings for what's left of the term. It makes sense for the two of you to move into my place. I've had a stairlift fitted, an' we've even managed to prise Thora Hird off it, so everything is ready for you to come and get settled in as soon as the doctors give you the green light.' He coughed to cover his embarrassment at the unintended reference to the traffic accident that had brought all this about in the first place, but continued. 'Amanda, Marion, and Ronnie are only moving a couple of miles away. They'll be round all the time. It'll be like they've never left!'

Sheila looked over at Joseph. Their relationship still felt tentative and new, and she needed to know he understood her situation. Davy was a friend. He had been the closest thing Jamie had to a father figure, but how would it look if she moved into his house? Would Joseph disapprove? Then she saw him nod at her and felt as though the sun had come out.

'Oh, I don't know why you're looking so happy, Mum. You haven't tasted Davy's cooking yet.'

'Oi, you! I worked my fingers to the bone scraping that toast for you, and this is the thanks I get?' He aimed a playful swipe towards Jamie's head.

Marion nodded. 'Well, I'll thank you, Davy. All you've done for us... are still doing for us... I thank the Lord for you every night.'

'Ach, no bother, hen.' He stuttered, 'I'm just bloody thankful you and I are still here to see...'

Marion moved over to hold her brother by the arm. 'We're all glad, Davy.' She glanced at Ronnie. 'We all have a lot to be thankful for.' Her hand moved to cover her belly. 'It's still early days, but, well, there is another reason that we need to move to a bigger place.'

21 /
peckham, london, england, december 1990

AMANDA WATCHED AS THE THREE-YEAR-OLD POURED PRETEND TEA into the tiny cups. Her face was setting into a scowl, and she felt it deepen as the adults pantomimed their delight.

'Who's Daddy's clever girl, then?' he asked and swept his daughter onto his lap as the whole room laughed. Daddy's girl? She wasn't just *Daddy's* little darling; the whole world revolved around this tiny person who had pushed Amanda into the shadows of the household. She'd never been cuddled by her daddy, never had the chance, thanks to her mother's selfishness. What right did she have to shut down her need to find her father, her dad? All her life there had been a gap. A hole where her dad should have been. Now everything she had missed as a child was being paraded in front of her, taunting her with the perfect childhood she'd never had. She needed to get away from this blissful scene before she screamed.

'Make yourself useful, Amanda. Clear away some of those dishes, will you?'

'In a minute.'

'Now, please. Just put them by the sink. I'll do them later.'

Do the dishes, sweep the floor, make the beds. Just call me Cinder-

bloody-ella, why don't you? She held a precariously balanced pile of dirty plates and cutlery. With a hefty kick, she opened the door, and it banged back on its hinges with a thunk.

'What is it with you?' Jamie had followed a scowling Amanda into the kitchen when she grudgingly agreed to clear the dishes. 'Your face has been tripping you all afternoon.'

'It's her!' She ground out each syllable and tipped her head towards the lounge. Even as the words left her mouth, she knew how grumpy and spoiled she sounded, but she couldn't stop herself. 'Oh, look.' She stuck out her bottom lip and affected a petted, babyish voice. 'She doesn't like her trifle! Aww, isn't that adorable!'

'Oh, grow up, Amanda! She's only three years old. You're supposed to be an adult. Time you started behaving like one.'

'Just listen to you! You sound like an old man. In fact, you sound like my uncle Davy. If you don't like what I have to say, then don't speak to me. It's as simple as that.'

'Right, I bloody well won't speak to you. I'd been so looking forward to coming here for Christmas. Not to see everyone else, but hoping that we might get some time to ourselves. I've missed you since I've been away at uni.' He saw Amanda's face soften. When he leaned in towards her and lowered his voice to a more conspiratorial whisper and said, 'It's good to get you on your own for a few minutes,' her heart leapt, and her eyes opened wide.

'I wanted to talk to you about Claire. We're thinking of moving in together next term.'

Instantly, Amanda pulled back, curled her lip, and sighed an exasperated 'Fooph.' She shook her head and pushed past him, reaching for the apron on the side of the cupboard door.

'What do you mean, *fooph*? You're a girl, I wanted your advice. Is it too soon, do you think?'

'*Too soon?*' Amanda heard the shrillness in her voice and tried for a little more control. 'I don't know if it's too soon to ask your girlfriend to move in with you, but it's certainly too late to be coming to me for advice.' She could see bewilderment on Jamie's face. Honest to God. Boys! They didn't have a clue. She and Jamie had been so close growing up – one had always known what the other was thinking – and now, when she so needed his understanding, there was nothing.

She turned to face him, tied the apron round her middle, and stood with her hands on her hips, waiting. For a few moments, they conducted a short version of the staring contests they had challenged each other to when they were younger. Then Amanda decided it was beneath her dignity to behave like this. She could feel tears threatening. They were tears of frustration, but Jamie wouldn't know that. Her tears were her ultimate weapon in a conflict with anyone, but especially with Jamie. She knew she would get him around to her way of thinking if he saw her getting upset. She deliberately stumbled over her words as a reinforcement tactic.

First, she looked at her feet. 'I've missed you, too, Jamie… more than you know.' A sniff to show she was bravely fighting back tears. Now, raising her eyes, she gazed at him from under thick, dark lashes. 'You always knew when I was feeling… upset. It was you who could make me feel better… no one else.'

Full gaze now, and a step forward to be within his arms' reach. But to her astonishment Jamie took a step backwards, away from her.

'No, Amanda. No.' His hand was held towards her, but with his palm flat, as if warding her off. 'No way are you going to manipulate me again. I'm wise to your little tricks.'

'What do you mean?' The tears miraculously dried up, and she stood her full height, chin up and brows raised in innocence. 'I've never tricked you, Jamie. You're the one person I could always be myself with.' The shock in her voice was genuine. She had never failed to bring Jamie around to her way of thinking before.

'Yeah, and being yourself means getting me to do exactly what you want. But no more. I can see right through you now.'

'Oh, really? I suppose that your *darling Claire* helped polish your view, did she?'

'Don't start on Claire. She would never behave like a spoiled brat, and she would never be jealous of a three-year-old.'

'I am not jealous!' Amanda shook her head with such force, her hair whipped across her face, obscuring her view. She used both hands to clear it away and looked again at this boy-man she had always had in her life. 'Look, the three of them are this nice little family unit. She's Ronnie's daughter. I'm not.' He was really paying attention to her now, so she continued. 'I get it. She's three, she's cute, and everything she does is *a-ma-zing*!' They both laughed a little at this. 'But I'm seventeen, spotty, and everything I do is bloomin' tragic!' She grew serious once again. 'I know Mum loves me an' all that… but I'm growing up. I want to find out who I am. Not just Mum's daughter or Amy's big sister. Me, Amanda Barr, a person in my own right.'

'So… how do you do that?'

'Well, for a start, I want to find my father. Find out who I came from. All I know is that he was American and was stationed in Dunoon. Oh… and he's black!'

'Leave it, Amanda. Don't go down that road. You don't need to find him to know who *you* are.' He reached over and took her hand in his. 'I know about my father, and he was American, stationed in Dunoon, and black, but that doesn't change who I am.'

'No? Well, good for you, Jamie. You know who you are and what you want. You're a basketball star, you're a blooming maths genius, and you're Claire's boyfriend. It's all there for you. But me? I'm not good at anything. I'm not skinny or gorgeous. No boys are chasing me…'

'Well, chasing a ghost won't give you the answers you want.

You'll still be you. All that will happen is that your dreams will be broken.'

'You don't know that. He could be aching to meet his daughter.'

'He probably doesn't even know he has a child, let alone be aching to meet you. I'm warning you, leave well alone. No good will come of it.'

'No good will come of it? You sound like Davy again. What the hell do you know about him?'

'I know enough to tell you not to do this. Anyway, you can't do anything till after you turn eighteen, so stop tormenting yourself with stupid dreams and enjoy yourself. You don't know when you're well off.'

Amanda's frustration boiled over, and she realised he was still holding her hand. Yanking hers away, she mimicked holding a walking stick and stooped her body over her exaggeratedly shaking hand.

'Oh, dear me, Grandpa, you are such a wise old fart. Thank goodness I can go to my grave safe in the knowledge that I took your advice and didn't take the chance to meet my own flesh and blood while he was still alive!' The wavering parody of a voice gave way to a loud rage. 'I don't care if you don't need to meet your father. I *have* to meet mine if there's any possible way I can. You can bugger off back to uni and your simpering little cheerleader. *Give me a B! Give me an I! Give me a T! Give me a C-H, and what have you got? Claire!*'

Jamie raised his hand to motion her to stop, just as he had earlier. At that exact moment, a cluster of adults burst into the kitchen.

'Jamie!' He heard his mother's voice amongst a chorus of gasps, and his wrist was caught in a strong, tight grasp and swiftly pulled behind his back, forcing a yelp of pain and shock from him.

'I wasn't going to hit her. Let me go. I wasn't going to hit her, I wouldn't! I just wanted her to shut up!'

He turned to see a furious Ronnie still gripping his wrist and glaring into his eyes. 'I don't care what you said or she did. Don't you ever raise your hand to anyone in my family again.' Taking a deep breath, Ronnie let go of Jamie's wrist, stepped back, and held his arm outstretched to indicate that Jamie should leave the kitchen.

Glancing back at Amanda as he walked out, straight to the front door, Jamie shook his head. 'Sorry, okay? I'm sorry.' He lifted his jacket and left.

They all stood and listened to the sound of the door closing. Marion put an arm around Amanda's shoulder and guided her towards the couch in the front room. They sat down together.

'Right, we've got the place to ourselves now. Talk to me. Please, darlin', you can tell me. What was the fight with Jamie really about?'

Amanda shrugged.

'Come on, love… What is it? You've been a right misery guts since you came down for the holidays. Has something happened at uni?'

'No, nothing's happened. Right! Nothing.'

Marion stroked Amanda's arm. 'You're all worked up, so it's not *nothing*. What is it?'

'What is it?' Amanda shook her head in disbelief and stared at the ceiling. 'How could you bring me up and not know what *it* is?'

'But I don't, so tell me. Just tell me.'

'I want to know who I am. You know who you are, whose wife you are, whose mother, and who both your parents were. I don't know. I only have half a history. I don't understand why you still won't tell me about my father!'

Marion took a deep breath. Her arm was still around

Amanda's shoulder, and she pulled her in and softly kissed her forehead. Slowly, she shook her head and shrugged her shoulder. 'I can't tell you, pet. Dunoon was... well, it was a world away. I was just young. Young and stupid. I worked hard, but I played hard too. There were all sorts of things going on, bad stuff. Girls were all after the Americans. God, they were coming from miles away to catch themselves a sailor. The big dream was to get a boyfriend and get pregnant so you could get married and have a bright shiny new life in the States. It worked for some of them.'

'Is that what you were trying to do? Would my father not marry you? Is that it? You're mad at him for not standing by you?'

'No, honestly that's not it. Look, there were... Christ, all sorts of stuff getting used. Cough mixtures then had codeine in them. Mixed with some cheap spirits and knocked back before you went out... well, let's just say things were pretty uninhibited.'

Amanda looked directly at her mother, waiting for her to continue. She'd never heard her talk about that time in her life before.

'Yes, I tried it, but only once. I hated it. Everything was blurred, and the next day I woke up feeling horrible, sick and disgusted with myself. I never did that again, but I saw plenty of others that did. The American boys loved it. Some of them really took advantage. Don't get me wrong, Amanda. I was no saint, but when I realised I was expecting you...'

Marion rose from the couch and walked over to the window. She continued talking with her back to Amanda. 'I wanted away from there. A fresh start, away from all the seediness, the violence. I didn't want my child contaminated by all that. You have always been wanted, Amanda. You are my child. No one else's.'

She faced her daughter. Her eyes were clear and focused on Amanda. 'That's it. That's all you need to know.'

Amanda couldn't speak. Her throat was tight, an anger was building, and a headache was clouding her vision. She shook her head at her mother and strode to the door. Holding it ajar, she rested her head against the edge and swallowed hard. 'I am going to find him, you know.'

Marion watched the door close and heard the determined tread of her daughter walking upstairs. 'I bloody hope not,' she whispered.

22 /
london, england, july 1993

Jamie watched his mother adjust the collection of feathers and stuff that she called a fascinator. He couldn't see what was so fascinating, but she was happy and did look nice. She turned to her left, then to the right, checking whether the hem of her dress sufficiently concealed her prosthetic, and smiled. Then, holding her arms out from her sides, she asked, 'Well, what do you say, Jamie? Will I pass muster?'

He walked over and took hold of her outstretched hands. 'You look beautiful, Mum. Joseph Cairns is a very lucky man.' He kissed her cheek, careful to avoid spoiling her make-up.

'You've scrubbed up pretty well yourself, son. Have I told you how proud I am of you? Because I am. So proud my heart could burst.' She gave a quavering smile and bit her lip against her emotion.

'Of course you're proud of me, Mum. I'm the man you made me.' He gulped and turned to look out of the window. 'Right, come on, bride-to-be. Let's get a grip of ourselves. The car will be here any minute, and we're not going to be blubbing into our hankies when it arrives.'

Jamie crooked his elbow. Slipping her arm through it, Sheila smiled and nuzzled his chest.

'Hey! Mind your make-up, Mum! We don't want you walking down the aisle with a smudged face, do we?' He bent down and softly kissed the top of her ear. 'Love you.'

Sheila tilted her head back to look at this boy of hers, this man who had been her whole life since the moment he was born.

'I know you do, Jamie. I love you, too, and I thank God every day for giving you to me.'

They both stepped forward and out to the waiting car.

The small wedding went beautifully. Jamie gave his mum away to Joseph in a ceremony conducted by their own minister and friend, Tony Barbour. Marion was matron of honour, and Joseph's cousin Jim was his best man. Many of the congregation had come along to see the marriage, but the reception was a meal for only twelve at a local hotel where a small private room had been hired.

Jamie and Amanda couldn't avoid each other, and any lingering antagonism dissolved further with each glass of champagne.

It had been three years since they were last together. Not by deliberate effort; their lives had moved in different directions as they pursued their studies and career paths. While Jamie qualified in sports science and his mother and Davy proudly applauded as he stepped up to receive his degree, Amanda decided to move up to Scotland and study in Glasgow. She'd made no secret of the fact that she wanted to move as far away from her mother and Ronnie's home as she could. But Jamie strongly suspected she'd chosen Glasgow as a way of beginning to search for her father.

Sheila had made a huge effort to persuade Jamie to wear a kilt to give her away. Jamie had finally agreed to a compromise: a smart blue suit with a waistcoat and tie in the modern Forsythe tartan. He had thought he would feel overdressed and foolish in such colourful clothes, but the suit felt good when he tried it on, and now he was glad he'd let his mum represent her family roots in some small way. Neither of his grandparents had ever set eyes on him. Banishing Sheila from their home when she found out she was pregnant had been their final contact with their only child. She had tried sending letters and photographs several times over the years, but they were always returned unopened.

Jamie looked at Amanda wearing a flowing orange, green, and yellow print dress with a matching headwrap that allowed her hair to spill down her neck and bare shoulders. She looked so different from the awkward girl he had grown up with. For the first time, Jamie saw a desirable woman. He wanted to get to know this new Amanda, wanted to get to know her well.

He lifted two fresh glasses of champagne from the tray and walked to where she stood waving his mother and Joseph off. Handing her one, he smiled and nodded towards her dress.

'I see you've adopted a Jamaican heritage now.'

Amanda took the glass and sipped, avoiding his eyes.

'It suits you, though,' he continued. 'You look beautiful. Stunning, actually.' He pushed his hair from his forehead with an affected sweeping gesture and attempted a Bob Marley–ish accent. '*I was thinking of going for the dreadlocks look myself, mon!* What do you think, Amanda? Could I pull it off?'

She began to giggle at his clowning around, but the champagne went up instead of down and she began to cough. The drink spurted from her nose. Bent double, she held her napkin over her nose and mouth to cover her undignified reaction. Once she had regained her composure, she looked at him.

'Look what you did to me, Jamie Forsythe. I would *never* waste champagne like that!'

He lifted a clean napkin from the table and dabbed Amanda's lips and cheek, then let it rest there while he looked straight into her eyes. 'I've missed you.'

She nodded. 'Me too.'

23 / peckham rye, london, england, december 1997

Amanda let Jamie carry the big white box in from the car, and she brought the bags containing the brightly wrapped gifts. She smiled as a bouncy little girl ran out and threw her arms around Jamie.

'Hey, sweetie, let us get in before you jump all over us! You wouldn't want Jamie to drop your birthday cake before you've even seen it, would you?'

He was holding the box above his head, away from the danger zone around an excited ten-year-old. Amanda kissed her mother's cheek as she handed her the carriers, and they laughed to see the happy youngster dance and chatter with Jamie.

Marion gently guided her elder daughter toward the living room. 'Come in and get yourself warmed up. It's freezing out there. How far away did you have to go to get parked?'

'Oh, we were lucky today. A big van just pulled out of a space as we came into the road. We're only about five doors away.'

The sitting room had a large sparkling Christmas tree in the corner, and on the couch across from it were Jamie's mother and Joseph. Amanda bent to give Sheila a hug.

Behind her, a deep, gravelly voice boomed out. 'Aye, you better have some of those hugs left for me, miss!'

She turned to cuddle her uncle Davy, who had arrived only moments after them. He enveloped her in his arms and kissed the top of her head.

'It's good to see you, hen. I hope that big boyfriend of yours is looking after you.'

Just then Amy came running in, carrying an armful of parcels, and stood in front of the tree. 'Mum says I can open them once everyone's settled. So could everyone please hurry up and get settled then? *Please*?'

'Here, I'll take the coats.' Jamie had come through behind Amy and began gathering up the coats and jackets.

'No, let me,' Amanda said, then, leaning close to Jamie, added in a whisper, 'I need to go to the loo anyway.'

As she was about to leave the sitting room, Davy plucked at the tinsel branches of the artificial tree. 'What's this phoney stuff all about? You can't beat the real thing.'

Amy's girlish tones chimed, 'It's a birthday tree, Uncle Davy. Tomorrow it can be a Christmas tree. A real one wouldn't last long enough.'

Amanda left them to debate the merits of real versus artificial and took the bags and coats up to the spare room.

Back downstairs, she saw someone approach the door and opened it before they rang the bell. It was a neighbour of her mother's. The old lady was holding her coat tight around her, and clasped in her hand was a large white envelope.

'Oh, Amanda dear, sorry, I was just going to slip this card through the door. It was delivered to me by mistake. Our usual postman would have recognised your mum's name, but these temporary workers just jam the letters in without a thought…'

'Okay, Mrs Harris, I'll give it to her. Thanks.'

'Merry Christmas, Amanda.'

'Yes, merry Christmas to you, too, Mrs Harris.'

Closing the door, she glanced at the envelope. On the top left corner was a little printed label with the sender's name and address. Mrs A. Bissell, Castle House Hotel, Dixon Esplanade, Dunoon PA23 4PE. Her stomach flipped as she read it. 'Dunoon!' She hadn't meant to say it out loud, but they were all giggling and chatting in the living room, so no one had heard. This must be the place where Mum lived when she met him! Over the years, she'd seen Christmas cards from Mrs Bissell. A long time ago she'd even asked her mother who would sign a card 'Mrs Somebody', not with their first name.

Her mother had laughed and told her, 'Oh she's an older lady, quite proper, a second cousin of my dad's or something. Anyway, I always called her Mrs Bissell…' The explanation went on, but Amanda tuned out by then. There had been no mention of Dunoon, though; she was certain of that.

This might be the best Christmas present she could hope for. A starting point, someone to go to and ask, 'What's my father's name?' Obviously, she wouldn't put it as bluntly as that, but… She hugged herself with excitement. Castle House Hotel was going to get a visit very soon.

24 /
dunoon, scotland, february 1998

AMANDA COULDN'T QUITE BELIEVE IT WAS EARLY FEBRUARY IN Scotland and the sun was out. Her recent memories of Scottish winters were of freezing in draughty digs in Glasgow, or more vaguely, of being a child, cuddled and warm in front of a blasting gas fire in Uncle Davy's old house. North of the border didn't often see sunshine early in the year, so two full days of warm, mild weather seemed like a good omen.

There, right in front of her, was Castle House Hotel. The gate at the end of the front path was painted royal blue, and a pristine white sign to the side proudly announced that all rooms were en suite, with colour TV and tea-making facilities.

A strange tingle of déjà vu passed through Amanda as she opened the gate and walked along the path to the door.

She'd been to Dunoon before. During her time at university in Glasgow she had taken the train through, trying to find clues to her father's identity. By then, the Americans had gone, the bars had changed hands, and few people wanted to talk of the time the Americans had dominated all that went on there. Now the genteel facade had returned. Dunoon hadn't quite become a sleepy backwater, but it was perhaps a little drowsy.

She rang the bell. A smiling young woman, wearing a large white apron, opened the huge blue door.

'Yes? Can I help you?'

'Em... I'm looking for Mrs Bissell. I was hoping to have a word with her... I think we might be distantly related... My mum worked here a long time ago. She might remember her. Marion Barr?'

'Oh, right. I'll go and find her. Why don't you come in? Have a seat over there. I won't be long.'

Amanda nodded her thanks and willed herself to keep calm and not show the excitement and impatience she felt coursing through her body.

The woman had indicated a chair with its back to the wall, facing a wide staircase. Amanda sat and looked around. The carpet and furnishings were old fashioned but of good quality and immaculately clean. She could clearly see the first landing, where a painting of the Holy Loch hung mounted in an ornate golden frame.

'Marion Barr's your mother, is she?'

The voice belonged to a smartly dressed lady with white hair and rimless spectacles who had appeared in the doorway beside her.

'Oh!' Amanda jumped up and held her hand out. 'Yes, she's my mum. I thought I would drop in when I was up here visiting. I hope you don't mind. It was a sort of a spur-of-the-moment thing.'

Mrs Bissell shook her hand and nodded. 'I'm delighted, dear. Sorry I startled you. Tell me your name, though. I can't call you Marion's daughter all the time, can I?'

'It's Amanda. Amanda Barr.'

'Ah, yes, of course it is. I was a Barr, too, you know? My maiden name, before I met my dear husband.'

· · ·

Just One Little Pill

Agnes Rose Bissell might have been well into her eighties, but her mind was still clear, and she prided herself on her ability to keep her own counsel. Discretion was the hallmark of a good hotelier. There was no denying she and her friends at the Seniors Club could spend many a happy hour discussing all the goings-on of the Dunoon folk, but never would she divulge anything that happened within the four walls of Castle House Hotel. Oh, yes, there were tales she could tell – her late husband had often said she should write a book – but she had her own moral code, and all that had happened within her domain would pass from this world when she did. Nowadays most of her time was spent in her cosy lounge looking out of the large picture window. She saw all that went on in the street and could even see over to the dark water as it flowed out to the Firth of Clyde.

She had watched as the coloured girl walked up the hill with her gaze firmly focused on the hotel and paused at the gate. Instinctively, she had known that this was not someone looking for lodgings. When she heard Marion's name, she was shrewd enough to guess the young woman had come looking for answers. Well, she would not get them from her. No names, no pack drill: she'd learned that in the war. Living under threat of invasion gave one a discipline the younger generation would never understand.

Despite this, she had enjoyed meeting the bright girl, and it gave her a rare chance to reminisce about days gone by. Certainly, she had romanticised the splendour of the hotel back in the seventies, but where was the harm in that? Amanda had tried several times to bring the conversation back to the names of the boys her mother had dated. It was easy to appear vague and forgetful, just as is expected from people of a certain age. It had been fun, although she did feel a little sorry for the girl as she watched her walk towards the ferry terminal, head down and disappointment showing in every line of her body.

. . .

Amanda braced herself against the chill wind coming from the water. The sun might have been shining, but it was still February after all. Others stood waiting to board as the ferry neared the Dunoon Pier.

A woman was looking in her direction but made no move towards her. Amanda smiled and gave a small nod, but the woman stayed leaning on the fence.

On board, Amanda seated herself beside a window and stared, hypnotised by the light dancing on the ripples and the gulls swooping like children playing tag.

She felt someone touch her arm and turned to see the woman from the terminal sitting beside her.

'Are you Marion Barr's daughter?'

The question was abrupt. The woman's face was scowled into deep lines, and she was scrutinising Amanda through narrowed eyes.

Taken by surprise, Amanda didn't answer but gave her a quizzical look.

'You are, aren't you?' She nodded and jabbed a finger towards her. 'Aye, you've your mother's features. His colouring' – she gave a dry laugh – 'but I can see your mother in you. We used to be pals, years ago. I'm Betty, Betty Lundahl.'

Amanda's disappointment dissolved, and she smiled and held out her hand. 'Pleased to meet you, Betty. Yes, I'm Amanda. Amanda Barr.'

'Aye, you kept your mother's name, did you?'

'It wasn't really up to me.'

She managed to keep her voice level even though her heart was pounding with excitement.

Years of wondering, crying, pleading with her mother. Searching bars and cafés in her time off from uni. Following false leads. Only to find out from a chance encounter on the Dunoon ferry! He hadn't been in the navy; he'd been a marine, a marine called Howard Odoms. Her father's name was Howard Odoms!

25 /
london, england, january 1999

Huddled in his jacket against the cold wind, Jamie looked up towards the window, hoping that Amanda would be home before him. Seeing the warm light shining through the blinds cheered him, and he picked up his pace, anxious to get into the warm and see her.

He was pushing his key into the lock when the door was wrenched from his grasp by Amanda, who stood, eyes shining, brandishing something wildly in the air.

'It's come!' She waved the letter above her head like an Olympic torch.

'What? Wait, let me get inside first.' He wiggled his key loose and stepped inside. Amanda was still trying to thrust the letter towards him. 'Right, just a minute, let me see.' He shrugged his jacket off and let it fall as he took the letter from her. He couldn't look up once he'd read it in case she saw the anxiety and fear in his expression. He pushed an enthusiastic note into his voice and managed to say, 'Great. That's good news, Amanda.'

'I know, I know!' Amanda took the paper out of his hands and danced her way into the sitting room, holding it against her chest. Jamie stayed in the hall, head down, staring at his empty hands.

What Amanda had dreamed of and he had dreaded had come a huge step closer. This wasn't the time to spoil her joy. Let her be happy at this confirmation of her parentage, but please God, please, let it be enough just to know. Don't let her want to meet him. Not him, not the man who had broken hearts, damaged lives, and then just walked away.

With each measured step in the search for her birth father, Amanda's patience had thinned. Jamie had spent many nights consoling her frustration and calming her rage at the bureaucratic barriers she'd had to overcome. He'd tried so hard to subtly encourage her to leave it be, to give up at each hurdle, telling her she'd done all she could and that it was becoming an impossible task.

Davy had tried to persuade him it would be kinder to help her. He'd said she needed to know who she was and would always wonder, maybe build her father into a hero. If she met him in person, then she could judge for herself.

Jamie wouldn't do it. There was a fear in him about that man. Things he remembered from his childhood, his mum's whispered prayers, and vague memories of overheard conversations between their two mothers. He'd seen letters when he was younger. Marion had tried to trace him long, long ago, but he knew why she had stopped the search. Amanda's birth father had gotten away with murder.

No matter what he said, Amanda wouldn't be dissuaded. Her single-minded determination had shielded her from his hints and advice, and now here she was on the threshold of connecting with him. The reality would meet the fantasy, and Jamie couldn't bear to see the destruction it might cause. Most of all he wanted to spare Amanda from being hurt.

. . .

'I can't believe it, Jamie! It took so long to find out *who* he is, and now finally I know *where* he is too.' Her voice got higher with every breath. On tiptoe, she began kissing his face. Small fast pecks, running up his cheek, over his nose, coming to his lips in a full passionate kiss, arms stretching up behind his head to pull it towards her.

Jamie gladly pushed all his fears from his mind and returned her embrace. With their arms still wrapped around each other, he walked backwards towards the bedroom with Amanda matching him step by step. As they reached the bed, Jamie released his hold to unfasten his jeans, and she simultaneously lifted her skirt and pulled off her pants and tights in one quick sweep, stamping on them to free her feet and kicking them away. They slid to a halt beside the discarded letter.

Still fully dressed from the waist up, they tumbled onto the bed.

'Slow down, what's the rush?'

'I can't. Come on, Jamie, let me do this.' Breathlessly, she climbed on top of him, sitting astride and supporting herself with her hands on his shoulders, then walking them back till she was sitting upright. She pushed back so he was deep inside her and started rocking her hips. He watched her expression change. Her eyes closed, and her breath came faster with each thrust.

Her orgasm happened in just a few moments, and he quickly rolled her onto her back, intending to slow things down and extend the pleasure, but within a few strokes he felt himself climax.

Amanda laughed. 'Now what's *your* rush, Jamie?' She turned on her side and he lay behind, wrapping his arms around her and kissing her neck and shoulders. 'I'm so happy, Jamie. I can't remember the last time I ever felt this... well, content, I suppose. Yes, I feel content.' She wriggled round to face him. Her eyes were bright, and she was grinning so hard he wondered if it hurt.

'It's good you're so happy.' He kissed her, his eyes closed tight so she couldn't see the worry in his face.

Later they picked up their clothing from where it had been scattered. As Amanda lifted her tights from the floor, she saw the letter beside them. Hugging it to her chest, she squealed with renewed excitement, then waggled the paper at Jamie. 'Isn't it great?'

Then her eyes opened wider, all the joy suddenly lost from her expression. 'Mum! Oh God! How do I tell her? Or do I tell her?'

'Well, it might be quite a shock. After all, you kept the entire search hidden from her.'

'Yeah, but it might make her open up a bit… knowing that I managed to track him down on my own… What's she got to lose?'

'What about Amy… and Ronnie? I'm pretty sure they know even less than you about her life up in Scotland. You can't just go in and start blurting stuff out. There are other people to consider.'

Even as he said this, his mind was scurrying in different directions. Perhaps he should encourage her to tell Marion. Most of this was her doing anyway. A lifetime of secrets. Maybe if she'd explained why she'd been so determined to keep the damn man a secret all these years, it would have stopped Amanda from… No, that was a stupid thought. Nothing in this world was going to stop her going through with this, not after all this time. There had to be another way. He needed to talk to Davy.

Amanda moved the cutlery to one side of the table and wiped away the wet ring under her water glass. She rearranged the knife, fork, and spoon again, then checked her watch for the tenth time in as many minutes. She looked around for the waitress and waved her over to ask for more paper napkins.

With her elbows on the table, she rested her chin on her clasped hands and closed her eyes. *Christ,* she thought, *anyone watching me would think I was praying. Well, too bad. I need to calm down and decide how I'm going to play this.* At least the café was neutral ground, a public place. They couldn't end up in one of their screaming matches, as they so often had before. Although, to be fair, it wasn't her mother who did the screaming. Marion always managed to keep her voice calm, even though it was her words that inflamed the situation in the first place. "No, leave it, you don't need to know. I won't discuss this again, Amanda…" Stonewall, stonewall, stonewall!

This time she would *have* to talk to her, because now she had the information her mother had denied her for all those years. She didn't need her mother to tell her the name of her father, but she did want to find out her reasons for keeping it quiet. Surely when she knew they were probably going to meet… if there was anything bad, she would tell her. Surely now her mother would treat her like the adult she was and discuss her past properly.

Marion peered through the window before she opened the door to the café. She waved at her eldest daughter as she made her way over to the small booth.

They kissed each other on the cheek, and Amanda pushed a large glass of white wine towards her mother as she sat down.

'I told you it was my treat, so I got our drinks up before you arrived. It saves us fighting over who's paying.' With that, she raised her glass and said, 'Slainte!'

'Slainte!' said Marion, and she too took a sip of her wine. 'Mmm, nice. So, what brought this on, Amanda? I can't remember the last time it was just the two of us.'

'Well, exactly! We were overdue to have a bit of mother/daughter time. Catch up and see how the other's doing. How's Ronnie? Still enjoying being the big boss at his new place?'

Marion nodded. 'Yes. He's working all hours just now, though. He's taken Amy to the cinema this afternoon. We get mum and daughter time, and Amy gets some time with her dad. Now that's what I call a well-balanced family.' They both laughed.

'Funnily enough, that's sort of… well, kind of what I wanted to let you know about.' She took a large gulp of her wine; she could feel her mother staring at her. 'I've tracked my father down. Howard Odoms. I've found him.'

Her mother's expression froze, colour draining from her face.

'You knew I wanted to find him. I've been looking for years. You knew that!' She realised her voice had risen and she was hunched over the table. In an effort to calm herself, she sat back, dropped her shoulders, and breathed out slowly. Marion still hadn't said a word.

In a softer voice, Amanda continued. 'You wouldn't help me to find him. I get that. You don't think much of him, okay, but that doesn't mean I can just forget he existed. Half of me comes from him. You chose him, let him father your child—'

'Stop. Yes, okay, I understand. But the thing is, Amanda… I found out things about him after that, *after* you'd been conceived, that made me see him differently.' She fiddled with the stem of the glass but still didn't drink from it. 'It was over before I actually knew I was expecting you. Even though I wanted you, wanted my baby, I felt so differently about him by then that… Well, it wasn't…' She paused to sip her drink. 'He's a cold, selfish… a user. I walked away. Contacted your aunt Sheila and came down here before he, or anyone, knew I was pregnant.' She wrapped her arms around herself before continuing. 'I'd been blind to what he was really like, but even at that, I could have let him know he had a daughter… maybe… I don't know. I adored you, Amanda, from the moment I had you. I'm not sure I would have wanted to share you, no matter what I thought of your father.'

'But Mum, doesn't that make *you* the selfish one?'

Marion shrugged. 'It didn't matter. When you were just a tiny baby, I found out more about him. Stuff that I just want to forget. That's when I made up my mind.'

'I'm a big girl now, Mum. I can take care of myself. I want to know him, and the fact that you didn't want me to know who he was has probably just added to the mystery and made me all the more determined to find him. So, your plotting really just backfired on you.'

Marion shook her head. 'I guess so. Listen, Amanda, I know you, perhaps better than you know yourself. You're going to find him and talk to him regardless of what I want, probably whether he wants to or not, so just remember this: I'm your mother. I've always been there for you, always loved you, and always will.'

'I know that!' Amanda's voice rose in exasperation that her mother still couldn't let go of her prejudice against her father. 'Finding my father has nothing to do with how I feel about you. It doesn't take away from our relationship, but it took the two of you to make me. Why is it so hard for you to understand that I need to find my other parent?'

'Amanda, you're expecting to walk into the life of a good, loving man who will welcome you with open arms. I think Howard Odoms will, at best, disappoint you, maybe even hurt you with rejection. Please believe me, he is capable of it.'

'You don't know that! Twenty-seven years have passed. He'll have changed. He won't be the same man who hurt you.'

'Right. Have it your own way, Amanda. I don't want to argue with you. Just… please, don't expect too much.' Marion lifted the menu and held it in front of her face as tears filled her eyes. 'I wonder what soup they've got on today?'

'Don't change the subject, Mum. Tell me what it was you

found out about him that made you so determined to keep me from him.'

Marion shook her head again. 'The girl he was seeing after me… She came to harm… at his hands. I don't know all the details, Amanda, and I don't want to make up the gaps in between what I do know. But what he did to her, he would have… could have done to me.' She raised her head and looked her daughter straight in the eye. 'I couldn't put you in harm's way. I just couldn't risk it. I only wish I could make you see that you're better off without him.'

Amanda narrowed her eyes and shook her head in denial. 'So, despite all the facts that you didn't know, you appointed yourself judge and jury? I'm all grown up now, Mum. I don't need you to protect me. I'm going to meet him and find out for myself.'

26 /
arizona, october 1999

day 5

Early next morning she settled her motel bill. She had hired a car to drive to Phoenix, and she hoisted her suitcase into the boot and looked back at the motel one last time. The contrast between her optimism when she arrived and her deep disappointment only four days later made her feel shaken and foolish. Her return ticket wasn't for another three days, but she wanted to try arranging an earlier flight back to London. She desperately wanted to talk to Jamie but decided to wait till she was at the airport, when she could message him her new arrival date and time. All she longed for now was to have him hold her so she could feel safe and wanted. Weeks and months of chasing her phantom father had revealed a shallow, bitter person that she was ashamed to share a bloodline with.

The young man at the British Airways desk was efficient and helpful. There was a small charge to change her homeward-bound flight, but a seat was found for her on the London flight late that afternoon. Amanda found a chair in a quieter corner of the airport and checked the time. It was almost nine o'clock in the morning here in Arizona. If she sent Jamie a message now, it would be teatime in Britain. That would give him time to get organised and come out to meet her at the airport tomorrow morning. She typed in her message, giving her flight number and arrival time, but kept the reasons for her early return brief. Tomorrow she would be in Jamie's arms and could tell him everything in person.

She made herself comfortable, using her suitcase as a footstool, and settled down with her book and music to help pass the hours until she could check in her luggage.

Amanda, eyes closed, nodded in time to the Boyzone hit on her CD player. Carried away, she didn't hear the two men approach her.

'Amanda! Amanda, why are you back at the airport? What's happened?' She looked up just as the younger of the two men reached her, then jumped with shock.

'Jamie!' She yanked the headphones from her ears and pulled away as if he were a stranger.

He tried to put his arms round her, but she resisted, puzzled by his unexpected appearance.

'What's going on? What are you doing here? How did you get here so fast?' Her heart was pounding, and seeing her uncle behind him added to her bewilderment.

Davy was out of breath and holding his chest, but he was the first to speak. 'Right, it's a bit of a surprise for you, hen, but there's no way we... Jamie was going to let you come away over here on your own. Christ, anything could happen, but you wouldn't have it. Stubborn as bloody always.' His smile took the sting out of his rebuke, but Amanda was not in the least placated. If anything, growing anger replaced her confusion.

'What the fuck do you mean, you weren't going to let me?' She turned to Jamie, who was holding his hands up, palms towards her in surrender.

'Yeah, sorry, love. You were adamant you wanted to meet him on your own, and I get that. We kept our distance. Let you go it alone. But come on, we needed to make sure you were safe.'

Davy was nodding his agreement, and Amanda whirled round and confronted him. 'And what about you, old man? What's your excuse for traipsing thousands of miles, wheezing and dragging your bad leg? What were you planning to do if there was some sort of showdown? Cough on him?"

Jamie leapt to defend him. 'That's enough, Amanda. Davy paid for our tickets, hotels, everything. Who do think bought us the mobile phones so we could keep in touch?'

Amanda stood, mouth opening and closing as if she wanted to say more, but instead she grabbed her bags and stormed off towards the coffee bar, leaving Jamie and Davy to trail behind like two rebuked little boys.

Anger was choking her. A fury of disappointment at her father's inadequacy found an outlet in the direction of the two men who cared most about her. Somewhere inside, a voice was telling her to stop her tirade, but the shock of finding them secretly guarding her made her feel undermined, and that was a layer too far.

Thirty minutes and two coffees later, the two men were left staring at each other across the table. Amanda marched up and down the sidewalk outside the airport, hoping the physical activity would burn away the last few degrees of her rage.

Finally, she returned and sat beside them, pursing her lips and heaving a deep sigh.

'Right, what's happening? I've changed my flight so I can go home today. When are your flights?'

Davy nodded towards the holdall where they had stored their tickets, and Jamie slid them out of the front pocket. 'We're not due out for another few days, but we can try to get them changed and go home on the same flight as you.' There was a hopeful lift to Jamie's voice as he looked at Amanda with a tentative smile.

Davy stood and took the tickets. 'Let me go and see what I can do.' And he walked off to find the British Airways desk.

Jamie reached over and took Amanda's hand. She didn't hold his, but neither did she remove her hand from his gentle grasp. He took that to be a good sign.

'It didn't seem like you hit it off with your father. Was he *that* bad?' Amanda shrugged and looked away without replying. He pushed on, hoping to soften her resistance.

'Did he look like you?'

Nothing.

'You must have found something in common. You are half him, after all.'

She crushed his progress with a raised eyebrow and contemptuous curl of her lip. He quickly retreated to safer ground.

'Thank God your mum gave you all your good strong genes.' A nervous laugh caught in his throat. 'At least you've put your curiosity to rest. No more wondering what he might be like.'

Amanda's expression changed, but he wasn't sure what it meant.

'Jamie? Are you scared of me?'

'Scared? Scared of your temper? Well, it's quite a temper, but I'm not frightened of it or you. What I hate is the way you let it take over. You don't often get really angry, but when you do… well, it's as if it submerges the real you. It's hurtful, sometimes even vicious. Think what you said to Davy back there. Vicious, and to a man who loves you and has done everything he could to help and protect you.'

Amanda nodded, but with closed eyes and pursed lips. Then she looked straight at Jamie. 'That's *his* genes. There's been times, over the years, when I kind of… lose myself. I hear myself saying things that I hate, but they come blurting out of my mouth.' She shook her head again and looked down at the table. 'I saw it in him. No, I recognised it in him.'

She felt Jamie stroke the back of her hand with his thumb. 'I think that's why he felt so familiar to me early on. I'd already identified some of his traits in me. I'm sorry, Jamie.' She began to laugh, and then, seeing Jamie startled, she turned her hand over and clasped both of his in her own. 'Don't worry, I'm not going mad. I was just thinking, maybe we could get your mum to recommend a good exorcist! Chase that black devil out of me.'

'No way! I like you just as you are. I don't want any part of you chased away. Yes, you've got a temper, but it just goes to make you who you are, and I love all of it, even the Odoms part!'

'Good. I love you, too, Jamie Forsythe. I don't love Howard Odoms, though. I wanted to, really wanted to, and I tried hard. Honestly, Jamie, I did try, but… I don't know… Christ, he's not even easy to like, never mind love!'

'You've spent most of your life wondering about him, building up a picture in your mind. I doubt anyone could live up to that. I've never really given any thought to meeting my father. I was told who he was and what happened and accepted it. He'll be dead now, anyway, but he never had any image to live up to in my mind. Not like your father. Do you think if you gave it a bit more time? You know, write, phone each other… take things a bit slower. Maybe then you would find a connection.'

Amanda shook her head and leaned in to cuddle closer to him. 'No, I'm done, over it. He's got his life and I've got mine. This has been pretty tough, emotionally, but I'm starting to feel better. Now that there's not an empty space where a father should be, it's as if I've got a fresh start.'

Davy stood at the side of the chilled cabinet. He hadn't wanted to interrupt their conversation, and he was glad he'd held back and listened. This was what he had waited all these years for. He'd quietly encouraged Amanda to track her father down, but now she wanted him out of her life. Well, he would help with that. He would exorcise the evil bastard. Not just for Amanda; at last he could do it for Diane and for his Ina, for all the women he'd loved. That black-hearted, evil bastard would have his day of reckoning.

They both stood looking through the glass doors that led out of the Departures area of the airport.

'That was weird, wasn't it?' Jamie turned to Amanda for confirmation.

'It was. I thought maybe it was just me, but it wasn't. He's not… not himself. He's not behaving like my uncle Davy.' She shook her head to clear her confusion.

They remained silent for a few minutes, still looking out where Davy had hurried off.

Finally, Amanda gazed down at the clutch of twenty-dollar bills he had thrust into her hands before he left.

'What's he up to?' Although she spoke aloud, her voice was as far away as her thoughts. There was no response from Jamie. His body was rooted to the spot while his mind clicked through snippets of conversations he had shared with the man he regarded as his ally, his guardian, his friend – yes, most of all his friend. A cold dread congealed in his chest. He turned to Amanda but couldn't speak. He couldn't answer the question in her eyes. If his fears were right, then Jamie himself had been the unwitting supplier. He had confided in Davy, had unburdened himself of overheard conversations, whispered prayers, and most of all his own speculations about Amanda's father. He now recognised little seeds Davy had dropped into conversations. Even when he had been just a kid, Jamie had unburdened himself to Davy, told him all his fears about Amanda's father.

Once contact had been made and Amanda had decided to travel to Arizona, Davy had encouraged her while at the same time reassuring Jamie that under no circumstances would she be alone over there, meeting this stranger. His financial and emotional support had facilitated the whole trip. Never once had Jamie suspected a hidden agenda. Now he felt stupid, naive, and overwhelmingly foolish.

He grasped Amanda firmly round the top of her arm. 'Come on. You need to check in.'

'But… Wait, Jamie, what are you doing? Davy changed your ticket to the same flight as me.'

'I'm staying here. You need to get on that plane. I'm going to get Davy.'

She pulled back from him and took in his clenched fists, narrowed eyes, and set jaw. She caught his fear without knowing its cause.

'I'm not going anywhere without you. Whatever you think he might be up to, I'm coming to find out with you. It won't take long to change these tickets back, and we can hire a car again.' They lifted their bags and headed towards the desk. 'Where do you think he's going?'

'Well, there's not many places he could go, is there? He's going to Tombstone.'

After over thirty minutes at the airline desk, Amanda and Jamie took the shuttle bus to the car rental service on the outskirts of the airport.

'You have *a lot* of explaining to do, Jamie!' Her irritation was clear, and Amanda was not the most patient of people at the best of times. Throughout the long wait in the line, she had stood with arms folded and toes tapping, which wound Jamie up even more.

Jamie reckoned they must be about an hour behind Davy by the time they were in their rental car and on the road. He was increasingly jittery and continued to make excuses not to reveal the cause to Amanda. 'Not now, shh. I'll tell you later when things have calmed down a bit. Just trust me, will you?'

Ten miles later they were on the long, straight highway that would eventually lead to Tombstone. Although Davy could still sense her bristling resentment, Amanda had stayed silent, allowing him to focus on negotiating the confusing twist of junctions leading from Sky Harbor Airport onto the long route south. Now he was trying to prepare himself for the inevitable questions.

Amanda didn't wait any longer. 'Right. I want to know everything, and I want to know it right now! Do you hear me, Jamie Forsythe?'

'Hear you? Of course I hear you. How could I avoid hearing you? There's only the two of us in the car. You do realise that I didn't get to question your decision to travel six thousand miles and meet with a stranger with a questionable past, but you can demand that I tell you right now what the hell Davy and I are doing by looking out for your welfare? Honest to God, talk about double standards, Amanda.'

'It's not the same thing, and you know it. Anyway, it's why we're chasing after my uncle Davy that I want you to tell me about. We were both booked onto this afternoon's flight home, and now we're careering back to Tombstone. It makes no sense!'

Jamie peered straight ahead, asking himself the very same question. His voice quietened to a whisper as he answered. 'I'll be honest, Amanda, I'm not a hundred per cent sure myself. I'm scared. There's such a feeling right deep in my gut that Davy is up to something… something frightening, maybe even dangerous. What I do know is that we need to go and find him, and I think we'll find him in Tombstone.'

Davy scanned the highway stretching before him. The hire car was an automatic, and with the lack of junctions and only light traffic, he could allow his mind to wander. There was no real plan in his mind, simply an outcome. Getting to this point had always just been a fluid *one day* feeling in his gut. All the times he'd directed conversations to what had happened in Dunoon, he'd intended to get at the truth. What he would do with that truth had always been shrouded from his conscious mind. Of course there had been Amanda to consider. Odoms was her father, and Davy had to hold back until she knew who this ghost from her past really was.

If Odoms had welcomed her with open arms, if they had found some bond between them and wanted to be family, what would Davy have done? Maybe nothing. But when he saw that Amanda didn't want anything more to do with that man, then the feeling of release, of *victory*, engulfed him. More than a quarter of a century since they lost Diane, since their lives were broken, and now he could break his life. Christ, he had played the long game. The first years had given him nothing but a sick, angry wife. As terrible as losing Ina had been, it had also given him freedom. Marion and Amanda became a reason to keep going. Planning to move to London and help them had given him direction, focus, something positive. Amanda especially meant so much to him; then Jamie too. That big awkward boy had turned into such a great man, and he and Amanda were made for each other. Through all his dark thoughts, a chuckle escaped. Bloody Jamie. Jeez, that boy! God, he'd been a bundle of trouble when he was younger. He didn't keep bad company – no, he was the bad company! The other kids all looked up to him. If Jamie thought they should do something, then they did it. All small-time then, but if Davy hadn't been there, it could have gone on to the really bad stuff. He knew two of the boys Jamie had hung around with were already in jail, and there were others who had died. Drugs, bloody poison! Aye, poison. So many different drugs; so many ways they could do harm.

All that trouble with Jamie, him getting out of control – it had all been starting when Davy and Sheila had been in that crash. Strange how looking back gives you such a different perspective. He'd suffered deep grinding guilt for months, years, afterwards. The police, the cameras, and witnesses had all said it was the other guy's fault. Seeing the amber light and putting his foot down to try and make it through – but he hadn't, in any sense, poor bastard. But Davy had long wondered: if he hadn't been upset and rubbing his eyes, if... Could he have maybe seen him coming and not moved forward? But now... now he thought it might have been God's plan all along. Terrible what Sheila had to go through, but he'd moved in with Jamie and saw what the boy was getting into. Then moving him over to Peckham: well, that had taken Jamie on a new path, the one that made him the fine man he was today.

Ever since Amanda found Odoms, possibilities had been bubbling in the back of Davy's mind. Half-formed ideas about what he might say and do to punish this man. In his dark fantasies, he had stabbed, strangled, bludgeoned, and tortured a faceless black man. The man wasn't going to be faceless any longer. Davy was going to see a human being, flesh and blood, and that made a difference.

What he wanted more than anything was to make Odoms realise what he'd taken. He wanted not to *take* this man's life but to change it as devastatingly as his own had been changed. He wanted, even needed, to see him cry, beg forgiveness, realise the enormity of Diane's loss and the denial of all her future had promised. She had been only seventeen. So much more life was ahead for her, and Howard Odoms had taken it away.

At sixty-four years old, Davy Barr wasn't ancient, but neither was he physically able to challenge a younger ex-marine. He knew he would have to come up with a plan that would play to the few advantages he did have.

War movies and books or spy stories had always been his favourite entertainment. They showed how the element of surprise put you ahead of the game. He knew who Howard Odoms was and where he lived and worked. Odoms didn't have a clue about Davy's existence, much less that he was here in Arizona and coming for him.

Amanda had been meticulous in reporting all her movements to Jamie while she was with her father. It had been a firm condition that Jamie had insisted on before agreeing that Amanda could meet her father without him.

Davy saw the signs for Tucson a few miles ahead. It was beginning to get dark, and it had been a long day. There were only about eighty miles more to Tombstone, but he wasn't sure if he should charge ahead or rest here. Abruptly, he pulled into the cut-off lane and headed into Tucson. He knew he wouldn't sleep, but he checked into the first motel he came to, knowing he needed to think through what he was going to do and how he would manage to do it. He'd waited a long time for this. He wasn't going to mess it up now.

His flight home was still booked for three days from now. Time to take a breath and plan.

• • •

It was easier to talk to Amanda when she was sitting at his side than if she had been facing him, eyes boring into his, demanding answers.

Slowly he gave her the little snapshots of conversations Davy had had with him over the years. He wanted to let her join the dots herself, hoping that his conclusions were wrong and the result of watching too many television dramas.

He began with the conversation between their two mothers when he was a little boy. That experience, or at least a version of it, had become a recurring nightmare throughout his childhood. Whenever he'd been ill, he would dream the bad man was coming for him, wanting to poison him. Without fail he would waken vomiting and shaking, often with a wet puddle in the bed, too, although he edited that bit out of his recollections.

As he reached adolescence, the nightmares faded, but a feeling of foreboding remained. He knew it was all centred around Amanda's father. Looking back to explain everything to Amanda, he was shocked to suddenly realise how relentless Davy's pursuit of information had been. When his mum had been in hospital after the accident, Davy had gone with him to the flat so he could pack his things and stay with him in Peckham till his mum was better. He'd needed his birth certificate so he could be enrolled in school over there, and searching deep in the layers of the old black toolbox that served as their family safe, he'd found that big brown envelope.

Seeing the insignia for the US Marines had taken his breath away. Initially he'd thought it was his own father's whereabouts the letters were referring to, but then he saw Marion's name and address. Why they should be in his mother's possession, he wasn't sure, but it was clear that this was an attempt to trace Amanda's father. And now his own personal bogeyman had a name – Howard Odoms.

Davy had been at his back. Slowly he'd reached over and took the papers from him. His face had become contorted. Mouth twisting, eyes squeezed tightly shut, fists clenching and unclenching. Then he'd taken one last look, folded all the papers along their original creases, and replaced them in the envelope. He'd given them back to Jamie, telling him to put them back and forget he'd ever seen them.

Silence was an unusual state for Amanda, but throughout Jamie's unfolding of the secrets of the past, she stayed quiet, staring out the windshield at the dusty terrain. Jamie faltered many times during the telling, especially when revealing that he'd known her father's name for all those years when she'd spent so much time searching for it.

At that point in his story, Amanda gripped his arm. 'What! You knew his name? All those years… you knew his name?'

Jamie glanced over at her. 'Let me finish, okay?' She could yell and scream at him some other time; right now there was more at stake, and he must make her see that. He went on to explain his fears for her safety and Davy's plan to quietly stay in the background and watch out for her. He had paid for their flights, motels, everything.

'I was never suspicious of his motives because I know how much he loves you. Why else would he go to so much trouble and expense?'

'Well, he lost his daughter… Oh God! No, no, do you think…' Amanda tipped her head back and closed her eyes, exhaling deeply. 'Jamie, I think the girl… the one Mum said was poisoned… I think it was my cousin.' Her voice was small. Only her lips moved.

'What?' Jamie glanced over, looking for an explanation.

Amanda turned to look directly at Jamie. 'Diane, my cousin. I've seen photos of her. So have you. Davy's got them in his room, and there's the one on the telly of him with Auntie Ina and their daughter. Diane. She went to Dunoon to work beside my mum.'

'What about her?' His stomach was shrinking. He already knew what.

Amanda turned to face him. 'The girl who died. I think they meant Davy's daughter, Diane. He thinks Howard poisoned her.' Her hands went to cover her face. 'But she died in hospital from a miscarriage. She bled out from losing her baby.' Bringing her hands down, she gripped Jamie's arm. 'Could it… You don't think it could have been Howard's baby, do you?'

Jamie shook his head in denial, not convincing either of them. That joined the dots, all right. Damn it!

It was dark when they reached Tombstone. Amanda suggested leaving the car parked beside the American Legion; she hoped Howard might be at work this evening. That would mean Davy would have trouble confronting him.

The door opened to a bright comfortable room with a bar at the top end, tables and chairs in the centre, and couched seating built along the walls. Flags, badges, and photographs covered almost every available inch. Every branch of the American military services was represented. Howard was not in evidence, and Amanda excused herself after spotting the sign for the restrooms over an alcove on the opposite wall.

At the bar, Jamie asked for a Coke. The barman nodded and went to the far end of the bar, where he lifted a glass to the soda taps. As he finished pouring, he glanced up at the tall, thin black man sitting alone at the top corner of the bar.

'What about you, Samuel? Are you ready for another?'

Jamie looked up and saw the man smile broadly at the barman.

'Yes, sir!' he replied. 'I'll have a Pepsi-Cola. Why would I drink anything else?'

'Yeah, yeah, I know, your grandpappy was saved by the sign.'

Jamie froze. He looked more closely at the man. He had tightly cropped grey hair, and one side of his face was lower than the other. The left eye was clearly damaged and drooped at the outside edge, but his right eye was bright and clear. He took the glass of soda from the barman with his right hand, but the other arm lay heavily on the bar, unmoving.

Jamie knew. Right then, he just knew. It wasn't hearing Samuel's name or about the grandpappy, although that's what had drawn his attention. No, it had been a… a what? A recognition? A feeling, kinship, blood ties? Whatever. Crawling round his insides was a warm, light feeling. This man, this damaged soul, was Samuel. The same Samuel who had loved his mother and been cruelly ripped from her all those years ago in Dunoon. This was *his* father. How could this be? They were in Tombstone, Arizona, for God's sake! How could Jamie be sitting in the same room as a man he'd thought to be dead long ago?

His heartbeat sped up till he thought it might pound its way out of his chest. He reached into his glass for a fistful of ice and held it till the ice melted and his hands were cold; then he placed his palms over his eyes, finally sliding them around to the back of his neck. The coolness helped calm him. Again, he looked over to where the tall man sat, sipping his drink and looking round the hall with an expression of wonderment on his face. This was a man he'd been told had suffered and died, yet here he was. Damaged, yes, but alive, very much alive.

Jamie lifted his glass but put it back on the counter when his hand trembled, slopping cold cola over the rim. Sitting upright on the bar stool, he straightened his back, placed his hands on his knees, and inhaled deeply, then slowly blew his breath out to steady himself. He stood and felt his legs shake so badly he had to grip the bar to keep his balance.

The barman came over to him, eyes narrowed in suspicion. 'You okay, bud?'

Jamie could only nod. He felt winded. His breath was shallow and fast. He sat on the stool again, heavily, and still with a firm hold on the bar.

Finally, he tried standing again, and his legs felt more like his own this time. He walked towards the older man. 'Samuel?' His voice was little more than a whisper.

'Yes, Samuel, yes, that's me.' He nodded and smiled as the tall young man approached.

Jamie spoke in a gentle voice. 'Hi, may I join you?' And before Samuel had a chance to answer, he continued, 'I hear you like Pepsi-Cola. That's my favourite drink too.'

Amanda surveyed the whole room from under the alcove as she returned from the restroom. Howard wasn't there. Jamie had moved to the end of the bar and was talking to another man. She could only see the top of his head; Jamie had his back to her, obscuring the rest of the man from her view. The barman was nearer to her end of the bar and was washing glasses under the counter but watching Jamie and the man as he did so. Amanda decided it would be easier to approach him and ask if he knew where Howard might be.

'Excuse me.'

He looked up at her. 'Yes? What can I get for you, miss?'

'We're hoping to catch up with Howard Odoms this evening, and I wondered if you were expecting him in to work?'

The barman looked uncomfortable, glancing round the room as if to check whether anyone else was going to answer her question. Then he looked back at Amanda.

'Eh, well, he wasn't scheduled to work at all this week, then I heard he might be back.' He glanced over to the man Jamie was talking to as he said this. 'But now...' He blew out his lips, making a horse-like noise, and shrugged indecisively.

Big help, thought Amanda, but she smiled and thanked him before moving towards Jamie.

Just then the door opened, and a tall, immaculately dressed black woman strode in, turning all heads in the bar towards her. She headed straight for the corner where Jamie and the man were still deep in conversation. The man stood quickly and stumbled a little. Jamie steadied him, and the woman transferred her phone to her other hand and used her free arm to offer him support.

'Vanessa!' he called out with surprise and delight in his voice. As he stood, Amanda could see he too was very tall, almost as tall as Jamie, although he was a little stooped. His face looked odd, as if one side was lower than the other.

'Why, Vanessa, I would know you anywhere. It's so good to see you, Nessa, real good.'

'Okay, well, we need to go now, Samuel. Come on. Take my arm.' Looking up at the barman, she shook her head. 'He's not going to make bail till morning, fool that he is.'

The barman made another horsey blow with his mouth and turned away. Then, suddenly remembering Amanda's enquiry, he moved closer to Vanessa. Amanda couldn't hear what he told her, but Vanessa looked over at her and asked, 'You looking for Howard Odoms?'

Amanda nodded, and Jamie turned in his chair, seeing her for the first time since they had entered.

'Well, he won't be in here tonight. You might get him tomorrow, okay?' She turned to the stooped man. 'It's okay, Samuel, we'll come back tomorrow.' She began to guide him towards the door but stopped, turned, and looked Jamie up and down. He moved forward and held the door open for them, steadily meeting her gaze. Her eyes narrowed as though she wanted to say something, but instead she continued through the door and helped her brother into her car, which she had parked at the entrance. A blue badge was displayed prominently in the windscreen. Jamie still held the door and watched as the engine purred into life and they drove away. Samuel looked out the window at Jamie until they had driven out of sight.

Jamie and Amanda found a room at the Rose Tree Inn and booked in overnight. It wouldn't merit many stars, despite having the rooms named after famous movie cowboys, but it wasn't luxury they were after as they tried to make themselves comfortable in the Kirk Douglas Room. Framed photographs of scenes from the movies decorated the room. A thick woven throw on the bed and the floor rug were, according to the notice on the dresser, handcrafted by Native Americans and available to buy at reception.

Neither of them gave the room more than a cursory glance. Jamie stretched his back against the door to ease the tension and closed his eyes with a deep sigh.

From a young age he had known all he needed to about his father. There had been no curiosity, no desperation to try and track him down. From all his mother had told him, he had been a nice guy who had suffered terrible injuries before he had any idea that he had fathered a child – in fact, before she herself knew she was pregnant. His condition had been critical, and visiting him would not have been possible, even if Sheila had been able. She was told he'd been sent home to the marine hospital in Charleston and would be on life support, if he survived at all.

Yet Jamie had seen him. Sitting in Tombstone, Arizona, drinking Pepsi-Cola!

He looked over at Amanda, who had taken her shoes off and was sitting on the end of the bed, rubbing her temples. She had been quiet. He felt apprehension ripple through him. He knew she was waiting for an opportunity to vent her frustration about his part in the attempt to foil her search for Howard Odoms. He couldn't deal with that now. Shock and confusion at seeing the man who seemed to be his father were smothering every other concern.

Amanda looked up at him from the bed. 'What will you say to your mum?' Her voice was tight.

He shook his head and shrugged. 'No idea. First I need to make sure he is who I think he is.'

Her only response was to roll her eyes.

'Leave it, Amanda. Will you just leave it for now?'

Pursing her lips, she lay back on the bed and rolled onto her side, facing away from him.

Jamie couldn't settle. He tried lying down; he tried sitting in the chair. He'd had a long hot shower but still couldn't relax or get any sleep. Amanda drowsed off once or twice, but by four in the morning they were both wide awake.

'Jamie?'

'What?' He turned to Amanda, a snap of irritation in his voice.

'Hey! All I was going to say was if we can't sleep, maybe we should talk.'

'Okay, so talk, but don't start a fight with me just now, Amanda.'

'Your mum... What are you going to say to her?'

'I don't know. God, I really don't. Maybe I shouldn't tell her?'

'You have to, don't you?'

'What are *you* going to tell your mum? What will she say now you've found *your* father? Maybe she was right all along and you shouldn't have chased him down!' He felt better deflecting attention from his problems.

'I don't need to tell her. She doesn't care whether he's alive or dead. It's different for your mum. She loved Samuel. She was broken-hearted about what happened. My mum just walked away, chose not to tell him she was pregnant. Your mum didn't have those choices.'

'Shut up, Amanda. I can't think about these things just now. I shouldn't have let them leave without talking to them last night. What if they don't come to the Legion tomorrow? What if I've found him only to lose him again?' His voice had gotten higher, and Amanda knelt on the bed and pulled him down beside her.

'Shh, shh, it'll be okay. The barman knew him. Howard must know him too. They were friends when they were in the marines. Maybe that's why Samuel is here in Tombstone.'

Jamie nodded, seeing the sense in her logic. He lay down and held out his arms, hoping she would let him hold her. Amanda took his hand and stroked it but remained kneeling on the bed, leaving a distance between them.

27 /
tucson, arizona, october 1999

day 6

Davy woke at six the following morning, surprised to find he had slept for over four hours and feeling unexpectedly calm and focused. Complimentary coffee and donuts from reception passed for breakfast, and he took them to his room, where he studied the motel's directory of local services.

A large shopping mall was only a few blocks away, but the stores didn't open until 10 a.m. Slowly and meticulously, he showered, shaved, and dressed. He put on pale grey trousers and a light shirt, keeping himself as nondescript as possible. Then, to pass the remaining time, he bought a pack of cigarettes from the machine at reception and stood on the balcony, smoking and watching the morning rush hour slow to the more leisurely traffic of mid-morning.

He went to Hillards first. In their sports department, he found the hunting and fishing equipment near the back. There was a variety of knives on display. He examined the individual knives in turn and decided on one just as an assistant approached him.

'Can I help you, sir?' It was a young male assistant, but he was a little bit too flirty for Davy's taste.

'Yes, I want a good knife for gutting fish. It's for my mate… friend… for his birthday…' Davy avoided eye contact with the assistant, simply continuing to read the information on the display.

'Oh, well, sir, you can't go wrong with this one. It has a lifetime guarantee, and it's a bargain, at a forty per cent discount as our manager's special. It's a real dependable blade.' As he spoke, the young boy tried to lean in to Davy's line of vision.

'Mmm… Okay. I think I'll go with this one. Can you gift wrap it?'

'Certainly, sir. If you'll just come over to the register, we'll get it all organised for you.' Dropping his voice, he abandoned the efficient shop script and added, 'I just love your accent. Are you Irish? My grandmother was from Ireland, County Cork. She was a McMonagle. Do you know them?'

Davy was startled at this attempt to engage him in conversation. It was what he had hoped to avoid, and yet he knew that everywhere he and Jamie had gone in Arizona, their accents had been commented on. Most had hazarded a guess at their nationality as British, but very few had pinned it down to Scotland. One receptionist had gone for South African, another for Australian, so he was happy to let the Irish identity continue. It was easier to shrug and shake his head than speak and give him more to work with.

The assistant dropped the boxed knife into a carrier bag and handed it over to Davy. He paid with a fifty-dollar bill and nodded towards the charity box on the counter when the assistant offered him a few dollars in change.

'Well, thank you, sir. You have a nice day now!'

In the car, Davy placed his purchase on the front passenger seat and started the engine. Throughout the short journey back to the motel, he kept glancing at the carrier as if looking for confirmation that he really had bought a knife, had taken another step on this strange path.

Once inside his room, he locked the door and closed the blinds on the small window. The temperature outside was well into the nineties. They expected it to go into the hundreds in the next day or so, which was unusual this late in the year.

The digital clock on the bedside table showed one thirty. His plan was to set off late afternoon and arrive in Tombstone as dusk was falling. He lay on the bed and closed his eyes.

Ina was berating him. 'You need to do this, Davy Barr. I don't think you've got the bottle for it, but somehow you need to find it in yourself to step up. For our Diane, for me. Get us justice, for God's sake. Davy, don't chicken out.'

He wakened to see the dusk already falling. Four o'clock! How had he slept the afternoon away? He rose and went to the bathroom, where he splashed cold water on his face. Lifting his head, he considered the face in the mirror.

He saw a tired, grey man with sagging jowls, eyebrows wildly sprouting over his pale, watery eyes. A deep sigh left him, and he looked at his hands, resting on either side of the washbasin. Long fingers, high blue veins, uneven nails disappearing into the scabbed cuticles where he had bitten down to the flesh. Were these hands that could maim, perhaps even murder? Hands that had worked, supported his family, held his child, caressed his wife – could they grasp a knife and plunge into the flesh of another body?

In his first year at high school, his biology class had been expected to pin out a dead rat for dissection. He could see it now, plump, white, lying limply on the board. He'd held the pin, placed it against the thick pads of a paw. Everyone else had made noises, but they'd done it. Pressed and pushed through the poor wee beast's flesh and stretched him, spreadeagled like a crucifixion victim. Davy alone remained standing, the pin in his shaking hand. He could hear others snigger; Billy Payne called him a jessie; more sniggering. Auld McNab strode over, his cape billowing, and grabbed his hand, fingers pinching over the top of his, and pushed. The skin broke, and he felt the point slice through till it was secured on the dissection board. After the initial shock, he became somehow separate from the gruesome aspects of the lesson and was absorbed in the anatomy of the task. A lesson learned.

He stared into the eyes of his reflection. *Get over the first hurdle and you can do this.* Find justice. Make him understand the grief, the pain he caused. Use the knife to make him listen. But he needs to know you'll use it if you have to. Tell him you know what he did. Make him confess, apologise, beg forgiveness, show remorse. He needs to *deserve* mercy.

Stowed in the boot of his hired car were his suitcase and holdall with his passport and flight tickets. If both he and Odoms survived what was ahead, then it would be one's word against the other's. If Odoms didn't survive, then he would be back in Phoenix, hopefully on a return flight to London, before anyone knew he'd been there. Of course, if Davy himself didn't survive, then it would make no odds to him at all. He was quite prepared for that. In some ways, it might be better.

28 /
tombstone, arizona, october 1999

Jamie and Amanda were seated inside the Legion. They had arrived as it opened and taken the booth nearest the bar, facing the door. Jamie wanted to see Samuel as soon as he came in. He'd heard Vanessa say they would be back today, but she hadn't mentioned a time.

They arrived just before five o'clock. First came Vanessa, who held the door for Samuel to enter, supported by a very downcast Howard. Jamie almost jumped out of his seat, but Amanda held his arm, urging him to wait. Howard helped Samuel onto a stool at the end of the bar, and Vanessa dumped her briefcase on the counter.

Howard slumped against the bar without taking any notice of the rest of the room. Amanda felt sick. Right now, she wanted to be anywhere except where he was, but this was for Jamie. She nodded to Jamie, and together they walked over.

'Howard.' She spoke quietly, and he looked up, studying her silently for a few moments.

'I thought you'd gone.'

She nodded. 'I tried to, but…' She turned and clasped Jamie's hand. 'Look who I found at the airport. Jamie, this is

Howard.' She nodded from one to the other and back again. 'Howard, this is Jamie.' Each acknowledged the other with a slight nod.

Vanessa had watched this exchange closely, and Jamie looked at her and spoke.

'I was in here last night. I was chatting with Samuel just before you arrived and took him home.'

She nodded and continued to stare at him as Jamie went on. 'Samuel remembers some things about his time stationed in Scotland, don't you, Samuel?'

Samuel nodded, a happy grin still on his face.

'He remembers Sheila, the girl he was keen on in the bar they used to go to.'

'Sheila? Where is she? Isn't Sheila working tonight?' Samuel's grin faltered.

'This isn't the place where Sheila worked, honey. This is where Howard works. You like it here.' Vanessa spoke in a soothing voice and slipped a protective arm around her brother's shoulders.

Jamie looked at Vanessa. 'I'm Sheila's son.'

Vanessa hugged her brother tightly, burying her face in his neck trying to hide her tears from him, but he realised she was upset and became quite agitated. She grabbed a paper napkin from the bar, dabbed her tears carefully, and drew herself up to her full height.

'I saw you last night, and felt… strange, like I was having a flashback. They say everyone has a double, don't they? You were a stranger, and I would have looked like a crazy person asking you if…'

'What's wrong? Vanessa?' Samuel was grabbing at his sister's arm, trying to get her attention back to him.

'Nothing's wrong, Samuel. These are nice people, and I want to talk to them. Okay?'

'Oh, okay.' He sat down again, but his grin had gone, and he looked almost ready to cry.

'Look, he's had a long day. He's tired. I need to take him home and let him get some rest.'

'He could go have a sleep in the trailer,' Howard offered, taking part in the conversation for the first time.

'No, I don't think so. I want him home with me tonight.' Vanessa's tone had become crisp and sharp. 'You need to get to your trailer and clean yourself up.' She then spoke to Jamie in a softer tone. 'Do you two have transport?'

Jamie nodded. 'We have a rental. It's parked just outside.'

Vanessa had slipped back into the assertive role she was comfortable with. 'Okay, why don't you follow me in your car. My home is about a thirty-minute drive from here.'

No one had looked at Howard to include him, but he explained his plans as though they had.

'I'm going to stay and have a coffee and a bite to eat. There's no food at home, and I haven't eaten since this morning. Amanda, d'you want to stay here?'

She shook her head and took Jamie's hand. 'No, Howard. I'm going with Jamie. Bye, Howard.'

'Goodbye, Amanda.' He turned away.

Just outside, Amanda stopped and asked Jamie to wait. She turned and went back inside, to where Howard was ordering food.

'You knew, didn't you?'

He turned and looked at her, a half smile on his face.

'Knew? Knew what?'

'You knew Samuel was alive. You knew he was Jamie's dad. You knew Sheila was pregnant before you ever left Dunoon.'

Howard shrugged.

'I told you about me and Jamie, about his mum, Sheila, being friends with my mum… you knew and didn't say a word. You really are a shit, Howard Odoms, a deep-rooted arsehole.'

'You're gonna think the worst of me no matter what I do or say, missy. What the hell good would it have done to tell you about Samuel? He can't be a father to anyone. He'll forget he's even met you or Jamie five minutes after you leave the room. What's the point of getting everyone all worked up?'

Amanda shook her head in resignation, then thought she should mention Davy. 'Listen, you need to look out for—'

'Amanda! Come on!' Jamie stood holding the door open to urge her along. Amanda looked at the uninterested expression on Howard's face and, without another word, turned and ran to catch up with Jamie.

The route to Tombstone was mostly straight, well signposted and uncomplicated. By five thirty Davy had parked in a quiet, poorly lit street on the edge of the small town. He passed only two people on his way to the trailer park, but neither one appeared to notice him as he walked past with his head down and both hands thrust deep inside the pockets of his zipped-up jacket. His right hand gripped the handle of the stout blade he'd bought that morning. Being honest with himself, he was concerned that the younger, fitter man might overpower him and turn the knife on him.

He'd chosen a fishing knife because he was at least slightly familiar with it – well, a long time ago he had been. When he was a young teenager, his da had taken him fishing in the river. In Glasgow, the water was filthy, with the industries on both banks flushing their waste straight into the Clyde. But his da would take him on the bus, upriver to some of the wee villages where the powerful river flowed clean and pure enough to drink. They had some great days fishing back then. Whatever you caught, you had to either cook and eat or, if it was too young, put it back and let it grow for another day and another angler. His da had taught him how to gut and fillet trout. When he caught one, they would cook it in a pan over the fire right there on the riverbank. Anything his da caught would always go back home for his ma and Marion. His sister was only young then, just a toddler, and Ma would flake the fish between her fingers to make sure she didn't get any of the bones.

Seeing the American Legion building up ahead chased the happy memories from his mind. He looked around the deserted street and over to the trailer park.

He knew from Amanda's texts that the red-and-white trailer at the front belonged to Odoms, and he could see part of it from the corner on the opposite side of the street. This was only a few yards along from the American Legion, where his quarry worked, so he could watch any comings and goings from both from where he stood. A standing, staring man was conspicuous, so Davy brought out a cigarette and lighter and leaned against the wall of the building in what he hoped was a nonchalant manner.

He puffed the smoke high in the air, occasionally glancing at his watch to indicate to any passers-by that he was waiting for someone, and indeed he was.

Odoms's truck was parked in its space, so he knew he had to be either in there or working in the Legion. He waited and smoked.

29 /
tombstone, arizona, october 1999

Vanessa's car turned into the driveway and straight into the open garage. On the street in front of her home, Jamie put the car into park and switched the engine off. He and Amanda looked at each other in silence; then she reached over and covered his hand with hers.

'It'll be all right. It will. I know you're nervous, but…' She didn't finish her sentence. Vanessa was now standing at her open door, beckoning to them.

Coming around to Amanda's side of the car, he helped her onto the sidewalk, and as they walked towards the door, she slipped her arm around his waist.

Vanessa stepped back and gestured for them to enter the sitting room. Samuel was sitting on one of the dining table chairs that had been turned to face the sofa where Jamie and Amanda sat down.

Everything was moving in slow motion for Jamie, and yet his mind was racing.

Samuel's normally smiling face was drooping. Vanessa crossed the room, stood behind him, and began rubbing his neck and shoulders.

'He's tired. He doesn't do too well when he has such a busy day.' She bent and spoke quietly into her brother's ear. 'Let's get you up to your room for a rest, Samuel.' Helping him up, she looked over at the couch and whispered, 'I'll get him settled and be right down. We can talk then.'

On their own in the room, Amanda and Jamie spoke in whispers.

'There's so much I want to ask her, but I don't know where to start.'

Amanda still had her arm round his waist, and she gave him a squeeze. 'Let's wait and take our lead from her. Just take it slow. Remember, this is all new to her as well.'

After a few minutes, Vanessa came back to the sitting room and walked straight up to Jamie with a broad smile.

'Hello, nephew.' She held her hands out to him and, rising, he took them. As he leaned toward her, their arms went around each other in a hug. They stepped back and regarded each other, both with tears in their eyes. Jamie gave a little self-conscious laugh.

'I always thought my father had died… long ago.' He coughed to clear the emotion from his voice. 'My mum thought he must have died after…'

'He almost did, several times.' Vanessa's face became solemn. 'But they brought him back. Well… not all of him, but he manages with a bit of help, and he's a happy soul.'

'He seems happy.' Jamie gulped and sat heavily on the chair behind him. 'That's good… My mum… She thinks he's dead. I think I have to tell her he's alive…' He looked up at Vanessa and saw she too was close to tears. He pressed on in a small hesitant voice. 'She prayed for him, you know, every night. When I was a child, I heard her ask God to look after him. "My lovely Samuel", she would say.'

Vanessa crouched in front of him and cradled his face in her hands. 'Well, he did. God answered her prayers and looked after him. Her lovely Samuel, my lovely big brother…'

She brushed Jamie's tears away with her thumbs, then, taking a deep breath, stood up. She was tall, like her brother, but when Jamie stood beside her, she only came up to his chin. They hugged and wept.

Amanda stood slightly behind him and rested her face against his shoulder. She too was crying, but silently.

She lost track of how long the three of them stayed in their sad little tableau. Finally, she took a breath and stepped to the side of the sofa.

'You know, we should be celebrating. This is more like a wake, but Samuel is alive. Resurrected, almost… Well, kind of, for you and your mum, anyway.'

Vanessa nodded, wiping her face with her hands. 'You're right. It's just… so emotional. Seeing you was… is scaring me. The more I look at you, the more I see Samuel before he was injured.' She turned to Amanda. 'You're right, though, this is a joyous day. But I don't know what to do. I never imagined Samuel might have a child. He is still so childlike himself in many ways. But… no, let's gather our thoughts. Shall we pray? Thank the Lord for bringing us all together?'

Amanda stepped forward, placing a hand behind each of them and steering them gently towards the kitchen. 'Maybe later we could pray, Vanessa. Right now, I think we should make some hot coffee and clear our minds.'

They spent the next hour in the kitchen, poring over photographs of Samuel and his family when they were growing up. They had lived near Macon, in Georgia, and only with the financial help of both her older brothers had Vanessa been able to afford to study at Mercer University there.

Samuel had been in hospital for a long time after he returned to Charleston, but once he was stable and physiotherapy had taken him as far along his recovery as it could, they had placed him in a nursing home. He had shared it mainly with elderly veterans with dementia and Alzheimer's. There had been no stimulus for him, and he became very withdrawn, especially as family could only rarely visit. After a long battle with authorities, he had been moved to a care home in Arizona so he was close to Vanessa, and that had helped him up to a point.

'I love my brother, and I owe him a lot,' she explained. 'Without him, I wouldn't have gotten to Mercer, got my degree, and met my husband. But my job is real demanding. Sure, I could bring Samuel out for short trips or an occasional weekend, but it broke my heart to see the depression set in as soon as I took him back to that place.' She looked at both Jamie and Amanda to see if they understood her position. 'Then one day Samuel sees Howard Odoms.'

Amanda looked startled. 'Howard was in a care home?'

'Not quite. Another part of the facility where Samuel was cared for rehab patients.' She bit her lip, clearly unsure of how much she should reveal about Howard.

'Howard is my father. I finally traced him just a few months ago. We arranged to come out here so I could meet him. That's why we're all the way out here in the Arizona desert. Ironic, isn't it? I come to meet my father, and Jamie discovers his.'

Vanessa sat back and stared hard at Amanda. 'Wow! Praise be! The Lord works in mysterious ways, does he not.'

'Oh, he does. He sure does.'

All three of them were laughing when noises came through the wall. Vanessa held her finger to her lips for them to quieten down.

'Samuel's awake. Let me go see to him.'

30 / tombstone, arizona, october 1999

Davy had been waiting there for only twenty minutes when he saw someone leave the Legion and cross to the trailer park opposite. At first, he didn't think it could be Odoms: this fellow was kind of short and walked with his head down, a dejected look about him. However, seeing him take his keys out and let himself into the red-and-white trailer confirmed to Davy that it was him.

He dropped the remains of his cigarette, mashed it into the dusty street with his shoe, and crossed the street to the park entrance for a better view of the whole trailer. The lights were now on inside, and the blinds closed. He waited and watched, seeing a shadow occasionally pass the windows as the man moved around inside.

It was still early in the evening. He was in no rush now. His quarry was in place, and he was ready to confront him. This was a time to savour having come this far. He contemplated Odoms's reaction when he revealed he was Diane's father. Shock? Well, surprise, certainly. It wasn't as if he would have any idea how doggedly Davy had pursued him for all these years. Fear? Probably not. His arrogance would override any possibility of emotional alarm, and physically he would never imagine himself losing out to a sickly older man. Of course, thought Davy, patting his pocket, the knife would rebalance that. Anger? Well, what the hell did Odoms have to be angry at? No. In the anger stakes, Davy knew he won on that score. Anger had been his fuel, and it was time to take aim at the man responsible.

He looked around. The streets were deserted of people, and only the lights of an occasional car passing on nearby streets broke the stillness.

As soon as he got inside, Howard kicked his sandals into the shoe box under the seat. He kept a tidy home. Military training had instilled the habit, and now his current accommodation demanded it if there was to be any semblance of order. He liked order. He'd had his fill of chaos in his younger days. Order made him feel secure, focused his mind, and stopped demons clawing at him. For years, he'd used alcohol to silence them, but that brought its own problems, more layers of disorder.

He stripped off his shorts and shirt, dropping them in the laundry basket concealed behind the wardrobe door. After lifting a clean folded towel from another shelf, he went to the small bathroom and turned on the shower.

Vanessa had been right to tell him to get cleaned up. The smell of the police cell was still with him. He poured a generous puddle of shower gel into his hand and scrubbed it vigorously over every surface of his body. The sharp citrus scent did its best to banish the fetid reminders of his hellish night in custody, and with eyes closed against the soap, Howard replayed the distress and humiliation of the previous twenty-four hours.

Those two cops wouldn't listen. Dumb bastards! He'd tried to make them understand he couldn't leave Samuel, but no, they had a warrant, and they were taking him in no matter what he said. For Chrissake! It was only a bump. No one got hurt. And the tickets – Christ, what were a few traffic tickets these days? Vanessa was supposed to take care of them for him. She hadn't paid him his full allowance for months. The rest of it should have gone to settle the goddamn fines. All those assholes out gawking at him as they tried to force him into the cop car. At least one of them had the sense to get Big Tony from the Legion to come get Samuel.

Finally, after lifting his face to the hot spray, he turned the shower off and shook himself free of excess water before reaching for the dry towel. He slipped on soft, clean shorts and one of his desert camouflage T-shirts.

Coffee, hot black coffee: that's what he needed. He filled the reservoir, added the filter paper, spooned in ten scoops of the dark Columbian grinds and sat back to watch the liquid drip into the glass pot.

He heard footsteps outside on the dry ground of the path and, nudging the blind to one side, looked through to see a man coming to his door. He stepped to the side and opened the door just as the stranger lifted his fist to knock.

'Who you lookin' for, buddy?'

'Odoms. Howard Odoms. That's you, isn't it?'

'Who are you? I don't believe I know you.'

'Can I come in? We need to talk.'

'I don't feel like talking, an' I'm not interested in anything you've got to say. Okay? Now just beat it.'

'You're Amanda's father, aren't you?'

Howard stopped talking. He studied the older man's face and replayed what he'd said, picking up on the Scottish accent for the first time.

For a long tense moment, a silence stretched between them. Then Howard stepped back and gestured for the man to come in.

. . .

Davy kept both hands in his jacket pockets, stepped inside, and stopped. Howard reached behind him to close the door.

'I've got fresh coffee here. D'ya want some?' He lifted a second mug from its hook and held it out.

Davy shook his head. 'I just want to talk.'

'So, how do you know Amanda? Has she asked you to come see me?'

'I'm her uncle.' Davy took a step further into the room and stood, well balanced, feet a little apart, knees slightly bent. Looking around, he asked Howard if he lived alone.

'Most times,' Odoms answered. 'I help look after an old buddy. Look, what is it you want?'

Davy shrugged. 'Just to talk. Amanda doesn't know I'm here. Nobody does. I want it to be just you and me. Man to man.'

'Okay, so talk.'

Davy nodded and, at a leisurely pace, stepped around the room. Howard narrowed his eyes and moved over to the door. Holding the handle, he shook his head.

'Okay, mister. I've had the day from hell, and I don't need this shit. Time to leave.'

Calmly, the older man walked over and, with his hand on Howard's shoulder, firmly pushed him away from the door.

'Sit down, Mr Odoms. You are going to hear what I've got to say. Then I'm going to listen to you.'

Howard allowed himself to be propelled back to the couch, where he settled in, arms outstretched and resting along the top of the seat, one leg bent up with his ankle on the other knee. It seemed like a determined attempt to look unconcerned, but Davy could see the apprehension building in his face.

'You're Amanda's father?'

Howard nodded.

Davy let a beat pass before leaning towards him. 'I'm Diane's father.'

A long silence followed.

He watched Howard shake his head, then nod. He opened his mouth and closed it again. Then, putting both feet on the floor, he leaned forward and buried his head in his hands.

'I did everything I could.' His voice fell leaden towards the floor. He lifted his head and looked Davy in the eyes. 'I got her to the hospital. What else could I have done? What else could I have done?'

'Tell me what happened before that. Tell me everything.' Davy sat across from this man who until now had only existed in his mind's eye, and now here he was, the man who brought his only child to her death. It felt unreal. Perhaps that was why he felt so calm, totally in control. Howard was rubbing his head with his hands, rocking forwards, then backwards, looking to the ceiling but not talking.

Without raising his voice, Davy issued a firm command. 'Now!'

Howard obeyed, just as he had been trained to do.

'We'd been listening to the radio. Sunday afternoon, nice lazy Sunday afternoon. We were sitting on the bed. I had my arms around her. That stupid song came on… "Old Dough"… "Mouldy Old Dough"! That was it! We did that creepy voice together when they sang that bit.' A smile formed at the memory, but it froze on his face when he looked over at Davy. 'When it had finished, she told me she was late. You know, her period? "A wee bit late".' He emphasised the Scottish accent, then shook his head. 'A *wee* bit? Maybe she'd been scared to tell me sooner. But I don't think so. She loved me, adored me. No one ever loved me like Diane. The very first time she laid eyes on me – pow! That was it. Man, she was smitten. That's some feeling, having someone just… adore you.' Again, he looked at Davy to be sure he understood, but the man's expression was fixed and grim.

'Anyway, when she told me she could be pregnant, I… well, I wasn't pleased. I had only two months left there before I got posted back here, to the States. Shit, man, I wanted out of that place so bad. *So* bad…' His face twisted as so many of the injustices and cruelties came back to mind. 'You have no idea what it was like for…'

'Not you. Diane. Just tell me about Diane.' The command was still in Davy's voice.

'Yeah, okay. Well, she knew I'd be going home at the end of the year, and I guess she didn't want to lose me. She might not have lost me, you know. I enjoyed being adored. She was the best thing that had happened to me the entire time I was in Scotland, maybe the best thing ever.' Davy nodded solemnly to spur him on.

'She must have been off the pill for months. Guess she thought if she was pregnant, I would need to do the right thing.' Then, sitting upright, he asked Davy, 'She shouldn't have waited so long before telling me, should she? She should've told me. She should have.'

He stood and began pacing. Then, turning back, he held out his arms and spoke to the air above Davy's head. 'She wanted to leave it till she was too far into the pregnancy to get a termination.' He leaned back against a cupboard door and slid all the way down to the floor, pulling his knees up and hugging them.

'Fucking ironic! The only reason we gave her something to stop the pregnancy was because I thought she was only a couple of weeks along!'

'What did you give her?'

A burst of cold realisation slapped him back from his speculations, and a shiver of fear rippled his body. He stuttered his denials.

'No, no, she'd been drinking. I wouldn't have let her drink if I'd known she was so far along. But she knew. She knew she was way into the pregnancy. She shouldn't have been drinking. I wouldn't have let her if I'd known.'

'What... did... you... give her?'

Moments passed before he continued, his voice small, reflective.

'I was mad. Real angry with her. She was trying to manipulate me. I'd told her to go on the pill right off. I didn't want a kid. I didn't want to get tied down. What I wanted most was to get the hell out of Scotland, and she was trying to keep me there.'

'What did you do?'

'I told my buddy when I got back to the base. He said it could be sorted.'

Davy fell. The couch was right behind him, and he hit it hard. He felt the wind go out of him. Whether it was from the impact of the fall or the confirmation of his darkest thoughts, he couldn't tell.

He looked down at Howard hugging himself on the floor and tried to imagine the young marine, the man that his Diane could have adored so completely. The image wouldn't form. For all Odoms said she'd fallen for him completely, she hadn't been sure he returned those feelings, or she wouldn't have secretly tried to get pregnant.

'How did you *sort* her?' He spat the words out. They tasted of the bile churning in his stomach. 'Tell me everything. It's time to bring it out in the open. Tell me it all.'

'It was a mess... a mess.' Howard's forehead rested on his knees, and he spoke without looking up. 'We'd gone dancing in Glasgow, but we had a room so we could stay overnight. It was cheap. They told me where to go. It wasn't supposed to be a big deal... a bit of a heavy... you know, but—'

'I don't know. I want you to tell me. Say all the words. Stop trying to hide from it.'

'Put the pill in her drink, they said. It will work in two hours. A bit of… It'll bring on her period, they said. Keep away from the base, away from Dunoon. Take some towels…' Howard looked up, shaking his head. 'I took the wrong towels. I didn't know what they meant.' Davy's stare bored into him, and he had to look down again. 'I trusted them. I thought they knew what they were doing. I did everything they told me…'

'What happened after you'd given her the pill?'

'We walked up to the room…' A shuddering sigh shook his body. 'We were only just in there when… she saw the blood.' He stopped talking. Both men sat in silence.

Davy stern and still, Howard shaking and burying his face in his T-shirt.

Finally, Davy broke the silence. He kicked Howard's foot and told him to go on.

Gulping air and rubbing his shirt over his eyes, Howard fought for enough self-control to continue.

'She was so upset, crying… crying for our baby. *Our baby*… I hadn't thought about a baby. Somehow, I didn't really make the connection between a pregnancy that was meant to push me into staying there, getting married… all that, and a child, my child.' He looked up at Davy, his eyes earnestly asking for understanding. 'It was only meant to be a late period, not a baby. She never told me she was having a baby, not till then… when it was too late!'

Howard swallowed hard, straightened his back, lifted his head until it rested against the wall and, with a soft, clear voice, told Davy about his daughter's last few hours.

'She wanted her mom. All she kept asking was for me to take her home. Even when she was so weak her voice was a whisper, that was what she was asking. "Take me home. Please, Howard, I want my mum." I did my best for her. I did. I stayed with her. Sure, I wanted to run, but I didn't. I stayed and helped her. I got her to the hospital. I got her help. It's not my fault if they couldn't save her.' Howard sensed Davy's mood change at these words. Anticipating a physical assault, Howard braced his back against the wall and stood to his full height. But first he defended himself with words. 'I told them your address. She'd told me on our way into Glasgow, pointed out your street and told me your address, 321 Jameston Road. I've never forgotten it. How else were they able to get you to the hospital? You wanted to be with her! I did that for you... for her, for Diane.'

Davy too was on his feet now but turned away, walking over to the sink and turning the tap to let water run into his cupped hands. He held his wet hands over his face and tried to take deep breaths. A deep, wheezing fit of coughing shook him, and he bent double, trying to catch his breath. Howard took a bottle of cold water from the refrigerator and handed it to the older man.

Davy coughed and struggled for breath. Leaning over the sink, he hawked and spat gobs of brown mucus. The cool water helped soothe his burning throat, and he slowly regained his composure. Afterwards, he rinsed the sink clean and cursed himself for those cigarettes he'd smoked earlier, blaming them for this latest episode. The coughing fit had lost him the upper hand in this confrontation. He watched Howard and saw some of his confidence resurface. His *confession* had been to vindicate his actions that night, but it was the announcement of his *gallantry* that had caught hard in Davy's throat. *I did that for you...* The phrase reverberated in his head, getting louder with each beat.

'You did that for me?' His voice was hoarse but sounded flat, emotionless.

'Yes, made sure they got your address. Without me, she would have lain in that room alone. Without me, they wouldn't have known how to find you.'

'Yeah, you're a hero. Christ, they should give you a fucking medal.' Davy's voice strengthened, deepened, and Howard heard the anger build. He stepped back just as Davy stepped forward. There was no room for pursuit. Davy reached into his jacket and pulled out the knife. Its sharp point jabbed Howard's chest. 'Yes, I'd pin it right here.' Jab, jab. 'Right here.' Jab, jab. 'Right at your great big hero's heart.'

Howard was against the window, pressing the blinds against the glass as he tried to back away. Davy knew Howard wasn't frightened of the knife. He knew he was unnerved at this rage, but driving a blade through skin, pushing through flesh and bending it past bone – well, it wasn't in him, and Howard seemed to sense that.

Instead, he exorcised his grief at the man responsible, wailed for his loss, screamed, spat, and cried out the pain he'd had to live with.

'My daughter, my beautiful girl…' The point of the knife was now resting on Howard's throat. Davy was leaning against his chest, and his forehead was pressed hard into Howard's face, but his voice quickly lost power. 'You don't know… I'm… lost…'

Howard reached up and gripped the wrist holding the knife. He pulled it outwards, away from his throat, and dropped the knife onto the surface, then pushed the weight of the man off him. Gently he eased him over to a stool, then leaned on the edge of the counter, still holding Davy's wrist.

'I've known loss. I know what you've had to go through.' He fixed his stare directly on Davy. 'All my life I've lost people I loved. Diane was one of them.'

'She was my child… Losing a child… it's different, unnatural. They're part of you. It rips away something inside. It killed Ina. I lost her too. We shouldn't have had to bury our child.' Davy closed his eyes.

A stillness fell over them both for a few moments.

Howard slowly leaned toward him and, in a calm voice, confessed. 'I buried my child.'

Davy's eyes opened, and he stared hard but said nothing.

'Our child, Diane's and mine. I buried him.'

Davy shook his head. 'Diane's baby?'

Howard nodded.

'How…' Davy cleared his throat. He began to cough again but stifled it to press for answers. 'Where… my grandchild… Diane's baby, where is he?'

'I couldn't leave him there. So tiny… perfect. I held him in the palm of my hand. Cleaned the mud from him with the sheet. He was cold. I tucked him inside my jacket, beside my heart.' He looked up at Davy. 'I couldn't just leave him in that wet field, could I?'

Davy raised his eyebrows to encourage him to go on.

'I wanted to keep him with me. I took him back to the base, but… I bathed him, warm water. My boy…'

'It was a boy?'

Howard shrugged. 'I felt like he was. My boy. My Sonny, but I couldn't keep him. He wanted his mama. I felt Diane tugging at me, telling me to give him back to her.'

Davy had stopped coughing. His shoulders dropped, and he became still. 'Where is…?'

Howard smiled. 'I put him where he belongs, with his mama. A day after her funeral, I went to Diane's grave. It was easy to lift the loose turf and dig into the wet soil. I couldn't go all the way down, but far enough.' Howard cupped his hands and looked at them, still smiling. 'I did right by him. I wrapped him in a little cloth and placed him in a box all padded with cotton. I didn't pray or nothin', but I talked to Diane. She was… not happy… but, you know, at peace. It was the right thing to do.' He nodded. 'Yeah, the right thing.' He paused and looked at Davy, who now had tears in his eyes. 'Yeah, it was only days before they shipped me back to the States, but I was glad I could do it. You know… for Diane, and for Sonny.'

Davy was shaking his head. 'No, no that canny be right.' He looked up and with narrowed eyes faced Howard. 'You're sure?'

'Sure? Of course I'm sure. Do you think it's something I would forget?' Leaning toward the older man, he jabbed his finger into his own forehead. 'It's damn well etched in here, etched in blood!'

Davy was still shaking his head. He stood and began to walk away from Howard, then turned back and faced him.

'You're a bloody liar.'

Howard's face creased in puzzlement. 'Liar? Jesusfuckinchrist Almighty! You're callin' me a liar?'

Davy strode to confront him and nodded. 'I buried my Ina in the same grave. There was no baby, no box, no nothin'.' He moved even closer and placed one hand on the wall, the other on the side of the sink, covering the handle of the knife where it had been left.

Howard looked to the ceiling of the trailer and rested the back of his head against the wall. 'I did bury him there…' He felt Davy stiffen and move towards him, so he put his hand out and firmly pushed his shoulder to stop his advance. 'Wait! I moved him. It didn't feel right. I couldn't leave my boy in that place. Diane was his mama, and she'd had time to say her goodbyes. Now it was my turn.'

Davy had stopped in his tracks, but his grip on the knife tightened, and when he spoke his voice was incredulous. 'You dug him up? You desecrated my daughter's grave… *twice*? You robbed her grave?'

'He was the son of a United States Marine. I gave him a proper burial. A burial that the son of a marine should have. His little body's in the ocean…'

Through the hand on Davy's shoulder, Howard could feel the other man's chest rise. Sensed his movement almost before he had made it.

Davy thrust the knife towards Howard's belly. The point cut his T-shirt and grazed the skin just as Howard pushed Davy away and his right hand swiftly came down to cover the older man's fist on the knife. The younger man was stronger but hemmed into the corner between the wall and sink. Davy closed in, struggling to keep control of the weapon. He realised Howard had gained the upper hand and had managed to turn the blade back towards him. Deliberately, he pushed forward with his full weight.

Even as Davy felt the blade pierce his skin, he kept the forward momentum going. Pressed flat against this man who had haunted his life, he smirked. His body relaxed, and he would have fallen had Howard not supported him with his other arm.

He felt himself being laid gently on the floor. His hand was still on the knife, and he tried to pull it out. Howard stopped him, his hand still covering Davy's.

'No, leave it. You'll bleed out. I'll get the medics. You'll be all right. We'll get help.'

'No.' Davy's voice was barely above a whisper. He struggled to not cough, knowing it would rob him of the chance to speak. 'No, I might be goin' to die, but you'll go to jail. You'll go to…' The urge to cough won through, and blood sprayed lightly over his chest as, with the last bit of strength he had, he pulled the blade from his body.

31 /
arizona, october 1999

day 6

They left Vanessa's house around nine, intending to go north and find a motel. Meeting Samuel the previous evening had taken their minds away from their original reason for going back to Tombstone.

They drove with little conversation, each needing to sort through their thoughts on the events of the day.

Amanda was first to break the silence. 'We should have asked Vanessa about a motel in Bisbee. It would have saved us this drive.'

'Yeah, I know, but I was worried she might insist on us staying at hers. I needed to get away for a bit. Sort things out in my head, you know. It's been a lot to take in.'

'Yes, it's been a lot, all right.' She pursed her lips, then, turning towards him, shook her head. 'Why didn't you tell me his name? You could have helped me years ago, but instead you decided to help Davy – and my mother – by keeping me in the dark. How could you, Jamie? How could you do that to me?'

'For Chrissake, Amanda! Could we *not* talk about you for

once? I've just had the biggest shock of my life, and you're still harping on about you, your search, your fucking needs! Give it a bloody rest, will you?'

Amanda sat back with her arms folded and stared out to the side of the car so Jamie couldn't see her expression.

'I'm sorry.' Jamie's voice was calmer now. 'I know you're due an explanation and a big apology, but just not now, okay?'

She didn't respond. Didn't move a muscle, simply continued to stare out at the darkness.

As they drove, she noticed a pulse of blue light on the horizon. It was over towards the town of Tombstone. Amanda's angry sulk began to change to a strange sense of foreboding.

'Look! Can you see that?'

Jamie nodded and peered over towards where Amanda was pointing.

'I don't like that, Jamie. It's something bad.' She looked over at him and could see he shared her concern. 'Where do you think my uncle Davy is?'

'He's fine. I was getting all jumpy thinking he'd head out to your father's place, but we saw Odoms. He was fine. Your uncle Davy wasn't there.' He paused, then added, 'Even today there was no sign of him. No, he's gone off to have a bit of fun. He'll have driven out to one of the casinos or something.' Although his words were confident, his tone was unsure, as if trying to convince them both.

'Mmm, I don't know, Jamie. Davy's no fool. He knows how to keep out of sight. Look how well he kept the two of you hidden from me.' Amanda pointed at the growing light. 'Go into Tombstone anyway. Just to put my mind at rest. We can always go back to the Rose Hotel again. One more night won't kill us.'

Jamie groaned. 'Okay, but it's only a small town. Chances are we'll run into Odoms again.'

She shrugged. 'Yeah, well, that'll upset him more than me. Let's go.'

As they came closer to the town, they could see the flashing lights of emergency vehicles.

'Oh God! Something has happened. I knew it. I knew it! Hurry, Jamie, hurry.'

Jamie accelerated and screeched to a halt beside the Legion. It was as close as he could get. They opened their doors and started to run. They had to push through the people clustered around the entrance to the trailer park, where a fire tender and a paramedic van were parked, their flashing beacons spreading spasms of light far into the black desert night.

Amanda's heart pounded. She wanted to call for Howard. The very thought startled her. Davy! She should be calling for Davy, not Howard. He meant nothing to her now, but Davy had always been there for her. She should scream his name.

Jamie caught her by the shoulders. 'Wait, let me find out what's happening.'

She nodded and stayed rooted to the ground, not calling for anyone.

She saw Howard's head and shoulders as he stepped from the trailer, and she felt herself breathe again. Pushing gently on the shoulders of the two women in front of her, she said loudly, 'Excuse me. Please, that's my father, excuse me.'

The small crowd parted to let her through, and she ran over to where he was standing on the step below his trailer door. She stopped just inches away from Howard and looked directly into his eyes. 'Are you okay?'

He nodded in response but looked away from her gaze and down at the ground.

She thought he looked smaller. He seemed to have shrunk since she'd confronted him in the Legion. She tried to shake off this unexpected concern for him and concentrate on her uncle.

'Davy?'

Howard tilted his head towards the ambulance.

'What happened? Did you hurt him? What did you do?'

'He came looking for me. He came to my home.' His voice was low and directed at the ground. 'Did you send him? Did you tell him where I lived? Was this all just one big set-up to get at me?'

'No!' Her voice was strident, but she took it down to a whisper, leaned towards her father and put her hand on his shoulder. 'I wanted to find you because you're my father. They… Jamie and Davy, they followed me. I didn't know. I swear, I thought they were still in London. None of this…' She took a shuddering breath, unable to continue. Only then did she become aware of someone standing right behind him. She looked up and gasped as she realised it was a policeman. He wasn't in uniform, but she was in no doubt, especially when she registered that Howard's hands were handcuffed behind his back.

Howard was pushed forward and ushered into the back seat of a police car which had been out of her sightline, parked behind the fire tender.

Amanda couldn't speak, couldn't move. Tears blinded her, and only when the paramedics' siren sounded was she startled into moving. After all three emergency vehicles left the trailer park, she spotted Jamie beckoning her from the car. He had managed to bring it closer to the trailer park now and was ready to follow the ambulance. He leaned over and held the passenger door open, keeping his voice calm as he delivered his news.

'Listen, Amanda, the paramedic said Davy's condition is critical. They'd been going to take him to the specialist unit in Tucson, but he needs to be stabilised first, and Bisbee is much closer.'

Amanda was crying and rocking in her seat, holding the strap of the seat belt out to prevent its restraint. Jamie concentrated on driving. His face was set, shoulders tight and tipped forward as if he could add to their momentum and get them there faster.

This was his fault. He had been the first link to weaken in the chain of secrecy. As soon as Davy sensed that, he had followed the trail, slowly but relentlessly. How could it come to this?

They almost passed Vanessa's house again on the way to the Copper Queen Hospital, where Davy was being taken.

Very little traffic was on the road, and they could follow the emergency vehicles' lights most of the way there. Inside the town, the hospital was well signposted. When they parked the car, Amanda grabbed the door handle to rush out, but Jamie reached over and held her fast.

'Wait, please, sweetheart. Take a deep breath. The doctors will do everything they can, but… maybe we should compose ourselves. Davy is in a bad way. It's his breathing…'

'No, don't, Jamie!' Pushing the heels of her hands against her eyes, she sighed. 'I know, but let's just go in and hope he knows we're there.' She lowered her hands and looked up at him. 'It's our turn to be there for him.'

32 / bisbee, arizona, october 1999

day 7

AT THREE O'CLOCK IN THE MORNING, JAMIE AND AMANDA WERE STILL waiting in the relatives' room. Endless cups of disgusting coffee, discarded magazines, hopeless attempts at napping or staring at the walls: anything to avoid talking to each other. Amanda stayed doggedly at the opposite side of the room from Jamie. When he asked if she wanted coffee or a magazine, her responses were only nods or shrugs. However, her body language was screaming anger and resentment towards him.

Only two days ago, he had been shocked but happy to have found Samuel, a man whom he had always thought to be dead. Now he was awash with guilt at his part in the events that brought Davy to the brink of death. Yet as awful as he felt about that, his fear of losing Amanda because of it troubled him more.

The eerie quiet of night-time in the hospital was broken when the doctor came through to speak to them. The operation had gone well, and although they still couldn't see him, they were heartened to hear that Davy had been stabilised and would be kept in the Bisbee hospital for the time being.

The doctor's face was solemn. 'The police are waiting to interview Mr Barr once he's conscious, but even that must be kept brief.' Focusing on Amanda, he continued, 'Your uncle will need a long recovery time, Miss Barr. Both his lungs were compromised even before this incident, and we have had to remove one lobe of his left lung in order to give him the best possible chance. The immediate first aid and the quick response of the paramedics kept him alive till we could operate. Without that, I'm afraid the outcome would have been very different.'

Amanda nodded and shook his hand. 'Thank you…' Unable to say more, she nodded again and stepped forward awkwardly to hug him.

The doctor patted her shoulder. 'You should try to get some rest, Miss Barr. There's a motel right beside the hospital that has twenty-four-hour reception.'

The small room was clean and comfortable, with twin beds separated by a small cabinet. Jamie sat on one bed, facing Amanda on the other.

'We need to phone your mum,' Jamie said to Amanda. She had been putting it off for hours, hoping to be able to say Davy was going to be okay.

'It'll be what… eleven in the morning there?'

She nodded sadly. 'God almighty, where will I start?'

The ring tone sounded strange in her ear. *Please don't answer, please don't answer,* she prayed.

'The Spencers' abode! Y'ello.'

Her relief at hearing Ronnie's joking voice inched her resolve up a notch. She took a deep breath.

'Ronnie? Hi, it's me, Amanda. Eh, I'm in America. I came over

Lorraine Queen

a few days ago. Jamie's here, too, and Uncle Davy...' She heard Ronnie laugh and try to speak. 'No, wait, Ronnie. There's been... em... an accident. Davy... He's in hospital. He's really ill.'

33 / arizona, october 1999

day 8

THEY WATCHED THE ARRIVALS DOOR INTENTLY. JAMIE WAS TALL enough to see over the crowds waiting to greet their visitors, but Amanda had to lean to each side and occasionally stand on tiptoe looking for a clear view. The arrivals slowed to a trickle and the crowd thinned before two familiar figures came through the doors to the long walkway towards them.

Sheila led the way, dragging her suitcase. She quickly spotted her son and broke into a warm smile at the sight of him.

'Jamie! Jamie, over here.' She waved and increased her speed. When she reached him, she abandoned her case and wrapped her arms around his chest, but only briefly before she turned to check on her friend. 'Come on, Marion, they're here.'

Marion had stopped in the walkway and was staring at Amanda. Sheila nudged Jamie forward, telling him to help Marion with her case before taking Amanda's hand.

'Oh, Amanda, this must have been terrible for you. Your poor mum can hardly take it all in. How's Davy doing now? Is he conscious I've been praying for him? Our whole congregation is too.'

She continued a stream of chatter as she put her arm round Amanda's shoulders and guided her out of the Arrivals area.

Jamie carried Marion's case with one hand and draped his other arm round her shoulders. Accompanied with a few gentle squeezes to her shoulder, he offered what he hoped was some reassurance with the well-worn phrases he'd heard others give. 'He'll be all right. Don't worry. He's made of tough stuff. He's making steady progress. Just give him time.'

Jamie drove, and Amanda sat in the front passenger seat, studiously looking out the window. Sheila was beginning to falter in her bid to fill the silence but then looked over to her friend and noticed the tears on her cheeks.

'No, Marion, don't cry again. You're making yourself ill. It'll all work out okay.'

Marion shook her head and spoke for the first time.

'No, it should never have come to this. It's my fault. I'm sorry, I'm so sorry.' She reached forward and put a hand on her daughter's shoulder. 'Amanda, I can't turn the clock back, but please believe me, everything I did was to try to protect you.'

Amanda inched her body towards the door, slipping her shoulder from her mother's reach. Marion withdrew her hand and slumped back with a deep sigh. Her friend pulled out a pack of tissues and handed one to her, giving an encouraging pat as she passed it over.

The long journey passed in excruciating silence. Several times, Jamie offered to stop for coffee or toilet breaks, but Sheila, gauging the mood of the others, urged him on: 'No, dear, let's just get there.'

. . .

Just One Little Pill

Howard pulled his truck into the parking lot at the Bisbee hospital and fumed inwardly as he tightened his grip on the steering column. Twice in as many days he'd been bundled into a police car and taken to the local jail. Twice Vanessa had come to represent him and arrange bail but had taken her own sweet time about it. The charges wouldn't stick, he knew that, but at least the old bastard had survived. Things would have been a lot more complicated if he'd died. It had been a near thing, though. The old man had wanted to die, deliberately forcing his weight onto the knife. Dumb sonofabitch! He rolled down the window and took a few deep breaths to calm himself. Now he needed to visit the old motherfucker to make sure he was going to be straight about the whole stupid mess.

Howard walked along the corridor, looking for room 3C. The nurse had directed him away from the ICU, where he'd thought Davy Barr would be, telling him the patient was now out of danger and breathing on his own.

The blind was closed on the room window, so Howard was unprepared for the sight of the people gathered around the bed. He recognised Marion first. Short blonde hair replaced the long dark locks he remembered, but otherwise he knew it was her within a second. The woman with her was matronly and middle-aged, but she began talking first, and as soon as he heard her voice, he realised this must be Sheila Forsythe.

'Howard, we must thank you for saving Davy's life.' And she stepped towards him, reaching forward as if to embrace him. Howard recoiled, and at the same time Davy growled from the bed.

'No, get out. Basta—' A bout of wheezing prevented him from continuing. He tried to remove the oxygen mask from his face, but Marion pushed his hand away and held the mask firmly in place. As she did so, she deliberately turned her back on Howard, who stood stock still in the doorway.

He turned to leave the room, glancing at Amanda, who was perched on the edge of the broad windowsill.

'I came to see how he was doin'.'

Amanda nodded, then followed him out to the corridor. 'Yes, they operated as soon as he got here.' She indicated Davy's room, then added, 'It was touch and go. They said if you hadn't acted so quickly, he would have…' Her voice dropped to a whisper. 'He probably wouldn't have made it.' She looked at Howard with narrowed eyes, but her words were soft. 'Are you all right?'

Howard shrugged. 'All right?' He snorted and shook his head. For a split second, he almost said more, but instead he turned and strode off towards the exit.

A few steps further on, he saw Jamie walking towards him. He glared up at the young man, daring him to say anything that would give him an excuse to vent his anger.

Jamie stopped directly in Howard's path. 'What are you doing here?'

'Leaving, why? You got something to say about that?'

'You shouldn't be here. This isn't the place, but I do want to talk to you about Amanda and…' He paused and took a shuddering breath. 'About my father.'

'What's to say? She's my daughter. You're Samuel's son. Yeah! So, we all live happily ever after? Except we don't. Amanda and I can't get along for more than five minutes, and Samuel forgets you exist ten seconds after you leave the room. The end.'

'No, there's more to it than that.'

'He's right, Jamie.' Amanda's voice startled them both. She walked towards them. 'Let it go, will you? You've interfered enough. You and Davy… pushing me, following me, manipulating… I've had it with all of you.' She sighed and ran past both of them towards the door leading outside.

At that same moment, Marion came through the door and saw her daughter run off. She strode over to Howard and stopped almost nose to nose with him. 'What did you say to her? Have you upset her?'

Before he had a chance to answer, Jamie turned and left. 'Wait, Amanda, wait up.'

Howard and Marion faced each other for the first time in almost thirty years. She was scowling, head jutting forward aggressively.

'What a fucking mess—' she began, but Howard interrupted in a harsh voice.

'Yeah, your mess. Don't think you can put this on me. You were the one that started all this. You got pregnant, then kept it hidden from me all these years. That's what started this whole sorry piece of crap off in the first place.'

'Oh, no you don't, Howard Odoms. Don't you dare try to lay all this on me. You killed Diane, or are you just blanking that bit out? Killed an innocent young girl just as her life was starting. That's what brought us all to this. Davy would never have been here, never have been involved, if you hadn't poisoned his daughter.'

'I saved his damn life! Or have you forgotten that? And Diane…' He stepped even closer to Marion and hissed, 'I did everything I could, everything. She loved me…'

'Well, she paid a bloody high price for that, didn't she?'

'Jesus Christ! That's what bothers you: I didn't love you. I walked away from you, and you kept Amanda a secret for fucking revenge, didn't you?'

Her eyebrows shot up till they disappeared under her fringe, and her voice came out in a falsetto. *'That's what bothers me?'* She lowered her voice to a growl. 'You weird, creepy bastard! You fed Diane the drugs that killed her, you tried to do away with the unborn child that you *did* know about – and you think *that's* what bothers me?'

'It was my baby, too, don't forget. What was I supposed to do with him? Huh? Leave him there—'

'You didn't give him the chance to be your son!' She was screaming now.

'No. No, *she* didn't give him the chance to be my son! She kept him secret from me too. She only told me she might be pregnant days before… before…'

Howard realised his hands were balled into fists. Exhaling, he forced himself to straighten his fingers and drop his shoulders. Standing upright, he squared his shoulders and lifted his chin as he gave Marion a last look. 'Bitch!' he said.

Outside in the small garden at the side of the hospital, Jamie was doing his best to hold a conversation with Amanda. She had turned and tried to walk away, but he followed her, continuing to talk. Soon she had managed to back herself into a small corner beside a seated area under a shaded canopy.

'Amanda, please sit down and let me explain…'

'Not now, all right? I don't want to do this just now.' She shook her head to emphasise her determination. 'Just go and bond with Samuel or whatever it is you want to do, but leave me out of it. I've had enough. I'm sick to my stomach with all the drama and disappointment. I just want to go home.'

'If you're going home, then I'm going too.'

'No!' She shrugged off his attempts to put his arms round her.

'I've always given in to you, Amanda.' He followed her as she tried to turn away from him. 'Ever since we were little, I always gave you your own way. Surely you can understand why, this one time, this one thing, I couldn't give you? I was scared to. Scared you would find out that your father was bad, maybe even evil… Then when we were… together… I was scared of how you would react towards me… because I had kept his name to myself all that time.' He spread his arms wide and bent to whisper to her. 'It's you and me that's important, Amanda. The rest of them—'

She didn't let him finish. 'You weren't supposed to be here at all. It was my search for my father. Nothing to do with you, but oh no, you've been sneaking behind my back… You and Davy, conspiring and manipulating me… Now look where we are! Davy fighting for his life, my father getting arrested…' She took a deep breath, then continued in a calmer voice. 'Look, Jamie, you need to do… whatever you need to with your father. I understand that, but just let me go back to London. I need to sort things out in my head, and it's better if I'm on my own. Everywhere I turn, I see people that I thought loved and supported me, only to realise every single one has kept secrets and conspired behind my back. Right now, I feel betrayed… by everyone, but most of all by you.'

'I was trying to protect you. All I did was to try to save you from getting hurt.'

Amanda was walking away but stopped and turned to face him, shaking her head.

'But you lied. For years you lied to me. I can't trust you, Jamie, and right now, I don't want you anywhere near me.'

She saw Howard leave the hospital main entrance and walk towards the car park.

'I mean it, Jamie. Leave me alone.' With that, she turned and ran to catch her father before he got to his truck. 'Howard, wait.' She'd reached him but had to gasp for breath before she could say any more. He stopped at the door but kept his back towards her.

'Can I get a lift?'

Howard was surprised at Amanda's request but quickly agreed. 'Sure.'

They drove in silence for the first mile. Then Howard asked, 'Where do you want me to take you?'

'Honestly? I don't know.' She buried her face in her hands and let the tears come. The sobs built up until they racked her body. She felt the truck come to a halt and heard a seat belt unclip.

Howard's arms were around her, and he whispered into her hair, 'Shh, let it all out, baby girl, let it all out…'

She felt exhausted. Her eyes were hot, probably red and swollen too. Howard handed her a bottle of water and spoke quietly.

'Here, you need to replace all those fluids. Arizona is no place to let yourself get dehydrated, little girl.'

She sipped the water slowly. It was warm but helped her dry throat, and she felt a little calmer.

Howard turned on the ignition and announced in a firm voice, 'Right. Let's take you back to Tombstone. You can freshen up at my place. After that you'll have a better idea of what you want to do.'

Amanda nodded, relieved not to have to make any decisions for now.

Howard had gone home after his release from jail, but he'd only had time to shower, change his clothes, and clear away the medical debris left by the paramedics. He realised he would have to do something with the rest of the mess before he could take Amanda there.

Amanda had been drowsing, so he spoke quietly and told her to give him just five minutes to tidy the place up a bit. She gave a little nod without opening her eyes, so he left the truck window open and walked quickly to his trailer.

Davy's blood had dried onto the carpet and splattered against the counter legs and seats. He sprayed liberal amounts of detergent over the non-porous surfaces and wiped them with paper towels. The stained carpet he covered with a rug from the bedroom, and he spread a bedcover over the seating. Glancing round the room, he decided that was the best he could do under the circumstances. He drove the truck into the parking spot and help guide Amanda into his home.

'Hey, why don't you go lie down for a while? You look beat.'

'Mmm, we didn't get much sleep last night.' After a moment she added, 'Nor the night before, come to think about it.'

He closed the blinds, switched on the air conditioning unit in Samuel's bedroom, and left her to rest. He spent the next two hours scrubbing the living area while she slept.

He had everything all ready to switch on as soon as she wakened. When he heard movements from the bedroom, he clicked on the coffee filter, pushed down the toaster lever, and turned the heat up full under the skillet with the butter, ready to add the beaten eggs.

He watched her face closely as she came into the kitchen and saw the table set for two, with orange juice, silverware, and even paper napkins – well, kitchen towel, but he knew it looked impressive.

Amanda's surprised expression quickly turned into a broad grin, and he felt rewarded.

When they had both finished, they sat back in their respective seats and stared out the window. Howard was first to speak.

'Feeling better now, kid?'

She nodded. 'Thank you.'

'Any idea what you want to do now? Just so you know, there's no pressure. You can stay here until you feel ready to do… whatever. It's up to you, baby girl.'

'Thanks.' She paused, then looked at him. 'I really didn't have any idea what I was going to do when I walked away from Jamie at the hospital. I just knew I had to get away. Then when I saw you at your truck…'

'Listen, I'm just glad I was there. Honestly, it's the first time

I've felt useful – needed – since this whole thing got started.' He began to clear the dishes. 'Just take your time. Feel better, and don't go makin' any hasty decisions. This past week has been…' He searched for a word, but instead threw his head back and made a noise like an explosion: 'Kaaaa-booom!'

Amanda laughed. 'Exactly! I couldn't have put it any better myself!'

Together they washed and tidied up the kitchen. Daylight had disappeared by the time they finished, and Howard asked if she wanted to watch some television.

'No, I don't think so. Could we just talk?' When he sat opposite her, she continued. 'Davy told me – us – what happened.'

'Look, let's just put that night behind us.'

'Yes, sure, I mean I appreciate you saved him, stemming the blood flow, keeping him alive till the paramedics got here… but I meant what you told him about… after Diane died, the baby. What you told him about the baby.'

He simply stared at her.

'Did you bury him in Diane's grave?'

'Look, it was a long time ago. We can't change anything now. I thought it would make him feel better. No harm in telling him what he wanted to hear, was there?'

'But he knew you were lying.'

'Yeah.' He shrugged. 'How the hell was I gonna know he put his wife in the same grave?'

'So you didn't bury the baby, then?'

He began to get agitated, sitting forward, spreading his fingers out on the table and studying them closely before speaking again.

'That was my baby too. A baby Diane had kept secret for months before she told me she *might* be pregnant. If she'd been upfront with me from the start, none of this would have happened.' Then he looked across at Amanda, shaking his head. 'Not you. You had already happened. But there's another secret that was kept from me! I didn't deserve that. I should have been told! Both of them, your mother and Diane, they should've told me.'

'And then what? You would have done away with me too?'

'No! I… I don't know what I would have done. The point was that I was never given the chance to have any say… make any decision, talk to your mother or Diane. No one told me anything.' He realised his hands were shaking.

He got up, strode over to the refrigerator, and pulled out a bottle of water. He offered it to Amanda. When she shook her head, he opened it and took a deep drink.

'I'm sorry. I shouldn't go off on you. It's not your fault. It's not you I'm angry about.'

'Okay, I know. Just tell me what did happen. The truth. You can be honest with me.'

He paused, then sat beside Amanda. 'I went to Diane's grave. Not during the funeral – I couldn't risk that. The next night. I had my boy, our boy, all wrapped up in the tin, but I was angry. Well, angry and sad. I told her I was sorry, told her I missed her and that I loved her. She knew that.' He looked at Amanda, and she nodded. 'But mostly I was angry. I… I yelled at her, at her grave. I told her I was taking my boy home. I wasn't leaving him in a foreign country. He was American, and he was coming home with me.'

He heard Amanda take a sharp breath and glared at her.

'What?' he demanded.

'No, nothing. I get it. I'm… I don't know, a bit shocked to think about it, but I understand, I really do. Did you bring him back… here to Tombstone?'

'Not to Tombstone. I was posted back to Jacksonville in North Carolina. I buried him near the veterans' cemetery there. It's by the beach. He can feel the beat of the ocean and know he's the son of a marine.' He looked at Amanda and lowered his voice to a whisper. 'My brother, Thomas, is buried there.'

Amanda took his hand, and they sat quietly together.

Howard was the first to break the silence. He took another drink of his water and went over to the kitchen area. Lifting the half-full coffee pot, he asked Amanda if she would like some.

'No, thanks, I feel pretty worn out, actually. Would it be okay if I spent the night here?'

'Sure it would. You know that.'

'Thank you, but then tomorrow…'

'Hey, let tomorrow take care of itself. Just take one day at a time.' He gave a snort. 'I believe I heard that somewhere, but it's good advice. You can stay here as long as you need, till you know exactly what you want.'

'I want to go home, Howard. I just want to go home.'

'Okay then. That's what we'll do. Tomorrow, right?'

34 / arizona, october 1999

day 9

Next morning Howard drove to the hospital car park and collected Amanda's holdall from Jamie. It contained her passport and a change of clothes. He could see the boy's anguish, but just as he had promised his daughter, he refused to give any information about Amanda other than yes, she was okay, and no, she wasn't ready to see him or talk to him. She had switched off her phone after texting Jamie with instructions on where to hand over her bag so he couldn't call or text her with questions or promises she couldn't cope with right now.

When Howard got back to his trailer and gave Amanda her holdall, she showered and dressed for the journey ahead.

'Okay, ready, Howard?'

'Sure, but please, Amanda, let me drive you to Sky Harbor. There's nothing else I need to do, nowhere I need to be…'

She shook her head. 'If you can take me to the bus station in Tucson, that's fine. I've asked a lot of you this past week, Howard, so please, just drop me in Tucson. It's time to stand on my own two feet. I need to take some control of my own life again.'

Lorraine Queen

. . .

When they reached the bus station, Howard parked his truck, and they both remained seated in the cabin.

Amanda turned to her father. 'I know this has been a mess, and I'm sorry for all I've put you through – what I've put everyone through – but I want you to know I'm glad we met. I'm happy that you're my father. I think you would have been a pretty good dad if you'd had the chance. Look how well you care for Samuel. Look how good you've been to me over the past couple of days. Thank you. I really mean it, Howard. Thank you.'

'I'm glad we met, too, baby girl.' He rested his hand on the side of her face and brushed his thumb across her cheekbone. 'I think you're pretty damn wonderful, and I'm grateful we've come through this mess on the upside – well, you and I have, at least. An' don't you go apologising for all the… anything!' His hand moved under her chin, and he gently nudged it upwards. 'You didn't make any of the crap happen. Me, your mom, your uncle, and even, God rest her, Diane all played a part in this. Out of all of us, you were the only one that was upfront and honest – okay, you were pretty single-minded about it, a force to be reckoned with, for sure, but that's nothin' to apologise about.'

They embraced and sat quietly for a moment.

'You look after yourself, baby girl. Let me know how you're doin', okay?'

Amanda nodded, kissed his cheek lightly, and thanked him again, then lifted her holdall. She left without looking back, blinking away the tears before they could fall.

She dismounted the bus outside Sky Harbor Airport, glad that she had only her holdall to carry. The rest of her clothes were in the suitcase, still in the rented car. She thought Jamie, her mother, or

Sheila might bring them when they returned home, but in all honesty, she didn't care.

She knew she was doing the right thing in leaving, but her stomach was feeling queasy. Little wonder, between time changes, the heat, and the emotional upheaval she'd been through in the last week. She bought a box of mints in an airport shop and sat, quietly enjoying the coolness of the air-conditioned lounge.

She fished out her CD player and headphones, trying to make herself as comfortable as possible for the three hours until boarding. Listening to music would stop her from running things through in her mind again. Soon she was lost in the steady stream of songs, and feeling calmer than she had in days, she even found herself dozing off once or twice.

Suddenly she was wide awake. The song that began playing was the one she and Jamie had danced to that first night they went to a club after his mum's wedding. Haddaway, who looked so like Jamie, singing "What Is Love?"

Amanda sat up with a jolt. Jamie had sung the words to her as they danced that night, begging her not to hurt him anymore.

Tears welled up, and her throat tightened. She had hurt him: bitchy, bossy, determined to have everything her own way. But God, he'd paid her back now! How could he? Plotting behind her back, following her... Through all her years of disappointment and frustration searching for Howard Odoms, Jamie had known all along, known the name and known there had been trouble with another girl... Christ! She felt betrayed. She needed to get away – from Jamie, her mum, Davy, even Sheila...

She looked up at the departures board. Her flight was boarding at gate nine. Gathering up her things, she felt her stomach churn once more. *Oh God*, she thought, *please, let this be a smooth flight. I don't think I could take any more upset.*

At least she had a window seat. Once on the plane, she lay her forehead against the window, and it cooled her skin. The mountaintops below were covered in snow, and yet they were only an hour into the flight away from the arid desert landscape.

The flight attendant had been round offering drinks and supper, but even thinking about eating set off an acid burn in her throat. Scrabbling in her holdall, she found the few remaining mints from the airport. The old lady in the next seat watched her and nodded.

'Heartburn, dear?'

Amanda shrugged. 'Could be. My tummy's been upset for days.'

'Here, try one of these. I get them for my acid reflux. They're very good.'

Amanda smiled her thanks, accepted one, and washed it down with a small drink. She prayed it would settle things quickly.

She must have slept after that, for she wakened to the attendant leaning over to touch her arm.

'The captain has put the seat belt sign on. He's expecting a bit of turbulence.'

Amanda had forgotten she'd unclipped her belt earlier to try and relieve her belly pain. Soon the plane began to bump: nothing too rocky, but Amanda could feel her insides lurching.

This was all she needed. Her mouth filled with saliva, and she began to retch. The old lady pressed a sick bag into her hands and began to gently rub her back.

'There, there, dear, you'll be fine soon.' She held Amanda's hair back from her face. 'I know it's horrible, but it usually goes after the first trimester. I was a midwife for almost forty years, and believe me when I tell you every mother I delivered felt it was all worth it.'

Amanda immediately stopped retching and stared at the kindly woman.

'No, no, it's a bug or something. I'm not preg…' She closed her eyes and did a quick calculation. Her head drooped, and she thought, *Oh, fuck!*

The three of them had been sitting in the visitors' room yesterday when Jamie had taken her hand and started talking about Howard. There had been lots of talk of Howard. Marion had been angry, then dumbfounded, then worried: deeply worried about Davy, about what the long-term effects on his health could be. Possibly even more worrying was how the police would view his part in the whole terrible episode.

Then Jamie had stroked her hand. She'd looked at him, then at Marion, wondering if he realised he should be telling her about how Howard had been through hard times, had turned to drink and maybe even drugs at one time but then managed to get his life sorted out.

Sheila patted his hand reassuringly. 'Yes, Jamie, but that is all in the past, dear.'

'No, wait, Mum. I need to tell you this.'

Still puzzled, she listened. She listened while Jamie told her of Howard's spell in the rehab unit of a big hospital. She listened when he told her he had been recognised by an old friend who was in another part of the same hospital and how Howard had cleaned up his act and spent much of his recent life caring for his friend, sharing the responsibility with the man's family.

'Well, good for him.' She turned to Marion. 'See, Marion, there's good in everyone. He cares for his sick friend, and he saved Davy. Can't you find it in your heart to forgive him?'

'Mum, wait, listen to me. The friend Howard looks after was his friend in the marines. He was in Dunoon with him. That's where he was hurt.' Now Jamie moved over and wrapped both his arms around her. 'Mum, the friend is my father. Samuel. It's Samuel. He's alive.'

. . .

Sheila heard a wail. Her mouth was open, and her breath was escaping noisily. She began to tremble; then it built up to a shaking that would have been more violent had Jamie not been holding her tightly. Marion joined their hug, but now Sheila felt stifled. She pushed away her friend and her son and walked to the window. So many questions whirled in her head as she looked out. Her Samuel, her lovely Samuel. *Dear God, you saved him.* But why had he never contacted her?

Jamie sat her down again and told her what he knew. That helped. She calmed herself. But one thing was certain: she had to see him.

35 / bisbee, arizona, october 1999

day 10

The car pulled up at the sidewalk, and she watched Vanessa and Howard get out. Vanessa held the door open, and Howard leaned in to unfasten the man's seat belt, then stood slightly to the side, ready to help.

The feet and legs came first, his body bent so she couldn't see his face.

She held her breath.

His arms reached out, and with one on top of the door and the other supported by Howard, he finally emerged and stood to his full height. He appeared a little bewildered until he fastened on Howard's expression. He smiled.

Sheila had both hands clasped against her mouth, thumbs pushing her lips closed. This was her defence, ready to capture and stifle any sounds before they could betray her. She wanted to close her eyes and pray, but the need to keep looking at him was stronger.

They began to walk towards the rest area, where gravel and cacti had been landscaped around two benches. The temperature was still warm and comfortable at this time of day. Once he was safely seated, she saw him lift his face to the morning sun.

In that moment, she saw the young Samuel, the boy who had loved her. She felt his lips kissing her, heard his voice teasing her and his arms embracing her. His laugh rang in her head. He had laughed easily and smiled in a special way that was just for her. Their love and youthful passion had been so intense and yet so brief.

She wore a large-brimmed sun hat to shade her face. She doubted he could recognise her as the young girl from thirty years ago, but the mind was a strange thing. As damaged as his memories were, he recognised Howard and Vanessa afresh whenever he saw them, and so she couldn't take the risk of him seeing her. If she could have been sure her appearance would trigger memories of the happy times they had shared, she wouldn't have hesitated. But neither she, Vanessa, or Howard was prepared to risk having his mind fall back to the last time he had seen her. Distance provided a safety net for her too. She had cherished her memories of Samuel. Then, as the years passed, those memories had become part of seeing Jamie grow. Everything their son did reminded her of Samuel: every inch he grew, every smile, laugh, and gesture – it all had blended until there was only Jamie. Samuel had faded from her mind as an individual. The facts of names, places, and dates were there, but the emotions attached to those facts had been neutralised. Or so she had thought.

Sheila felt breathless as the memory of those feelings hit her with a clarity she had not expected. Then, like a belly punch, came a different, fiercer emotion. Sheila rarely felt anger, but now it flooded her. She raged at the thugs who had robbed her and Samuel of the lives they could have had.

She had shed tears silently since seeing Samuel. Now angry sobs escaped, and she pulled further back into the shadows in case the sound alerted him to her presence. All the could-have, should-have, would-have thoughts that she'd tortured herself with in the weeks after the attack came back to punish her all over again.

It had been too late then, and it was certainly too late now. She prayed.

Time gave a different vantage point, she decided. Sometimes, looking back, you could see where God's hand had been at work. The Grant brothers and their evil deeds had been the Devil's doing. God had saved Samuel, kept him alive and wiped clean his memory of the horror. Then He'd let Samuel's seed grow so her life would have a purpose. Jamie was her reward for the trials she had been through.

Now she was content. Jamie had grown into a man she would always be proud of. She had a husband. They shared a real affection, not the tingling excitement she'd felt with Samuel. She'd been just a girl then; no, theirs was a relationship of adults. Their work with the parishioners gave her meaning and purpose.

Sheila stepped forward to catch one last glimpse of Samuel and blew a gentle kiss toward him. 'God bless, my dear, lovely Samuel.'

She wiped the tears from her face and walked slowly back to the car where Jamie and Marion waited. They both hugged her.

'Are you okay, Mum?'

She nodded. 'Yes, fine. I'll be fine.' She put her arm around her son and, looking to the sky, whispered, 'Thank you.'

epilogue
Arizona, October 2001

THE CHILD TODDLED TOWARDS THE TELEVISION, ARMS OUTSTRETCHED for balance, sticky fingers aiming straight for the colourful characters on the screen.

'No, Sammy! No, you don't!' Amanda dived forward to cut off his advance, and she heard the deep laughter of the man sitting in the opposite chair.

'Hey, little critter, you need to mind your momma.' He laughed again and looked round at the other adults to make sure they had seen what had happened. The man's deep voice caught the little one's attention, and he changed direction, making straight for the big man's knees. He placed both sticky hands on the man's trousers and looked up at him.

'Maah...' And he gave a big smile.

The man took each of the child's hands in his and began to sing. 'Twinkle, twinkle, little star, how I wonder what you are. Up above the sky so bright, like a diamond in the night. Twinkle, twinkle, little star, how I wonder what you are.'

Amanda and Howard looked at each other, amazed and delighted, both to hear Samuel sing with such confidence and to see the rapt expression on little Sammy's face.

Vanessa had come through from the kitchen and stood behind her brother, stroking his hair. 'He sang that song to me when we were kids. We would look out the window at the night sky, and he would point to the stars and sing.' Vanessa smiled. 'He used to call me Twinkle sometimes. I was only little, but I still remember it so clearly.'

Scooping her son into her arms, Amanda bent forward and kissed Vanessa lightly on the cheek. 'Thank you for a lovely afternoon, Vanessa. Sammy is a very lucky boy to be able to visit with his great-aunt and two papas.'

'Well, you are most welcome, my dear, as is your precious boy. We'll always be happy to see you. It means a lot to us that you undertook the journey with a toddler. It couldn't have been easy. I do hope you'll come again. Perhaps next year?'

'We'll see, Vanessa. I'd like to, but… Well, let's just play things by ear. I know Jamie has talked about coming back out to see his father and bringing Sammy with him, so I'm sure he'll soon come to know you all very well as he gets older.'

Howard rose and began collecting the bits and pieces that seemed necessary to traveling with a child these days.

'I'll put these in the car, Amanda.' He went over to Samuel, who was still smiling at the little boy. 'Okay, buddy. I'm goin' to head out now, but I'll see you soon.'

Samuel nodded and shook Howard's hand vigorously. 'Sure, buddy, sure.'

While Howard waited in the car for the long goodbyes to be over, he popped a pill from a blister pack and washed it down with a gulp of the water he always kept in the car. He had the air conditioning running so it was comfortable before Amanda strapped her son into his car seat. Nevertheless, she gave him a blanket and a pacifier before getting herself settled into the front seat.

'He'll be sound asleep before we reach the end of the road, wait till you see.'

They drove in silence for a few minutes. Then, glancing at the baby in the rear-view mirror, Howard nudged his daughter.

'Yup, he's fast asleep. Probably dreamin' up more ways to get into mischief!'

They had travelled several more miles towards Tombstone when Howard quietly asked, 'So, you and Jamie? You think you'll ever get back together? Properly, I mean, not just this shared-parenting caper?'

Amanda shook her head. 'It's not going to happen, Howard. Don't get me wrong. He's a wonderful dad, and neither of us regrets having little Samuel. But things between us can never be… *right* again. He can protest that his motives were all about protecting me… and he does, all the time, but the trust's gone.' She sighed deeply and hesitated before adding quietly, 'I felt, and still feel, betrayed.'

'Yeah, but come on. He was only a kid when he first heard bits of gossip about the big bad bogeyman! You might have done the same thing if roles were reversed.'

'Maybe at first, when we were children, but we were in an adult relationship. I thought we'd told each other everything, and yet… No, Howard. I would have told him. At some point I would have had to tell him. He watched me search for you, for your name, for years, and he still didn't tell me.'

She rested her head against the window and watched the shrubs and towering green cacti flash past her field of vision. For a moment, she wondered how the huge saguaro cacti could thrive in the fierce heat and drought of the desert and yet small bushes and shrubs began to shrivel and die so soon after opening their leaves. On her last visit, she had been startled to see tumbleweeds roll along the desert floor, sometimes crashing into the cars. Howard had explained that the wind ripped out the shallow-rooted shrubs and their edges broke off as they tumbled, until they became brittle spheres. Until then she had only been familiar with them from cowboy movies. Now, after only her second visit to this very foreign land, she realised she was beginning to understand how nature adapts, wins through, even in the unlikeliest circumstances. Looking at her father, then at her son, she shook her head in wonder at how they had all managed to come together, despite all the prejudices, the secrets, and the thousands of miles of separation.

Before long they pulled into the trailer park in Tombstone. Howard brought the bags inside and held the door open as Amanda carried her sleeping son. She took him to the bedroom and laid him gently in the travel cot beside her bed. Sammy gave a little snort and stretched his arms above his head until he almost filled the length of the cot. Howard watched from the doorway. Amanda tiptoed out and closed the door behind her.

'He'll need a proper bed soon. That cot just makes it and no more.'

'He's going to be as tall as Jamie, isn't he? He certainly doesn't take his height from our side.'

'No, but we all contributed plenty of other good genes, didn't we?'

'And a few not-so-good ones… He's got our temper, I'm afraid. You should hear him when he doesn't get his own way! It's pretty fierce, I can tell you.'

'Yeah, well, as long as he can stand up for himself, that's no bad thing.' He offered the pot of coffee.

'No thanks. I think I've had my caffeine quota for the day. Vanessa kept refilling my cup, and boy, it was strong stuff!'

Although he was still living in the same trailer, her father had refreshed the flooring, blinds, and couch covering so everything looked brighter, more inviting than on Amanda's last stay there. He had rented the car seat, travel cot, and pushchair before Amanda and Sammy's visit and insisted on covering the cost.

Vanessa had helped with their airfares and tried hard to persuade them to stay with her. Amanda was glad she had decided to stay with her father, gently telling Vanessa she would visit every day but wouldn't want to tire Samuel or have the little one disturb him when he was resting. The relationship with her father had become both comfortable and comforting after many telephone calls and letters. Howard was still awkward with video calls, but his letters had surprised her in both their frequency and their tenderness. All through her pregnancy and difficult break-up with Jamie and then after Sammy's birth, his letters had been supportive and encouraging. She had looked forward to each, and he had sent at least one every week. They were never long letters but always said enough to give her spirits a lift.

Earlier that day Amanda had insisted he let her cook dinner that evening. She had shopped in a large supermarket in Bisbee before driving to Vanessa's house, and she began to sort through the ingredients. Howard stood beside her and directed her to where he kept the pots and utensils. In such a compact space, she could have figured it out very quickly herself, but she liked working in partnership with him.

Afterward, they ate their meal quietly, both listening for any noise from the bedroom where Sammy slept. When they had finished, Amanda sat farther back on the couch and leaned against the window.

'The time has gone so quickly. Sammy only just adapted to the different time zone, and now when we get home he'll have to do it all over again.'

Howard nodded and glanced back towards the bedroom. 'It's been so great to see you and to meet my grandson. I never had any experience with kids, but he is real special. I didn't know they could be so much fun.' He hesitated before adding, 'I'm gonna miss you guys.'

'We'll be back, Howard. I might not be back for a while, but Jamie will come to see Samuel. He'll bring your grandson to visit too.'

With a sigh, Howard rose and began taking the dishes to the sink. Amanda attempted to help, but he told her to put her feet up and rest.

She shook her head. 'No, we'll get these dishes out of the way in no time. It's our last night here, and Sammy is sound asleep, so we've got a rare chance to just sit and talk.'

'Okay, you start.'

Amanda raised her eyebrows. 'The dishes or the talking?'

He laughed. 'The talking.'

'Don't I always?' She laughed. 'Well, his doting gran will be at the airport to meet us and smother her darling boy in kisses, no doubt!'

'Which one?'

'Which gran? Oh, my mum, although Sheila is just as besotted.'

'Is her brother still living with her?'

'Uncle Davy?' She shook her head and cast her eyes down. 'No, he stayed with Mum and Ronnie for almost a year, but his breathing got worse and worse. He needed round-the-clock care, and they just couldn't manage anymore. He's in a nursing home. Mum feels guilty, as if she let him down, but he's better off there. I go and visit when I can. So do Sheila and Joseph. Between all of us, he has company pretty regularly... but... I don't think he'll... you know. He's not got long left.'

Howard covered her hand with his and led her over to sit down by the window.

'Tell me about your plans. Are you enjoying being back at work?'

'Yes, in a way. It's good to get out and talk with other adults. Sammy loves his nursery, and Amy, you know, my little sister? Well, she's going to school near me and collects Sammy some days. In fact, most weekends she stays with us.' Throwing her head back, she laughed out loud. 'She's a riot. Keeps trying to get me to sign up to dating sites! Says she'll go as my chaperone if I meet them when Sammy's at his dad's.'

'Do you go?' he asked in a quiet voice.

'God, no! I'm a respectable mother and pillar of society these days.'

'Don't you want to meet someone… a guy? If you're sure you don't want to get back with Jamie, then what's stopping you?'

Amanda held her hands up and shrugged. 'I'm just not ready. Don't know if I ever will be.'

'You're too young to give up on a relationship.'

'Well! Get you, giving advice to the lovelorn.'

They both laughed. Then, looking at the clock, Amanda said, 'Right. Time for bed, I think. We've got a long way to go tomorrow.'

Howard watched as she gathered up her things. She leaned over to kiss him lightly on the cheek before slipping quietly into the same bedroom as her sleeping son. Going to the refrigerator, he took out the box of pills from his pocket, then washed two down with the ice-cold water. There were only four pills left. He made a mental note to pick up a new prescription on his way home from the airport.

The toddler slept for much of the drive to Phoenix, waking only as they reached the outskirts of the city. Amanda had been singing nursery songs to him for the last twenty minutes to keep him amused. Howard picked up the words in no time and was soon singing along to 'The Wheels on the Bus', much to Amanda's amusement.

Inside the terminal, Howard stayed with them as they checked their bags, then took them for something to eat. They went to a small café, the same one where he and Amanda had shared a coffee on the first day they met.

Little Sammy needed no encouragement to eat and devoured everything he was offered. Howard was glad of the happy distraction. He was determined not to start getting sentimental, certain it would set Amanda off too.

The line at security was long but moved quickly. Howard stayed with them until they reached the barrier. He gave Sammy a kiss on his curls, then turned to Amanda and put his arms around her. She rested her head on his shoulder for a moment, then kissed his cheek.

'Bye... Dad. I'll call you once we're home and settled. Thanks. Thanks for everything.'

When she and Sammy were safely through the security line, Amanda turned and waved to him. Waving back, he watched her walk away from him, Sammy's dark head nestling into the crook of her neck. Would *his* little son have looked like Sammy? As soon as he had set eyes on his grandson, he'd felt a familiarity, as if he'd known him already. Genes, he supposed, although it felt like more than that. His boy – Sonny – would be almost the same age as Amanda... if he had lived. If only Howard hadn't been so stupid. So young, and so damn stupid. Listening to everyone except himself. Taking others' advice... *What you need to do, buddy...* Sonny would be a grown man now. Maybe even have a family of his own. Instead, he was lying deep in the sand, thousands of miles away.

A shuddering breath escaped, and he looked down the corridor, but it was full of strangers. And now Amanda, his girl, was leaving too. He turned and walked slowly towards the exit. In his mind, he took each step as he had two years earlier, with his *new* daughter by his side. He remembered how she had looked. Her clothes, her laugh… even her temper!

Of the few things in his life he was grateful for, she was top of the list. She and Sammy. He put his hand in his pocket and pulled out the empty pill box. He was grateful, too, for these pills. The morphine had let him keep his secret from her. The last thing he wanted was to burden her with such a terrible prognosis as he'd been given. No, the cancer would finish its work soon. Who knew? Maybe he and old Davy would go at the same time. Now wouldn't that be funny. He gave a grim laugh.

acknowledgements

The journey of this novel has been complex.

Let me begin with admitting what a horrible child I was. I told my little sister terrifying tales as we lay in bed at night. I was amazed to discover that I could provoke an emotional reaction to something I had just made up.

Thank you for still talking to me all these years later, Lynne.

Amid the dozens of jobs I've had throughout my life, one employer made me realise that writing might be something I could do, or at least learn to do better. I had a small group of bosses who encouraged and enabled any idea I put forward. My thanks go to the marvellous Alex Howie, Jennifer Polson, and all the team who worked up in Aberdeen.

Friends Graham and Winnie Kerr coaxed me into trying one of the creative writing courses at the Centre for Lifelong Learning in the University of Strathclyde. I finally tried a short summer course and enjoyed it so much that I followed up with every course that I could attend. Two tutors gave such excellent advice and inspiration that I felt my confidence grow week on week. Thank you to David Pettigrew and Professor Linda Jackson.

Acknowledgements

In those classes a bond was forged among many of the students. Keen to keep our momentum going, several of us formed a group called Nibs United, which, although it didn't continue for more than a few months, provided valuable encouragement to us all to continue writing. Thanks to Gail Winters, who organised and ran that group.

Building on the Nibs United experience, another writing group was formed, which continues successfully to this day. Writing Wrongs meets twice monthly, and the members have played a vital role in helping keep me on track with this book. My sincere thanks to every one of the members past and present.

The seed for this story was sown by my older cousin Marie, who was one of the girls who went to Dunoon at weekends. I'm pleased to say she found her happy ever after, and she and her husband are at fifty-two years and counting.

My friend Rose was an enormous help in furnishing details of her rebellious youth, which she has come through with wit, wisdom, and warmth.

Having taken my first novel as far as I could, I wanted to be sure it looked professional when I published it. Scrolling through CIEP's list of professional editors and proofreaders, I was very lucky to find someone who had grown up in Arizona and now lives in Scotland. It seemed almost predestined that Elyse would be the one to screen my outdated spelling, punctuation, and grammar. Her attention to detail is fantastic, and throughout her task she has treated me with patience and understanding.

My own life has often been tumultuous, and I've so often had cause to lean on a wonderful circle of dear friends and family, whose support I will always be grateful for.

Last, but never least, my long-suffering husband, Derek, has been trying for decades to get me to write. Over the years he has given me a typewriter, a word processor, and recently a very fancy

Acknowledgements

laptop (which I still haven't fully mastered), plus books on how to write… Well, we did it! Here we are with *Just One Little Pill* ready to go. It would never have happened without you at my back.